THE HOUSE IN THE WOODS

Arthur Henry

Foreword and Afterword
Donald T. Oakes

Introduction
Alf Evers

Preface
Neda M. Westlake

BLACK·DOME

Published by
Black Dome Press Corp.
1011 Route 296
Hensonville, New York 12439
Tel: (518) 734-6357
Fax: (518) 734-5802
blackdomepress.com

Library of Congress Cataloging-in-Publication Data:

Henry, Arthur, 1867-1934.
   The house in the woods / by Arthur Henry ; foreword, afterword, and annotation by
Donald T. Oakes ; introduction by Alf Evers ; preface by Neda M. Westlake.
      p. cm.
   ISBN 1-883789-24-9
   1. Henry, Arthur, 1867-1934--Homes and haunts--New York (State)--Catskill
Mountains Region. 2. Country life--New York (State)--Catskill Mountains Region.
3. Catskill Mountains Region (N.Y.)--Social life and customs. 4. Authors, American--
20th century--Biography. I. Oakes, Donald Thomas, 1923- II. Title.

PS3515.E578 Z465 2000
813'.54--dc21

                                                                    00-026232

Cover illustration Michael McCurdy
Photo reproduction Walter H. Scott

Permission from The Dreiser Trust to quote passages from A Gallery of Women,
by Theodore Dreiser, is gratefully acknowledged.

Design Artemisia, Inc.

Printed in the USA

TABLE OF CONTENTS

Arthur Henry

INTRODUCTION

The House, The Mountain Top, and The Catskills

In *The House in the Woods*, Arthur Henry managed to capture and preserve the spirit of a time and place while trying to do something very different: he set out to tell the story of the building of a house in the country by a pair of eager amateurs, but succeeded in giving us an absorbing and instructive picture of a turn of the century Catskill Mountain Top community in its complex relationships of soil, water, bedrock, plants, and people.

In the Catskills, "The Mountain Top" is the local name for a large division of the region from which, because of its elevated position, streams radiate in many directions. The valley at the head of one of these streams, the Plattekill, became the site of the house which Henry's book celebrates. It was there, in what they felt as a magical valley, that Henry and the people who helped him began trying to convert reality into a Utopian dream.

They arrived on the Mountain Top borne on the wind of a contemporary enthusiasm for what was then called "the simple life". For a time blinded to many of the facts of rural existence, they soon found themselves struggling with rocks, roots, and hardpan, chickens, pigs, and cows—and in the process won their way to an understanding of the land and the people of the straggling hamlet of Platte Clove. Their willingness to learn and to adapt got their House in the Woods built, and earned them a warm (if often baffled) acceptance by their Platte Clove neighbors.

Today, no one who wants to appreciate the charm and richness of life on the Mountain Top at the dawn of the Twentieth Century can afford to overlook *The House in the Woods*.

During the almost two centuries before Arthur Henry first touched earth in Platte Clove, the place had achieved a little niche of its own in local history. In 1708, colonial governor Lord Cornbury had conveyed it from Indian to white ownership as part of the vast Hardenbergh Patent. By the time the

American Revolution ended, it was still owned by absentee landlords, and was beginning to emerge from wilderness into settlement. The western part was in the hands of the landlords whose agents negotiated leases with settlers, while the eastern part was slackly managed and attracted the kind of unauthorized pioneers known as "squatters". By about 1820, a sawmill was at work near the head of the great clove or ravine down which the Plattekill plunges, and squatters were struggling to maintain a footing amid the debris of deforestation.

Talented amateur natural historian James Pierce of Catskill described the Mountain Top as he saw it in 1822:

> Unfortunately, most of the residents of this part of the mountain area are not proprietors of the soil. They prefer stripping the land of its best timber rather than resort to the regular toils of agriculture. A considerable portion live in log huts without floors or furniture. Bread is rarely seen among them; and but few have gardens. Their principal food, in addition to wild meats and fish occasionally obtained, consists of potatoes and pumpkins.

These people had come as close in their daily lives to living the simple life as was possible given their place and time. To the west of the squatters' neighborhood, Pierce noted some fairly good farms properly leased from absentee landlord John Hunter of New Rochelle, New York. It was on the fringes of one of these that Arthur Henry's House in the Woods was built.

By the time James Pierce visited Platte Clove, land speculators, lumbermen, and settlers were sharing the Catskills with people of different interests. These new arrivals admired distant views, waterfalls and rocky cliffs, deep tangles of forest, and lonely lakes. A new attitude toward nature was changing the way people saw the Catskills. Before long, Washington Irving's Rip Van Winkle would become a hero of the Catskills. Thomas Cole and others would follow Rip as celebrators of the Catskills' romantic charm. Eventually tourists would arrive and fill summer hotels and farm boarding houses.

In 1840, Thomas Cole and poet-editor William Cullen Bryant walked through Platte Clove from the Stony Clove to the northwest. Unlike Pierce, they saw the vicinity as one of ravishing beauty, and exclaimed over waterfalls and views of mountains. It may well be that the most famous of Hudson River School paintings, Asher B. Durand's *Kindred Spirits*, was painted to commemorate this expedition.

During the infant years of the Twentieth Century, Arthur Henry learned much about the trees of the Catskills as he laboriously processed them for use in building. He learned too about what went on under the surface of the Mountain Top's scanty earth. He was reminded at the same time that his little bit of the Catskills formed part of the bustling resort region of the mountains. He came to realize that hikers, admirers of waterfalls and scenic vistas, trout fishermen, painters with their easels and umbrellas, and urban boarders awkwardly helping out with the haying as one of the pleasures of a farmhouse vacation all trooped through his magical valley.

He learned from his neighbors about the bluestone quarries which were making ugly scars on the mountainsides, about the past ravages of the region's tanners, about the "parks" built by prosperous city people eager to immerse themselves in the romantic glamor of the Catskills while yet avoiding contact with the thousands of recently-arrived immigrants who had found that the Catskills could offer a cheap summer respite from the dinginess of their urban lives.

He was aware of all this, yet he put it aside in a secluded corner of his mind as he concentrated on pursuing his hope of living close to nature and setting up a subsistence farm on which he and those close to him might live independent lives in freedom from the irrational notions of the society into which they had been born.

The book ends on a mixed note: of *triumph*—at having succeeded in building his House in the Woods and becoming part of the Platte Clove community; of *warning*—"if we run from the vexations of the city we will find the vexations of the country in wait for us".

Arthur Henry transformed the vexations he encountered on the Mountain Top and the idealism with which he entered his magical valley into a book of lasting value—not only as entertainment, but also as a help in our understanding of the social history of the Catskills.

Alf Evers
Shady, New York

PREFACE

You are to me my other self, a very excellent Dreiser minus some of my defects, & plus many laughable errors which I would not have. If I could not be what I am, I would be you.

Theodore Dreiser

This new edition of *The House In The Woods*, first pubished in 1904, has an Introduction by Alf Evers that emphasizes the importance of the book in the history of the Catskills. Donald Oakes has provided a Foreword and Afterword that explore the life of the author, with illuminating backward glances, after more than ninety years, at the circumstances that provoked the book and at the associations of its author, Arthur Henry. This Preface is primarily directed toward one of those associations: his friendship with Theodore Dreiser.

Mr. Oakes has made a genuine and creative contribution to Dreiser studies by adding new material to what has been known and, by his imaginative research, he has thrown fresh light on that friendship. The Afterword reads like a novel that Dreiser might have wished he had written.

Theodore Dreiser's comment quoted above in a letter of 23 July 1900 from Montgomery City, Missouri, to Arthur Henry in New York epitomizes the friendship between the two men at a crucial period in Dreiser's career. *Sister Carrie*, his first novel, had been accepted by Doubleday, Page, but the firm was reluctant to publish the book, fearing critical reception. Arthur Henry, who had been closely involved in the writing of the story, urged Dreiser to hold Doubleday to the contract, a persuasion that agreed with Dreiser's view. The book was published in November of 1900.

The meeting of Dreiser and Henry, perhaps in Chicago in the later 1880's, but certainly in Toledo, Ohio, in 1894, their subsequent contacts in New

York, and the disintegration of their friendship have been touched on else-where, but the Afterword provides fresh insights into the relationship that was so important to both men.

Arthur Henry's participation in the creation of Sister Carrie was funda-mental, from his urging Dreiser to write a novel, to his editorial work on the manuscript, to his support during negotiations with the publisher. The novel was first offered to Harpers but rejected on the grounds that it would be offen-sive to women readers. When Frank Norris, then a reader for Doubleday, praised the work, it was accepted, but many changes were demanded.

Dreiser, his wife, and Henry then worked over the manuscript, shortening the narrative, removing offensive phrases or details of the plot. Their distinc-tive hands are clearly evident in the various alterations in the manuscript. The plain truth is that Sister Carrie, as it was written, would not have been acceptable to any American publisher in 1900, and the three participants should not be anathematized for altering a text which otherwise would be unpublishable. The full and unexpurgated text was produced by the University of Pennsylvania Press in 1981.

From their meeting in Toledo in 1894 when Dreiser was twenty-three and Henry was twenty-seven, the two young men became a mutual admiration society, attested by Dreiser in his autobiography and correspondence. After a summer visit with Arthur Henry and his first wife in Maumee, Ohio, in 1899, the Dreisers, with Henry in tow, returned to New York, and the collaboration between the two aspiring writers began in earnest, Henry working on his novel, A Princess of Arcady and Dreiser on Sister Carrie. The Afterword to this volume gives fresh details of that association, with an informed analysis of the ups and downs of the relationship that was partially broken by Henry's An Island Cabin, published in 1902, in which Dreiser is thinly disguised as the vis-itor who grumbled about the primitive living conditions on the little offshore Connecticut island, a fictionalized account of an episode that occurred in Noank. In a letter to Dreiser in 1904, Henry tells him that the friendship was doomed before his book was written. The Afterword gives credence to that remark by describing the involved relationships of Dreiser, Henry, and Anna Mallon, Henry's second wife whom he married in 1904. Dreiser's retaliation was "Rona Murtha," an episode in A Gallery of Women, published in 1929, in which he gives a scathing analysis of the ambiguities and romanticism of the male protagonist, an obvious Arthur Henry.

The Afterword, by use of hitherto unpublished documents, fills out the story not provided by either An Island Cabin nor A Gallery of Women. The reminiscences of Maude Wood Henry, Henry's first wife, tell as much about Dreiser as about him. The full account of the tragic life of Anna Mallon, Henry's second wife, supplies answers to many questions about this literary friendship and suggests why it may have been headed for disaster from the beginning.

"You ... are a very excellent Dreiser minus some of my defects, & plus many laughable errors which I would not have." Some five years after their association began, Dreiser suggests an ambivalence in his feeling about his friend who both delighted and exasperated him. In the Afterword, there is ample evidence, for the first time fully exposed, for this ambivalence. No friendship rides constantly on a lofty road of complete commitment; both Dreiser and Henry were complicated personalities with all too many contradictions, and in the Afterword, Mr. Oakes has contributed an absorbing analysis of a relationship that was vital to both men.

Neda M. Westlake, General Editor
Sister Carrie, The Pennsylvania Edition

ACKNOWLEDGMENTS

The recognition of those whose interest, encouragement, shared memories, and generous advice has made possible the writing of this saga is tinged with sadness that so many names have been lost with the passage of time—librarians at the New York Public Library, directors of historical societies, newspaper archivists, Dreiser scholars with whom research was shared, the Henrys in Yakima who responded to a blanket plea for family anecdotes, countless on the Mountain Top who willingly shared memorabilia and memories, and more.

Breast pounded thrice and *mea culpas* intoned, let me then speak of those who are yet remembered before they, too, are swallowed in memory's dark recesses:

Elsie Shaver, who started me down the Platte Clove road with her suggestion that I might find *The House in the Woods* an interesting read; *Beverly Gore,* who introduced me to the Mountain Top and shared in the early years of the search for the real Arthur Henry; *Martin J. Farrell,* for making available the Anna Mallon/Delia Farrell letters that transformed the chronicle of the House into a tale worth telling; *Alf Evers,* who saw beneath the book's romantic portrayals and found contributions that added new dimensions to Mountain Top history and culture; the *Directors of the Mountain Top Historical Society* whose patience and support provided the incentive to complete what had begun so many years earlier.

Professor *Robert Elias,* for sharing archival data and photographs accumulated for his biography of Theodore Dreiser, but equally for his correspondence with Maude Wood Henry which continued beyond that book's publication until her death; *Neda Westlake,* whose instant recognition that research into Arthur Henry could be of value to Dreiser scholarship, but chiefly for wise counsel that just as quickly was transformed into valued friendship; *Richard Lingeman,* distinguished Dreiser biographer, whose attribution of this work "as a labor of love by that vanishing breed, the dedicated amateur scholar" made my chest swell with a humility hardly distinguishable from pride.

Others on the near side of the manuscript's completion made valued contributions to its publication: *Michael McCurdy*, friend of some years standing, for the print that seemed destined in its creation to grace this book's cover; *Walter Hilton Scott*, friend and collaborator on other publishing projects, who photographed and enhanced every image collected relating to *The House in the Woods*, including all appearing in this volume; *Penelope N. Lord*, who was not fazed by the daunting task of transcribing the text of the 1904 book, faithfully adhering to its often archaic grammar, spelling, punctuation, and usage; *Lori Anander, Matina Billias, Patricia Davis, Susan Hartung* and *Steven Hoare*, copyeditors *extraordinaire*, whose obsessive diligence has made both Arthur Henry and me seem better writers than we were; and *Debbie Allen* of Black Dome Press, whose personal attention, lavished I'm sure on all her titles, but for *The House in the Woods* and this writer it seemed as though no others existed. My sincere thanks to these, co-workers in bringing *The House in the Woods* to publication.

and finally...

My wife, *Betty*, whose love of the Catskills and the Mountain Top came to reflect (and often exceed) my own enthusiasms, whose patient assurance of the value of the research made impossible that it not be brought to completion, and who rarely saw in me reflections of Arthur Henry—for which I am and will continue to be grateful.

Justine Hommel, who is surpassed by none as the reigning and unchallenged scholar of the Mountain Top and upper Catskills. I consider her worthy of designation as a national treasure. As with all who have dared to write of Mountain Top history and lore, I too have received from her knowledge, direction, advice, and encouragement. I count as a special gift, however, a friendship that has remained firm and unwavering for more than a quarter of a century.

Donald T. Oakes
Stockbridge, Mass.
May 1, 2000

FOREWORD

My involvement with *The House in the Woods* and its author began simply enough. The year was 1975. A Catskills neighbor, aware of the time and energy I had invested in the restoration of a former summer cottage, suggested that I read the charming memoir of a young writer's not dissimilar struggles to build a house on Tannersville's Platte Clove road seventy or so years earlier. Not only would I be comforted by the knowledge that it had ever been thus for amateur builders, she said, but also that I would enjoy his perceptive insights into turn-of-the-century Tannersville; for, among many things, the book was an affectionate cataloguing of neighbors, tradesmen, and craftsmen who travelled the Platte Clove road, familiar names and families that have continued into the present.

When some weeks later I came upon *The House in the Woods* in the depths of a local used book repository, my curiosity whetted by her enthusiasms, I purchased it, read the volume in one sitting, and the quest had begun.

Now, more than two decades later, it is apparent that what had begun as merely a casual curiosity about a brief, romantic moment in the long history of the Catskills' Mountain Top became the start of a journey that was to encompass the breadth of our nation—from Noank, Connecticut, to Yakima, Washington—and that my first innocent conversation with a local librarian/historian would lead to countless others with newspaper editors and archivists, with university scholars, librarians, and authors, with the President of the Women's Christian Temperance Union, and even with the granddaughter of the book's author. And, if the search is ended, it is not because there is not more to learn, but because for me the time has come to leave the quest to others.

The details of the search can be found in the Afterword. For the moment, however, the reader will best be served by approaching the volume as the author intended it should be read and appreciated, and accepting him as he represents himself. Certainly it was on these terms and conditions that my enthusiasms were kindled.

The outline of the book is deceptively simple: the author identifies him-self as a struggling and unpublished writer who is invited to share an early fall vacation with two dear friends—Nancy and Elizabeth—at Meadow Lawn, the farm and boarding house of Thomas Seifferth and his wife, Sydney, on the Platte Clove road. "Now," says Arthur Henry, "at this time I received fifty dollars for my first magazine article—an unexpected success after more than fifteen years of disappointment. Three hours after the money was in my hands I was on the train for the mountains."[1] The year was 1899.

Later that fall, captivated by the magic of the Catskills and the beauty of the Valley of the Plattekill, Arthur Henry purchased two and a half acres from the Seifferths for two hundred and fifty dollars, and made a commitment to build a house worth at least eight hundred dollars within two years. The down-payment was provided by Nancy, a successful New York City business-woman, head of her own "copying office" (i.e., secretarial service). Immediately, ground was cleared, a chimney built for one hundred and twen-ty-five dollars (undoubtedly again underwritten by Nancy), and the shell of the House in the Woods started. Work is still underway when the trio leaves the Catskills for a three-year absence, not to return until the spring of 1903.

In this interim, the three had become two—Arthur Henry and Nancy—with only a brief, cryptic explanation offered for the third member's absence: "During these three years ... we had lost Elizabeth."[2]

Between Arthur's growing success as a writer and Nancy's continuing suc-cess in her copying office, more than seven thousand dollars had been saved between them, enough for Nancy to take an extended vacation so that she and Arthur could spend at least the next year realizing their postponed dream of a house in the woods where they could " ... watch the sun drop behind Hunter Mountain, listen to the call of men, the barking of dogs from far and near as the cows of the country-side were driven home, see the forms of things swallowed by the darkness, and the lights of distant dwellings appear through the valley and part way up the mountain slopes."[3]

Concluded by a glorious chopping bee in the early winter of 1903, it is that year the book records. It was published in April 1904.

My enchantment with *The House in the Woods* was nurtured in a number of ways. On a most superficial level, I was intrigued that a book could be pub-lished at the turn of the century that described, even if discreetly, a *ménage a trois* that apparently elicited not the slightest reprobation from the rural folk who were neighbors and friends, traditionally the most conservative and morally reproving segment of our social structure. Although in the book he protected his companions by the use of their first names only, Arthur Henry could not possibly have shielded them from the myriad of casual or intimate encounters that would inevitably occur in the course of any given week; and yet their presence in the Platte Clove/Tannersville enclaves prompted no such response, no evidence of social outrage. Indeed, quite the opposite was the case. Reminiscences of the House in the Woods continue in the memories of those whose ancestors watched and assisted in its building in the shadow of High Peak, and they are for the most part gentle, affectionate recollections.

If titillation was intended as a minor objective, then I am convinced that Arthur Henry failed in this.

On another level, the deeper into the book I read the more I realized that the love for this place, for these mountains, which he expressed with such sensitivity, was that same emotion that some seventy years later churned within me; but, within me, it became a force that denied speech, as if to describe in words what the eye saw and the heart felt would rob it of its uniqueness. And so, it was with welcome abandon that I accepted Arthur Henry as my spokesman, confident in the knowledge that his eyes saw the very same mountains and valleys and streams, that the seasons changed no differently for him than for me, that we stared at the same night skies, that our vistas were often shrouded by the same mists, and I was grateful that he could express in words that which I could only feel. I do believe that few have written of the magic and majesty of the Mountain Top better than he.

Shortly before my introduction to *The House in the Woods* and its author, I made my first visit to the site of the Catskill Mountain House. As I stood there looking eastward over Palenville, past the silver ribbon that was the Hudson River, and into the Taconic and Berkshire Hills beyond, I felt overwhelmed, unable to assimilate all that lay before me. Two weeks or so later, still haunted by that first visit, I returned to the site with a friend, anxious to share with him what had been so compelling for me. The day was an even more glorious one; yet, somehow and in a way I could not explain, that second visit marred the integrity of the first. I wished I had not returned.

Still haunted by the strangeness of this response, I found I was set free by Arthur Henry's account of his, Nancy's, and Elizabeth's climb to the top of the timbered tower that then stood on High Peak:

I have never cared to visit High Peak again. One such appalling view of the world is enough for me. I am glad to know that our earth is but an insignificant speck of dust ... But for the few years here still left for me, I wish to feel that its land and seas, its gardens, its forests, and its fields are real; that in the spring the apple blossoms are rose-tinted, and in the fall one may pick up pippins by hunting in the grass; that my neighbors live near me; that there are pies in the pantry, oil in the lamps, wood in the woodshed, and a book open on the table where I laid it down. All this seems impossible on High Peak.[4]

I was buoyed by the knowledge that another was able to know and express that which I had felt so keenly, but so dumbly.

As evident in the above passage, however sensitive may be his descriptions of the world about him, above all else, Arthur Henry was a social animal, and his world view demanded friends and neighbors. Like the tree that exists only because there are ears to hear the sound of its falling, so I believe he would willingly defend the thesis that nature, the world, depends for its existence on people to live in it. *The House in the Woods* is dominated by his respect and genuine affection for all those whom he met and knew. Indeed, the word portraits of his friends and neighbors are the book's greatest treasure.

It would have been so easy for *The House in the Woods* to have become a turn-of-the-century *Mr. Blandings Builds His Dream House*, concentrating on the foibles and idiosyncracies of its cast of characters; or for Arthur Henry to have titillated his readers by playing the role of a 1904 Truman Capote, an aloof intellectual who eavesdrops on the lives of country folk. But the book is none of these things, for Arthur Henry presents himself as one who sees good in all men—far more so than are they able to see good in each other. "No one could have better neighbors than mine ... " he writes. "They have watched over this place as though it were their own, making no apologies for their advice, giving it directly and peremptorily, but always in a kindly spirit that has made it all inexpressibly pleasant ... And yet," he adds, "these people are not any too friendly among themselves."[5]

Because of this, he and Nancy saw their House in the Woods as a potential healing force in the Valley of the Plattekill, as a possible focal point for reconciliation:

[We] had built the House in the Woods. The country had brought a new balm to our lives. What could we bring to theirs? We knew the narrowness, the suspicions and jealousies which are bred of isolated life. The generation that once gave life to Platte Clove has grown old and more or less estranged by childish feuds, but we were a new family in the valley, and we fortunately escaped the influence of its warring elements. The House in the Woods was built in a friendly spirit, and when it was finished and thrown open [to] all the friendliness of the region it could serve as a common meeting-place for pleasure and not toil … [6]

Such was the vision to be realized, Arthur Henry might have rationalized, by the writing of a book that spoke ill of none.

If he spoke good of all, Arthur Henry spoke best of the Convery family. The Converys! How strange that this should be, for in my early research I was so often interrupted by a recurring rumor which had survived seven decades and at least three generations that an attempt had been made to halt publication of the book because it ridiculed the Convery clan. "That man said," the rumor ran, "that the Converys kept a pig in their kitchen." "Did they?" I would ask. "Well, yes," the reply inevitably would be, "but he shouldn't have written about it."

Arthur Henry did say that the Converys had a pig in their kitchen; more than that, he also said that there was a sick chicken under the stove and that their doorway was "swarming with chickens, ducks, geese, pigs, and calves. Sometimes, when a cold north wind is blowing, fifty or a hundred of these animals stand in the sunlight in the shelter of the house, as close to the south wall as may be. When the door opens, a chicken or a pig sometimes slips in." [7] But if this is the basis for the rumor, then it is apparent that the book had never been read by those who spread it, for it is on the Converys that Arthur Henry lavishes his most affectionate writing.

The disorder and disrepair of their house, in large part made of packing crates and scrap, obviously continued into the twenties at least, for one local resident told me, "When I was a kid, the Converys' place was the gauntlet— pigs or drinks, because they sold cider there during Prohibition." Yet, I must believe that the warmth and beauty of that almost outcast family continued as well, and that it conquered the gossip and rumor that could have exiled it. When John Convery, three years old at the time the book was written and the last survivor of the family that Arthur and Nancy knew, died not long before I began my search, he was acknowledged by all as "the best darned cabinetmaker on the Mountain Top," and always this was said with affectionate respect.

Arthur Henry describes a late afternoon spent with the Convery children waiting for their parents to return from haying. "Suddenly we heard someone whistling a tune … A little later we saw shadowy forms approaching down the road, and heard their muffled footsteps in the dust … They were close before they saw us. Hughie and Mrs. Convery walked hand in hand … Her feet were bare … Her waist was open at the throat. She wore no hat or bonnet, but on her gray hair was a cloth of gay colors, made something like a turban … "[8]

As Arthur Henry taught me to see what he saw, even today I cannot drive the Platte Clove road at dusk on a fall evening without expecting to see, coming around a bend, the Converys, walking hand in hand.

If *The House in the Woods* is a bridge to a cherished past, then one must wonder what it is that gives the book its contemporary quality, for it does not read as a work written almost a century ago. Perhaps it is because the world in which Arthur Henry wrote bears striking similarities to our own. Brainwashed by years of "Remember the Maine!" and Teddy Roosevelt's cavalry charge, we have forgotten how unpopular the Spanish-American War was. While not as extensive in time or casualties as the war in Vietnam, its impact on our national conscience—particularly on the conscience of youth —was hardly dissimilar. Arthur Henry records a conversation with Will Gillespie, whose later life as a recluse was merely an extension of a loss of confidence in society that began in his youth: "I guess I'm not patriotic," Will told him. "I don't sympathize with this country since the Spanish War. I can cut a good deal of wood in a day, but still, I don't seem to be strenuous enough for the life out there."[9]

Or, if our age at times has seemed under attack by rebellious youth, let us not forget that at the turn of the century the harbingers of social protest and change were the "Bohemians"; and their assault on cherished values bears striking similarity to the challenges associated with our "flower children" and "hippies". And, if the probings of latterday investigative reporters have given just cause for a loss of confidence and trust in our business and political leadership, let us not forget that Arthur Henry wrote in that time when the "Muckrakers" were making their appearance on the American scene, ferreting out corruption and dishonesty like avenging angels. (Indeed, it seems more than likely that Ida Tarbell's *History of the Standard Oil Company*, one of the classic muckraker exposés, was written in part in the House in the

Woods.)[10] Perhaps the book reads as if it were written yesterday because our worlds are so similar.

Or, perhaps it is that the idealism of Arthur Henry strikes a responsive chord deep inside each of us when he says: "Imprisoned youth forever longs to travel. All that we have hoped for, and that eludes us, exists in our imagination somewhere beyond our horizon … For everyone there is somewhere a portion of the earth, encompassed in a glance, where the power that created him … fashioned a living home … "[11]

That yearning is timeless, and historically has led men to shatter frontiers, even the frontiers of space; but particularly is it a yearning that afflicts modern man who lives in an age of mobility in which "belonging"—no longer intrinsic to our society—has become a goal to be attained. "Home towns", the mythic locale of belonging, the places men seek to return to, seem no longer to exist. Perhaps it is a book that reads as if it were written yesterday because it speaks to each of us of our yearning, of our hope, that somewhere there is a portion of earth where a living home can be fashioned, and that it will be found in time.

Perhaps all of this is why, in the book's final pages, Arthur Henry dedicates the volume: "To sincere pilgrims upon the dusty highways, and to those who, while caught in the tangle of the world's concerns, still cling to the dreams of youth, I offer these pages with confidence, for in them there is, at least, one true picture of possession in the Eden they long for."[12]

And so, pilgrim, read and enjoy.

CHAPTER I

THE DREAM

ANCY and Bob have just passed by me, on their way to our neighbor Jack's. They are taking our mail to him. It is Sunday, and Jack, who for thirty years has not missed a service, will take our mail with him to the church and give it to his son, who comes over every Sunday from Tannersville, four miles away. Such are the time-tables and messenger calls of the country.

Nancy, in her red jacket, and Bob, in his magnificent winter coat—the coat of a collie—have passed between the little balsams and tall clumps of withered fern, adding color and movement to this exquisite scene, and changing its inherent tenderness into something personal and profound for me.

It is difficult to keep awake in this sheltered spot. A group of balsams break the chill west wind, but through their branches I can dwell with indolent eye upon the valley of the Plaaterkill. It is a far view, between unobtrusive mountain ranges, inclosing fields by the river, now green with the aftergrass, and little hills covered with timber. The wind cannot reach me. It sings and sighs in the balsams, and I can hear its voice in the forest close at hand. In this particular spot there is a singular majesty even in its softest murmurs; for I lie upon the borderland between the world where God still reigns alone, and that portion of his domain which mankind has preempted—the wilderness and civilization, the unknown and the known.

I am on the edge of my meadow. Along the road that skirts it at the base of the hill I can see my neighbors—midgets in the distance—passing on their way to church. Among the trees just back of me—visible through the tentative clearings I have made—is the nest we have built. Not fifty feet farther begins abruptly a world of dense forest—vast in reality, covering thousands upon thousands of actual acres, and endless, to all purposes, because of the rocky ledges and entangled growth that make its recesses impenetrable. The sound of the wind that reaches me near at hand extends, I know, through all that mysterious wilderness. Each plaintive murmur or joyous gust carries me on long pilgrimages through those forest depths. The warm autumn sunshine falls upon me unbroken. I wake and doze, I meditate and dream. This is a little hour after months of toil—a tranquil hush in the midst of whirlwinds—a nugget of pure gold amid the litter of the mine, piled and scattered by days of incessant delving.

Not far away I can hear the noise of a hundred fussing chickens. This sunny hollow in the shelter of the balsams is one alcove in my palace of dreams. In another, not twenty feet away, are my pig-pens.

I am, in fact, upon a second borderland. Behind me lie the years of hope-vague, expectant, and intangible. Before is realization. All that life can mean to any one, this hillside is to me.

One very hot summer, some years ago, Nancy and Elizabeth deserted me, going for August and September into the mountains. I remained in New York alone, because I was too poor to follow them. Their occasional letters, read amidst the heat and noise and nervous tension of the city, tempted me with visions of cool forests and mountain brooks. I missed these companions dear to me.

In September, Nancy wrote that the summer boarders had gone; the mountains were beginning to assume their greatest beauty; the solemnity of the forests was no longer disturbed by voices. Peace lay upon the meadows of the valley. The days were the warm, lazy days of fall; the nights were cold.

This letter spoke to me with a familiar voice, friendly, tender, and beseeching.

Now, at this time I received fifty dollars for my first magazine article—an unexpected success after more than fifteen years of disappointment. Three hours after the money was in my hands I was on the train for the mountains. It was then hot in New York, but I had been warned to bring warm clothing. It was night when I stepped from the train in Tannersville, and a frosty air assailed my nostrils.

It was past the season when people flocked to the mountains, and I was the only passenger to alight. A rugged old man, your ideal of a farmer in these stormy altitudes, was revealed to me by the light of the lantern he carried. Thick locks of white hair and a heavy beard gave to his large head the look of a patriarch. His skin was as red and as wholesome as that of a winter apple. The wind flapped the tails of his thick ulster and slapped the brim of his slouch-hat sharply upon his cheeks. The light, hanging below his knees, cast his shadow heavenward, transforming him for a moment into a god of the weather. This was Thomas Seifferth, whom I was seeking. He led me to the stage. A heavy pair of black horses drew us swiftly from the station. There was no long drive through a city's streets. Immediately upon crossing the track, we passed over a brawling stream, ascended a sharp grade, and were rolling along a mountain road outside the village. The night was black around us, but though I could not see, I received an unmistakable sense of my surroundings. I could feel the tip of the vehicle and hear the grating of the brake as we passed down abrupt descents. I could feel the straining of the horses as we again ascended. The thin, frosty air laden with the perfume of the fir-trees, the distant sound of the wind in elevated forests, spoke unmistakably of the mountains.

Wrapped in my overcoat, in the back seat of the stage, I gazed wide-eyed into the night, pricked my ears to its weird noises, and experienced one of those thrilling periods of unreasoning rapture that come to happy men— unafraid, and still expectant, in their happiness. It is difficult to give tangible form to what this plunge into the heart of the Catskills meant to me. For every youth who reads there is a geography of the imagination, which, inch by inch, does battle with the atlas.

It was to Washington Irving that I owed my conception of the Catskill Mountains. In spite of the detailed knowledge and the actual experiences of later years, they had, until this time of my first visit, remained for me a portion of that far-off fantastic region containing Andalusia, the Bay of Naples, Loch Lomond, the Forest of Arden, and all the countless spots known to my youth, and yet unvisited.

Books were transparencies through which I beheld visions. I am no longer a dreamer. The years have wrought this change in me. Then imagination was everything; to-day reality is more. It is true that youth is illuminated by illusions—candles upon a shrine—and that age extinguishes them. There are unfortunates who, when these are all out, are in the dark. I am one of those who hold to my illusions until I can replace them by brighter realities. One by one, these candles have grown dim for me in the blaze of day.

For half an hour I could see nothing but the heroic outlines of the old man before me, and the immediate roadway, unevenly lighted by the swinging lantern hanging from the stage.

We followed the road around an abrupt turn. A dim light—that of a smoky lamp—shone from a corner window, revealing a tavern barroom. I afterward learned that this was Gaffey's Corner, named from the old innkeeper, and that here began the valley of the Plaaterkill. The frosty atmosphere and nipping wind, at first refreshing after the heat of the city, penetrated my clothes and sent a shiver through me. My surprised body began to ache with the cold. The road rose and fell over a constant succession of hills. At the foot of one of these declines we came upon a white farm-house so close to the roadway that our lantern disclosed its huge proportions. The upper stories were dark, but along its entire length, under the comfortable porches, the windows of the ground floor shone with a cheerful light.

To my delight, the horses stopped, and immediately a door of the house swung open.

"Did he come?" asked a familiar voice—Nancy's—clear and penetrating.

"Is it you?" asked Elizabeth, her softer tones scarcely reaching me because of a gust that swept between.

I should like to paint that doorway and the figures in it. The years, in passing, leave their pictures behind, and it is by these that we remember. Of them we select certain sacred ones, and make of them our Stations of the Cross. For me, at least, whose life has been a wandering one, the homing instinct has not attached itself to any place, but finds its satisfaction in the simple presence of affection.

It so chanced that the attitude of Nancy and Elizabeth—one of waiting in the doorway—gave a true expression to the spirit of peace and contentment that reposed in our companionship—peace and contentment, the blessed ones! Wherever Nancy, Elizabeth, and I might be together, these two invisible graces were also.

Elizabeth took my satchel—her soft brown eyes aglow. When Elizabeth is undisturbed by emotion, her face is grave with the gravity of a dreaming child; when she is pleased, delight plays over her countenance like a band of mischievous imps. The mouth, small in repose, becomes very large, the lips moist, full, and rosy. The quiet contour of her cheeks is broken by dimples.

I presume that up to this time, during the twenty-two years she had lived, Elizabeth had never restrained an impulse, and that, though at times impulsive, there had been no thought or act of hers that might not be exposed at noon of May-day, when all her native countryside make merry on the village green. It is seldom that you can look into a mature eye and see there no hint of withholding or of challenge, no play of question or reserve. The eyes of Elizabeth were never disturbed in their tranquillity except by the impulse of play; and then the spirit of mischief was no more subtle than that of a child hiding where it can readily be seen.

Elizabeth is as tall as I, heavily built, slow and easy in her ordinary moods and motions.

Nancy is very short. A heavy mass of hair, gathered as a crown upon her head, came scarcely to my chin as she stood before me, making unconscious and useless efforts to help me remove my coat; and yet in this small creature there are as many conflicting personalities as there are Elizabeths in the world.

Elizabeth has lived a singularly quiet life; Nancy, an active one. At the age of thirty-seven she seemed very old or very young, according to the spirit that possessed her. Fifteen years' daily association with the business life of New York had given her a knowledge of the world, which she used half in cynicism, half in regret at the loss of those illusions that haunted her romantic youth. The play of emotions in such a nature is too swift and discordant to catch and create a truthful image of them. In the space of a few hours, in the conduct of her copying-office in New York, I have seen her both tender and savage, generous and unjust. The years of business had clothed her with an outward personality made somewhat uniform by the grip with which a passionate nature and proud will sometimes seizes upon conflicting moods, and holds them quivering in the semblance of a form.

Commercially, she was shrewd, enlivening her autocratic methods by a nimble wit, and counteracting her wit by the gracious manner of its delivery. She was artful and faithful. Her word and her work could be relied upon. Her prices were enormous. She was at home in commercial New York, which is liberal and exacting.

In all of us, to begin with, there are conflicting spirits. For many, fifteen years are a sufficient time for one of these spirits, in active service, to dethrone the others, if not to obliterate them. Perhaps it was the amazing vitality of Nancy's nature that preserved its complexity intact. Deprived of exercise, almost unnoticed, all the gracious spirits of an aspiring, affectionate, and beauty-loving youth had remained with her, communing together in their seclusion, smiling in their sleep. Sometimes they would awaken and call to her whom they inhabited. It was because, in reality, these voices were the ones most appealing to her that Nancy, for fifteen years, had chafed at her surroundings. Quick to give and quick to resent, generous on impulse and not on principle, her friendship with women did not last.

Elizabeth, since she had parted from her brothers and sisters, had neither known or cared for any other companionship than Nancy's. Nancy, with an almost unlimited acquaintance, maintained a pleasant position in a friendly commercial world, but had few friends. When Nancy is alone with Elizabeth and me, she becomes youthful and sincere. Her features, then no longer sharp and aggressive, artful or elusive, are lost in their detail. It is her countenance alone I see, made winsome and companionable by those secluded spirits that come forth to visit me.

This was the Nancy and Elizabeth whom I found waiting in the door.

We do not usually analyze the people we meet. Most of us, busy only with our own desires, see that only in others which aids or hinders us, forming our likes and dislikes from this selfish standpoint. We penetrate other personalities so long as there is no resistance to our own, saying to ourselves, "These people are agreeable." We recoil at that in others which conflicts with ourselves. But whether those we meet are agreeable or disagreeable, it is of ourselves, and not of them, that we are thinking most. There is Myself and the rest of the world. I am an individual, well defined and of great importance. Those about me come and go in the multitude. That is why our neighbors—for the most of us—are ordinary people, and the characters we read about always seem unusual. It is the conduct of our neighbor that concerns us, and not his motives. We would rather judge than understand him. And how elemental is this judgement! We pronounce him good if he aids in our desires, and evil if he hinders them. It is in this that authors serve the world. They save us the trouble of forgetting ourselves, and help us to see our neighbor as he is.

I say all this, fearing that my brief analysis of Nancy and Elizabeth has made them seem unusual to you. The fact is, we were three very ordinary people, fond of each other, and glad to be together in this quiet place. We were like those acquaintances of yours you nod to and forget; like those in a multitude you pass by unnoticed.

Sentiment is very much the same anywhere. In so far as a man feels it and yields to it, his dreams and longings are the dreams and longings of the whole world. This is why a poem becomes popular, a song journeys from lip to lip; why whole audiences weep and laugh together.

If Nancy, Elizabeth, and I were unusual, it was not in our manners or appearance, in our desires or ideals, but in our devotion to that which seemed beautiful and good to us, and our disregard of the mere forms of propriety, of necessity and duty.

Most of those who fill the mountains in the summer believe that they love the country for its quiet beauty; and yet they go where the crowd is, creating for themselves a season of excitement, destroying the nature of the place they visit with their noise and bustle, driving the foxes to their holes.

Nancy, believing also that she loved the country for its quiet beauty, waited until the boarders were gone, and went to Seifferth's when its summer sign, "The Meadow Lawn," had been removed, and it became a fine old farmhouse in the heart of the valley of the Plaaterkill.

She went there usually in September, although this was the beginning of the busiest season in the year. Reckless in her expenses, extravagant the year around, possessing nothing of the money she had made—once in the country, she remained there for two and three months at a time, forgetful of the city she had left, caring nothing for the damage to her business, or the money she lost by her absence. For a successful woman this may have been unusual.

I thought little of all this as the girls greeted me on my arrival. I saw only before me the unchanging Elizabeth and the Nancy I love best to see.

They led me into a comfortable country sitting-room, made doubly so by the large box-stove that warmed it.

In the city, after a cold night ride, you may enter a warm room, and that is something; but you will miss the best of the reception I received. There is something more than warmth that issues from burning wood—something fragrant and soothing. The roar of the fire is a cheerful sound. A wood-box, heaping full, was in itself a picture of plenty and fine prospects. It had the air of a fat landlord, with a full bottle in his hand, saying, "Let's make a night of it, my friend."

There were three chairs close by the stove, two in which Nancy and Elizabeth had been waiting—the third for me. I held my numbed hands to the stove, and smiled into those eyes of brown and blue. Elizabeth yawned, laughed sheepishly, and yawned again.

"I was asleep," she said. She closed her eyes, and in a moment more was in the tranquil doze that readily came to her.

Nancy, wakeful and alive, sat close beside me, the hue of pleasure coloring her cheeks.

"How much is the board?" I asked.

"Well," said Nancy, "we have the three rooms I like best in the house, and Mrs. Seifferth said we could have them for seven dollars a week. It is after the season, you know."

"Well," said I, "I can stay six weeks."

"Think of it!" said Nancy, six thousand years of anticipation darkening her eyes.

"Or five weeks, anyway," I qualified.

"Oh!" said Nancy. "One week gone already!"

"Well, it might be six. I have a return ticket and about forty-three dollars. Six weeks would take forty-two."

"Of course," said Nancy, promptly, "there will be a dollar to Libbie and a dollar to the cook."

"That leaves me bankrupt and in debt."

I saw a familiar expression in Nancy's face. She was about to speak, caught my eye, hesitated, smiled, and was silent.

"No," I said; "you will not lend it to me. One magazine has accepted my article and it may take another. I have an article out with a second magazine and another with a third."

These prospects were certainties for Nancy. Anticipation, unlimited and sure, returned.

"You could not see the mountains," she said.

"No; it was very dark."

"The moon will rise at one o'clock."

We heard, in the hall outside, the thumping of a cane, the sound of slippers pushed slowly over the floor. I looked at Nancy.

"It is Mrs. Seifferth," she said; and then, in a whisper, "Rheumatism."

The door opened, and Mrs. Seifferth appeared, leaning on the door-knob and her cane. She was old, stooped, very fat, and suffering from a painful disease that crippled her; but with my first sight of her, none of these things, so evident to the eye, were noticed. The personality of this woman was neither old nor fat nor lame. It ignored age and infirmity. An indefinable impression of strength, of breadth, crude wisdom, shrewdness, and good sense, attended her.

"I guess you can find your room," she said. "I won't bother to sit up for you."

"Are they the ones I asked for?" asked Nancy.

"Take any ones you want," she replied good-naturedly. "You can arrange it between you. You can have breakfast when you get up."

I felt that I had been presented to her. With no other introduction than this, she closed the door, and we heard her laboriously climb the stairs.

"I thought Mr. Seifferth was a German," I said.

"He was born in Germany, and she in Ireland. They have been in this country for more than fifty years, and have lived together for about forty."

"And they live amiably?"

"Yes, very, it seems to me."

Comfort and contentment are insidious things. Some two hours later I awoke to find the fire burned out—Nancy and Elizabeth were both asleep.

I went into the hall and drew the front door open. The light from our sitting-room windows cut pathways through the darkness across a little patch of lawn, a roadway, a low brush fence, and was lost among the trunks of a dense forest just beyond. I could see indistinctly tall trees whose branches I could only imagine towering somewhere above the circle of light, and, close to the ground, the massive, somber foliage of the evergreens. More than this I could not have distinguished in the daytime; for though I loved the forest, it was unknown to me. I was like the lover who adores before he knows her name. This dark night, I thought, what does it conceal from me? Are these mountains austere, forbidding? Is their charm at hand? May I gaze on beauty idly here, or must I seek for it?

The wind in the forest made a partial answer. Its uneven gusts among the trees near by produced a familiar sound, such as I had heard in the groves and woodlands of the Middle States; but above these pleasing murmurs came an incessant roar as from an inconceivable distance, descending from far-off heights.

The desire of years rose to this sound, and held me thrilled and spellbound.

"It is the wind," said Nancy. She had been standing by me unnoticed for some time. I saw her trembling with the cold. Her eyes were heavy now with sleep.

"Come," I said; "let's go to bed."

"It is only an hour before the moon will rise."

"There will be other nights and moons, my dear. Let's go to bed."

We routed Elizabeth from her chair, and Nancy, taking the lamp from the mantel, led the way up-stairs, two flights.

"I asked for these three rooms," she said, "at the back, because they look out upon the valley and the mountains."

I scarcely remember getting into bed, for the wind and the warmth had finished me. I was awakened by Nancy's voice.

"The moon is up," she said. "Go to your window and look out."

The spectacle revealed by the moonlight was more like those we must sleep to see. Just beyond the meadow beneath me ran a succession of graceful mounds, and back of these what might have been a vast cloth of purple velvet flung here upon the earth, standing in huge, exquisite folds, maintaining its position by the thickness of its texture. Possessing all the majesty of the mountains, this range had none of their austerity. They were as comfortable as the undulations of a meadow. Impassable except through certain cloves, they gave no hint of imprisonment. They seemed entreating you to stay in this alluring valley. There was no coercion in their soft outlines.

A little above the meadow between my window and the mountains, clouds like silver dust passed down the valley.

There are two great instincts that have so far shaped the destinies of mankind—the instincts to pray and to wander. We are told that the one proves the existence of a God. What, then, does the other prove? The earth was discovered, piece by piece, by man seeking an Eldorado. Imprisoned youth forever longs to travel. All that we have hoped for, and that eludes us, exists in our imagination somewhere beyond our horizon. Does this instinct, as old at that of prayer, prove that for every one there is somewhere a portion of the earth, encompassed in a glance, where the power that created him has from the earth and sky fashioned a living home, where all things assume forms pleasing to the eye, where individual notes are melodious, and the multiple sounds make harmony; where the soil is friendly, and its fruits are sweet; where the sunshine and the rain alike bring health, and the year contentment?

If such a nook exists for me, I thought, it is here in this moonlit valley.

CHAPTER II

A Venture At Random

HERE were three windows in my room, and they were open. When I awoke in the morning my bed was flooded with sunlight, and I felt upon my face movements of air, cool, soft, and odorous. I heard the girls moving in the adjoining rooms.

"Hello!" I called.

"Hurry up," said Nancy; "we are going for a plunge."

I dragged my clothes to a window, dressing as I looked. The sun was about half an hour high, hanging just above the forest slope of High Peak. The long range I had seen in the moonlight, inclosing the valley to the south, shone, here and there, where the sides swelled outward in the morning light, revealing solid masses of rich foliage in many shades of green. The mighty hollows where the sun had not yet penetrated, and the sharp recesses that marked the individuals of this range, were of a uniform hue, their forests invisible through a purple veil of mist.

"All right," I called. "I am ready."

"Got your towel?" asked Nancy, at the same time entering and taking one from my wash-stand which she wrapped about her own and Elizabeth's.

"Where to?" I asked.

"I know a pool. We go there twice a day. In the morning for a plunge, and early in the afternoon, when it's warm, for a bath."

As we passed the open dining-room door I caught a whiff of breakfast from the kitchen beyond, and stood for a moment sniffing.

"Sausages and pancakes, I'll bet," I said.

"They are awful good, too," replied Elizabeth, who stood near me, sniffing sympathetically.

Outside we heard the noise of a chain-pump in rapid motion, and saw an angular young woman turning the crank. Her free left arm jerked violently, acting as a balance-wheel. She bent her knees and contorted her wiry body in abandonment to her task. I saw her thin face as she peered over her shoulder at us. I instantly recognized the type.

"Here is a homely woman," I thought, "who expects no consideration except what she earns. She is a slave of nature. She will wear her fingers to the bone in endless labor. She will run to do a favor. She expects nothing. She is brimming with good-will and a senseless, unreasoning joy."

"Libbie," said Nancy, "here he is."

She gave the wheel two more violent turns until the water, plunging from the spout, filled the pail. Then she wiped her hand on her apron and gave it to me, tittering like a school-girl.

"They've been looking for you awful keen," she said.

"Well, I'm glad to get here."

"I'll bet you are!"

"We'll be back in half an hour," said Nancy, pointing to her towels.

Libbie shivered and laughed.

"All right," she said, snatching up the pail; "I'll have a good breakfast for you."

She extended her scrawny left arm like a balancing-pole, and hurried to the house with the long, loping gait that keeps a full pail from slopping.

As we turned the corner of the house, I saw my patriarch coming across the meadow from the barn, carrying two milk-pails almost full. I heard the sound of a bell, and saw the cows pass slowly from the milking-yard down the road and turn into a hillside pasture-lot bounded in the distance by the forest-line. Behind the cows walked a man and a dog. In another portion of the great meadow surrounding us a number of calves were grazing. I heard the whinny of a horse in the barn. This early morning in the country, so expressive of its poetry, recalled the tenderest memories of my youth, and awoke the desires still strongest in me.

"Oh, me! oh, my!" I exclaimed; "why aren't we living this way?"

"Where you going?" asked Mr. Seifferth, a genial German nature speaking through his voice, his broad smile and kindly eyes.

"To the pool for a plunge," said Nancy.

"Oh, by tunner! now," he said; "I wouldn't do that."

"But we have been doing it right along."

"Well, well! Ain'd it cold?"

"It warms you up."

"Oh, I think it would kill me." He laughed at the idea.

We followed a winding path through the meadow, crossed a rushing brook by means of stepping-stones, and came to a second field, round, secluded, completely encircled by trees. The mountains rose about us like the sides of a bowl. At the opposite edge of the field we passed through an opening in the forest, made by an almost unused roadway. Turning to the right, by a path through the underbrush made by Nancy and Elizabeth, we came upon a small opening upon the bank of a creek which here formed a pool four feet deep in the center. A thick carpet of grass covered the bank. The place was completely screened by flowering weeds and underbrush. At this time in the morning it was shaded by the surrounding beech- and maple-trees, whose branches covered it like a canopy high overhead.

The slanting sunshine of early morning filtered through the foliage, tempering the chill of this dewy recess. Moist grass-blades and leaves moving in the light breeze, exposed and shaded by the overhanging boughs, flashed in the sunlight and grew dull again. In the half-light of dawn, I had stumbled on the bath-room of the wood-nymphs. There was a sense of stirring, of palpitation, as if our entrance had startled some belated ones not yet vanished for the day. At some distance from the pool I stopped and waited beyond the screen of underbrush. A moment later I heard the splash of water, gasps, a burst of laughter, stifled cries of "Oh! oh!" "Ouch!" and "Oh, me!" then a scrambling on the bank and exclamations of exhilaration and relief.

"Was it good?" I asked as the girls reappeared.

"Great!" said Nancy.

Elizabeth hung the towels on a bush to dry.

"Here is yours," she said; "we will wait for you in the sunshine."

I was chilled before I undressed, and when I stood naked on the edge of the pool my body, stiff and hidebound with the cold, shrank from the icy plunge. I ran up and down my stretch of inclosure, increasing my speed as my legs became limber. I turned handsprings; first one, then two, then three, then five, in succession. I was panting and warm. A sense of limitless strength thrilled my nerves. My muscles took command of me. Seizing a heavy stone, I hurled it across the creek. I leaped in the air and shouted. I longed to uproot a tree with my hands and send it crashing through the forest. For the moment I was a healthy savage, a true child of the wilderness, who survives nakedness and exposure, finding his joy as an animal in his prowess.

"My clothes enfeeble me," I thought. "Out of cold and nakedness I have wrested this exhilaration." Again I felt the frosty air. A slight chill passed over me. I was standing still. Naked, I might leap and run, pursue my food, delight in conquest, abandon myself to wild instincts; but if I wished to stand still and meditate, I must put on my clothes.

The clear, cold water of the pool no longer repelled, but invited me. My skin was smooth and moist and warm. I fell headlong from the bank, grazed the pebbly bottom, rose to the surface, made haste for the shore, and rolled out upon the grass before the heat had left my blood. Only my skin was cooled. Aglow from head to foot, I rubbed myself briskly and dressed. The frosty air seemed like a warm south wind to me. The sounds and odors of the forest were increased for my enlivened senses. I listened eagerly and felt again the familiar sorrow of my ignorance. What were these sounds, these odors? What was the nature of this forest world? I could not distinguish the different fir-trees. Even the maple, which I recognized, and the beech, the birch, the ash, I guessed at, were strangers to me. These conspicuous things, with pronounced forms, ever present to the eye, I knew nothing of.

"If this earth was made for us," I thought, "it has been thrown away. One of these gnats over my head must know as much as most of us, or he would die. There are innumerable voices in these woods, and they are only sounds to me."

Nancy, Elizabeth, and I are good companions, because, instinctively sympathetic, we do not disturb each other's moods, provided our moods are pleasant. Made exceedingly comfortable in my body by the exercise and plunge, I walked through the brush to the field, joined the girls, and strolled back to the farm-house, unconscious of myself and of them. I was lost in the midst of this forest world, its vast proportions made visible by the heights it covered. I was an insect crawling through a grassy path, with this difference, perhaps—there was longing, hope, and purpose in my eyes. As we neared the house, this difference vanished. I smelled my breakfast, and my eyes would have done credit to a wasp.

I shook from me all sense of awe and ignorance, and heard again the mundane voices of Nancy and Elizabeth. I was hungry, and would be fed. We trooped into the dining-room, called lustily to Libbie, and fell to upon the cakes and sausages.

During the meal she stood near us, exuberant, awkward, unrestrained, joining in all we said, giggling when she spoke. There was a joyous lilt in her voice. Her eyes were luminous. She watched our plates, hurried often to the kitchen, as if on a secret mission of delight, keeping a hot cake always before us. And this was after a hard season of boarders! Her ceaseless activity, the long hours of toil, kept her scrawny, but had not checked the flow of her good-will.

The soul of this creature, unconscious of hardship and neglect, was not troubled by them. I had met her like before. There are many Libbies in the world. If married, they make happy mothers; if not, they usually become unhappy ones.

"She is so lean," I thought, "so ugly, so poor, so affectionate, so generous, so simple, what chance has she?"

That evening, as we were sitting by the stove, for the nights were cold and windy, I heard a peremptory whistle outside, and a few moments later the rustle of a skirt, a light, nervous step, in the hall. The outer door opened and closed. It was midnight when we went to bed, and Libbie had not returned.

It had been a happy day. We spent the morning in the sunshine, lying prone in the meadow. One must have pleasant thoughts and serene companions to be happy through each idle, uneventful hour. Early in the afternoon we went again to the pool to bathe. The grass was dry, the sheltered inclosure warm, the water brilliant in the sunlight. When we reached the spot I said:

"Nancy, this cold water is not good for you girls, unless you go into it warm."

"I don't know why it is," she answered, ruefully. "I like the idea of doing it, and I persist, but I never have experienced that glow you read about."

Elizabeth, looking at the pool, humped her shoulders and shivered.

"I do it," she gleefully protested, "because Nancy does."

"You must exercise," I said. "We'll play 'Follow the Leader.'"

"What's that?"

I took off my coat and shoes and turned a handspring.

"Of course," I said, "you can't do that now; but we will begin with simple things like hop-skip-jump and ordinary somersaults."

The girls removed their skirts and shoes, pulled up their stockings, adjusted their bloomers at the knees, and were ready. We ran around the inclosure, jumped over low bushes, fell headlong into them, played leapfrog, and turned somersaults, until the girls were hot and breathless. Then I went beyond the screen of underbrush and waited my turn to bathe. This time I heard no sounds of dismay.

During the bath of about five minutes their voices, evenly modulated, were heard in pleasant, simultaneous converse, such as the nimble feminine intellect can follow and enjoy.

"I got the glow," said Nancy, cheerily, as she came through the shrubs.

"Yes," chimed in Elizabeth; "that was all right."

A little later I found them waiting for me at the edge of the field. They were asleep in a warm hollow, their bodies in the sunshine, their faces shaded by their hats. I, too, was drowsy and was soon asleep. Some two hours later the sun dropped below the neighboring trees and their chilling shadows wakened us.

"Oh," sighed Nancy, "if we could only live like this!"

There was truly an appealing calm, a commanding beauty, in this still valley, with its composing and graceful mountain-sides. It was comfortable in the sunshine. We remained in the meadow, retreating now and then, with the advance of the shadows, until, after a half-day's journey, we reached the house. We watched the sun drop behind Hunter Mountain, listened to the call of men, the barking of dogs from far and near as the cows of the countryside were driven home, saw the forms of things swallowed by the darkness, and the lights of distant dwellings appear through the valley and part way up the mountain slopes.

After supper we sat in the kitchen for a while talking with the old folks.

The kitchen is the heart of a farm-house. This one was large, well kept, and warm. The chairs were old-fashioned wooden arm-chairs with cushioned seats. There was a lounge in one corner by the stove. The opposite corner was occupied by Mrs. Seifferth. It was easy to see that this was her habitual place. It encompassed her and was imbued with her. It was satisfied when she was there, and would remind you of her when she was gone. But there was something unusual in the atmosphere of this room. It was at once cosmopolitan and homely, hospitable and secluded, companionable and composed. Above all, it was domestic. There was genius in all this. All the more because there was no premeditation or design. These two old people—the one, his broad-brimmed hat shading his eyes, half dozing on the lounge, the other reading in her corner—seemed at this season of the year to have no connection to the world outside this almost deserted valley, no personal concern except the life of their farm. And yet, during the three months just passed, they had kept a crowded, popular boarding-house. This horde had barely left them. A season of hubbub, of idle pleasure-seeking, of straining merriment closed but yesterday, and a winter of solitude was now begun. The transition was unnoticeable. All was composed. These, then, were strong personalities possessing the genius of aptitude.

Mr. Seifferth woke up upon our entrance and pushed his hat a little higher on his forehead. His eyes were warm in their welcome. He was seventy-two years old, ruddy, active, stalwart. His countenance beamed with benevolence. His laugh was hearty, sometimes roguish. He was one of those open natures that tell you early and at once all you wish to know. During the evening I became acquainted with his gawky, blundering, ambitious, and persistent youth, his wanderings, his courtship, marriage, the first foolish quarrels with his wife, their ventures in New York and in the West, and their final settlement on this mountain farm.

"That was thirty years ago," he said.

"I don't wonder that you stayed here."

"Ain'd it?" he replied, with genial warmth. "Yes; it was all wild country then. No prospects of nothing—except work. My gracious! the work we did, clearing brush, getting the stones out—it was wonderful! But I was young and strong, and it was just like fun. The farm out West was all right, but I couldn't stay there. I was never contented. When we first climbed up the mountains and come into this valley I said right out, 'I'll stay here.' It was all wild as anything. But such trees I never saw—beautiful, ain'd it? And the air—my gracious! it was the finest air I ever got into me."

He laughed at the recollection, throwing his head back and spreading out his arms in a gesture of whole-souled contentment.

Mrs. Seifferth followed the conversation closely, helping to complete the narrative with pregnant details, exhibiting a keen sense of humor, accurate observation, unlimited tolerance.

All this had been a delight to me. I was not seeking strenuous adventures. The melodrama is composed for those who require large print, who find little that is intelligible in life day by day, whose perceptions sleep until awakened by explosions and climaxes.

In my long search for a beautiful world, inhabited by people friendly and simple, I had found a hopeful prophecy in this tranquil day.

The incident that closed it was like a blow upon an old, old sore. That surreptitious whistle in the dark startled me. It jarred hideously upon our day of untrammeled companionship.

When my friend is away, I cannot enter. His door is locked, for there are thieves in the world. Circumspection is demanded of us all, because of those who are ulterior. But I will not yield to the despotism of libertines and thieves. I will leave my doors open and be indiscreet.

But there was nothing ulterior in Libbie. The night's adventure, whatever it contained, was innocent to her mind, at least. She appeared at breakfast-time the next morning as exuberant as ever. Her cheerful, bristling presence brought relief to me.

"You don't need much sleep," I ventured.

"Oh, say," she began eagerly, tittering and making nervous gestures as she talked. "We were off to a dance, last night. We stole the old man's horse out of the barn—yes, we did. And, say, we brought home a coon—it was in the bottom of a buggy in the shed. Don't you tell anybody that you had coon to eat here. They suspect us already, I'll bet—but they don't know."

She was thrilled by the importance of this great secret, and it kept her spirits dancing for several days. Such natures seem defenseless; but, in reality, they are impregnable. Used, abandoned, worn out and thrown away, they have, in spite of the world's rough treatment, feasted upon its choicest fruits. Calamity finds no hold upon them, for they are occupied.

In those days, when I was seeking beauty first in forms I had preconceived, I was anxious to pass by disturbing things. The whistle in the dark, and Libbie's quick response, assumed for me the colors of her own ingenuous nature, and were easily absorbed in the general impression of those weeks.

That was a time of pure romance for us, for we were three lovers, lost to the world we little understood, and at liberty in one where we might conjecture. We climbed the mountains, penetrated the forests up their precipitous sides until baffled by the dense growth, bathed in the mountain brooks as we discovered them, slept in the sunny openings, played together like children, and longed for a perpetual existence like this. The impending return to the city surrounded us like a lugubrious shadow creeping nearer.

It was our custom to leave the house without any definite plan, following at random the way that happened to tempt us. On the top of the hill just west of Seifferth's stands the house of the Farrells, neighbors of a lifetime. As we were passing this, one afternoon, Nancy said:

"Do you see that lane running past Mr. Farrell's barn, and through the fields beyond it?"

"Yes; what of it? It seems to be a road leading to that little house back there."

"That over there," she said, "is where the Gillespies live. This lane, here at Mr. Farrell's, I don't think leads there at all; but, anyhow, I know there is a path somewhere beyond these meadows that will take us to the forest past Round Top, across the ridge, and to the summit of High Peak."

"I wonder if we could get there," I said, "before the sunset."

Elizabeth turned eagerly to the lane.

Nancy and I find our greatest contentment in familiar things, but Elizabeth will probably never cease to expect happiness, indefinite but somehow perfect, in some place where she has not yet been. She believes in heaven.

We walked briskly, for High Peak in the distance appeared to be inaccessible from where we stood. Far away, it rose abruptly, an almost sheer ascent, and formed the center of a vast, dense forest extending nearly to our feet. The lane conducted us to the forest-line, and Nancy, after a little search, found an almost obliterated path through the trees and underbrush. Not ten feet from the opening the ascent began abruptly, over roots and stones, past intersecting limbs that had overgrown the path. We came out upon occasional openings filled with the sun of midday—little portions of June, forgotten, seemed to be hiding in these inclosures. The grass was green in patches. We heard the drone of insects among the flowering weeds. Between these openings our path lay obscure in the forest twilight.

I climbed through all this beauty in a wistful mood. The earth is our home; but, for most of us, home is merely where we eat and sleep.

We have bestowed what is best in us upon the fairies, sending them to live in the woodland for us. Men have said the earth is not sufficient for us all. There are too many without souls. Let us who possess these radiant beings place them in the safe-keeping of the fairies while we do battle for the earth. When we have destroyed the barbarians our souls shall return to us, with tambourines and garlands. Life will then be one long May-day, for we shall possess the earth in its fullness.

I said to Nancy: "The murmur of this forest seems to come from a single throat; and yet, if we listen, we can hear countless individual voices."

Nancy sighed. "In a few days we must go back to the roar of Broadway, the crowded cars, the struggle at the Brooklyn Bridge at night. Why was I not born a toad?"

"And yet," I answered, "the noise of the city is melodious at a distance. All the life in this forest is at war. If you are a toad, you must escape the snake and devour the insect."

"Well, anyhow, I am not a toad," said Nancy; "and I would like to live here as I am. Wouldn't you?"

"Yes," I answered, "I would."

"Let's do it, then," said Nancy.

The eyes of Elizabeth glowed with the unthinking expectation of a child. The idea, vague and impracticable as it was, appealed to all of us, assuming the shape of an assured reality to-morrow. Moved by a similar impulse, we sat down side by side upon a log, contemplating this vision in silent delight. Imperceptibly, its pleasant outlines faded, and we resumed our way, Nancy with a sigh.

We came to a tall brush fence, searched for a hole, forced our way through it, head first, crossed an open field, and skirted the edge of the forest where it began again, looking in vain for the pathway which the field had cut in two.

"Never mind," said Nancy; "I can find the way without it. The Lindsays live somewhere beyond these woods, and from their place there is a well-defined road going to High Peak. I know I can find the Lindsays."

I reminded Nancy of Long Branch, which she spent the night escaping and returning to, on one of our summer wheel rambles.

"But never mind," I said; "lead on, my little one. If we are lost, our problems will be solved for us."

For more than an hour we pushed through the tangled wilderness, until Nancy's look of assurance left her. She began to wabble as she walked; to look about her vacantly; to stumble over stones, and at last, abject and humble, she fell behind.

"Sit down," I said.

She did so, bowing her head in her hands.

"Nancy," I continued, "perhaps you will sometime learn that you are a woman, and that your greatest charm lies in your humility."

Nancy abruptly raised her head, and exclaimed: "I hear a dog."

In a moment her small figure was lost to us in the underbrush a little to the left ahead.

About half an hour later we came to a wide clearing, and saw a rambling, lonely house in the center, on the summit of a knoll. Its appearance of loneliness was intensified as, approaching it, we rose above the surrounding trees, and saw how distant was the world of other men. Far below lay the Plaaterkill and Hunter valleys—indistinct caverns between the opposite range and us.

A house in a lonely place is more awesome than the simple solitude. I remember that I approached this one with something of the feelings awakened when, in my books of adventure, I have stumbled upon the abode of moonshiners or brigands. We were about to pass by the house stealthily, when the door opened and a young woman appeared. She smiled when she saw us, and stood very much at home in her doorway. She was slender, graceful smiling.

"How do you do, Miss Lindsay?" said Nancy, transformed instantly, before my eyes, into that courteous, insidious, falsetto maiden I long to shake.

"I am Winnie Gillespie," said the young woman in the doorway.

"Oh!" said Nancy.

"I like to keep things straight," I said; "so tell me who the people are just back of Farrell's, since they are not the Gillespies."

"They must be the Lindsays, then," said Nancy. "I got them mixed because I used to pass you," she said to Winnie, "on my way over the hills to Tannersville."

This explanation seemed so satisfactory to both the girls that I let it pass.

I remember that Winnie brought us each a glass of milk, and when we renewed our way I carried with me a singular impression of the place; for the young woman, idly glanced at, had not entirely dispelled the first impression of outlawed desolation.

Some of the wild mountain people, I thought. It would be a good location for a romantic tale.

"She is a pretty girl," said Nancy.

"Perhaps we should have paid for the milk," I said; "for I presume these people get a portion of their living from those who climb High Peak."

I had a vision of round-eyed youths who served as guides, and of men with tangled hair, who trapped and hunted through the winter, and viewed the world below them with surly brows. Then I saw, in fancy, the blasé, gilded youth, with alpenstock and gaiters, chancing upon this mountain maiden in her doorway, submitting to her ingenuous charms, losing himself in these wild solitudes, meeting with adventures, and fleeing at last with the girl—or without her—pursued, in either case, by her savage kin.

If I had written it then, how different would have been my story of the mountains! If I had mimicked well, it might have found a fitting place on the shelves with my beloved Irving and my Cooper; but then you would not know Winnie, nor her people, as they are.

The Gillespies were the last hint of man between the valley and the top of the world. For some two hours we toiled the rocky road, through a forest of gigantic trees, encountering no opening, seldom feeling a direct ray of the sun. We passed just under the knob of Round Top, walked for some distance along the level ridge between it and High Peak, and clambered the remaining distance up an unbroken, steep ascent. We realized that we had loitered, and the day was passing. A distinct line of night was just beneath us, moving from tree to tree, in stealthy, invisible approach, gaining on us as we panted upward. We stole a moment to drink at a spring by the roadside, and, redoubling our efforts, broke through the trees and gained the small circular bare spot at the summit. In the center was a tower, built high, of spliced logs. We ascended this with our remaining breath.

I have never cared to visit High Peak again. One such appalling view of the world is enough for me. I am glad to know that our earth is but an insignificant speck of dust, in measureless spaces of air—because this it is. But for the few years still left for me, I wish to feel that its land and seas, its gardens, its forests, and its fields, are real; that in the spring the apple-blossoms are rose-tinted, and in the fall one may pick up pippins by hunting in the grass; that my neighbors live near me; that there are pies in the pantry, oil in the lamps, wood in the woodshed, and a book open on the table where I laid it down. All this seems impossible on High Peak.

When we reached the tower the immediate world was lost in an abyss of night, out of which we rose. Pale lights, phantom evidences of dwellings, twinkled far beneath us. Miles to the east, the earth lay in twilight, an indistinct patchwork. Daylight gilded the horizon, formed by the hills and mountains of other States.

"They do not know what time it is over there," said I; "or else these people below us have lit their lamps too soon."

As we looked, all the wide reach of lowland was overtaken by the shadows. Shadows crept up the mountains on the horizon, and they, too, were lost.

A few moments after the sun went down, the stars, which had begun to appear, grew dim again. The sky became lighter. A rosy flush tinted the passing clouds. A second twilight had begun—a thing we had grown familiar with in the mountains.

"Let us hurry," said Elizabeth, "and perhaps we can get out of these terrible woods while the light lasts."

We hastily descended the tower, ran across the open space, and, still running, plunged under the trees, down the steep descent. At first we had no wish to hurry, Nancy and I; for we did not dread the forest in the dark, but found an added pleasure in its weird sounds and mysterious aspect, even in the sudden palpitations we sometimes felt.

There was something exhilarating, however, in racing down this obscure path, over rocks and fallen limbs, slipping on the mossy roots, maintaining our footing by a hair.

Elizabeth lost her fear in the excitement of the run.

When we left the forest at Gillespie's clearing, we skirted the house some distance, in order to avoid the dogs, passing as swiftly and as silently as we could.

I doubt if either of these girls could run for an hour at this breakneck speed over a level road in the daylight; but, for some reason, they were able to do it down this rocky and impeded way, where one can scarcely walk at noon without stumbling.

Night fell in earnest as we reached the valley. Groping our way through the woods, we lost our path, and there, within hailing-distance of Seifferth's farm, we might have wandered in the underbrush until morning had not our shouts been heard. We did not realize our predicament, however, and were shouting for the echo. While we were listening to the mocking mountains we heard the voice of Mr. Seifferth, forced our way toward the sound, and came upon a cow-path, where he met us with a lantern.

The impression of the world from High Peak still haunted me, and I was glad to see his benevolent countenance, and to know, for sure, that a man might live upon this speck of dust, feeling the blood warm in his veins and the events of his day important after seventy years.

"I would like to live in the mountains," I said to Nancy, "but not on High Peak. That corner of the woods in the pasture-lot would be the place for me."

Nancy looked at me wistfully. As often as our eyes met that evening, they were full of dreams, of expectation, of vague assent.

We had found this spot in one of our rambles, and, little by little, as such things do, it had become the final Mecca of all our pilgrimages. It was on the hillside, some distance from the road—a corner of the forest that covers the sides of Round Top and High Peak—the beginning, in fact, of the foothills of these mountains. A chromo mountain brook, with still pools and noisy runs, came out of the woods at this point, between two interlocked hemlocks, and crept through a grassy bed down the open hillside. From here we could see the mountain ranges on both sides of the Plaaterkill, looking westward down the valley, beyond the bold line of Hunter Mountain, to an indistinct crossing range.

When our last day of gypsy life came, we bought this spot—bought it on a promise to pay, for we had no money, and left it behind us like an anchor in the haven we hoped for, disturbed alike by anticipation and fear in our venture.

Our night ride back to the city seemed like a flight after bearding the Impossible.

Was it the Impossible? We were embarked upon an adventure. Tales of those led astray by mirages of country life haunted us. Was the story of the House in the Woods to be one of realization or defeat?

CHAPTER III

THE HAND OF THE BUILDER

ROM the moment our two acres and a half were surveyed and the contract drawn, both Nancy and I felt as much of apprehension as of pleasure in our enterprise. Expectation is an irresponsible wight, and makes but a sorry hand around the treadmill. In the place of dreams we now had a contract to peruse. We were, in fact, to pay two hundred and fifty dollars for our land within six months, and to build a house worth not less than eight hundred dollars within two years.

To be out of debt had so far meant opulence to me. Nancy was beginning to make a good deal of money in her business, but, aside from her office furniture at this time, most of her assets were in a closet full of fancy shoes, innumerable hats and gowns she had scarcely worn, a clothes-basket full of silk stockings, a history of her times in gloves, and cobweb-covered chests packed with expensive underwear, almost unused.

Any one who is weary of the strain and noise and struggle of a city, and longs for the life of a farm, may gratify his desire if he wishes to. I assume that few such men of the city make less than a thousand dollars a year. I made this much in what is, at best, a barren field, and I was only beginning to be successful with the magazines. My pickings were less than the pay of the average reporter—the proverbial child of poverty. Of this I gave three hundred and fifty dollars to those who had certain claims. I lived on three hundred, and saved three hundred and fifty.

Most of those who own farms begin with less. Any one who longs for the country can do as well.

It may be true that men are creatures of circumstances; but if they are our masters, we have an unlimited choice of them.

At the end of a year we once more journeyed to the mountains—Nancy, Elizabeth, and I—with seven hundred dollars in our pockets. That evening, after supper, we gave Mr. Seifferth a balance of one hundred dollars due him, and put the notes he held in the stove to burn. It was a clear September night. Silently we left the house, walked a little way down the road, turned into a lane by which the cows passed the garden to the pasture-lot, crossed a tumultuous creek, and climbed the hill until we reached the corner of the woods that was now our own. We found the short stake, surrounded by its little pile of stones, which the surveyor had placed there the year before. Just inside of this we stood, and looked long upon the valley, dimly visible in the starlight. We were three people standing, for the first time, on the spot where we wished to live; and yet, as such things are ordinarily viewed, our wishes were impossible and our venture moonshine. The world is filled with books based upon desires thwarted, victims entangled in the social net, unhappy females misunderstood, heroes in hot water until the last few pages at the end; but this is not one of them.

In the morning I went to Tannersville and bought an ax and two hatchets for Nancy and Elizabeth. When I returned I met Mr. Seifferth on the porch. He took my ax from me, looked narrowly at it, held it close and at arm's length, balanced it, and gave it back to me. I realized then that there were all sorts of axes in the world. I had simply asked for an ax, and taken the first one offered me, walked home with it upon my shoulder—walked briskly, whistling, as it were, a careless tune. Now I glanced anxiously from it to the wise old eyes before me.

"Is it all right?" I questioned.

"I don't see anything wrong with it," he said. "It's a good ax, I guess. How much did you pay for it?"

"A dollar and a half."

"Well, that's all right if it is a good ax, and I guess it is. What are you going to do with it?"

"Make a clearing for a house."

My heart beat faster as I pronounced these words. Nancy and Elizabeth, holding their hatchets, laughed, and Mr. Seifferth beamed upon us benignly. One might have thought an inspired patriarch was sending his children into an enchanted forest for a fortune that was sure, so unfettered was imagination in this serene valley, so fair the autumn day. The house was in the meadow, the woods near by, the world of custom and of strict account remote, forgotten.

We ate our dinner in suppressed excitement, declined dessert, picked up our weapons from the floor where we had placed them, and hurried out.

"You had better grind your ax," called Mr. Seifferth as we were turning down the road.

"Does it need it?" I inquired sheepishly.

"Why, of course," he answered; "you can't cut with it the way it is. Can you turn a grindstone?"

He led me around the house to a group of apple-trees, where an aged grindstone was propped beneath the shade. A rusty tomato-can, half filled with water, was waiting on the frame.

For some time now I have had a grindstone of my own, and through many failures have learned to grind an ax without a bevel and not too thin, keeping the edge true to the shape that suits me best. That day, however, I only turned the crank, comprehending nothing of the grinder's art. My arms ached long before the job was done.

"Won't that do?" I ventured.

"No. You want to have it right," he said.

When I received my ax at last it had a keen and glittering edge. The old man smiled benignly, and I thanked him as I rubbed my arms.

"This stone is almost gone," he said, glancing, I thought, affectionately at the small, uneven wheel, worn almost to its iron hub. "I have thought some of getting a new one," he continued, more to himself than to me; "but I guess I won't now. I have used it a long time. It will last as long as I will, I guess. Ain'd it? And then," in a complacent murmur, "we might as well go together."

Whenever I approached Mr. Seifferth in those days I received only evidences of those qualities in his race that have produced its folk-lore, its mysticism, the notes of morning and of twilight in its music, its tender and ingenuous poems, its elfin songs.

I like to dwell upon these things now, for, having discovered that these qualities are there, I can, by appealing always to them, retain them for my communion, and so escape the surface irritations that constitute the social life of a neighborhood like this.

We owned no portion of the brook by which we had located, but our forest lot followed its windings along the edge of its western bank. Ordinarily when your purchase is bounded by a stream you own to the middle of it, but in our bargain with Mr. Seifferth he had expressly stipulated to the contrary. In fact, he hesitated a long time before selling us this particular spot, for during the open months of the year this stream supplied him with water. He showed us the little reservoir, encircled with sod, half-way down the hillside, from which his pipes extended to the house.

"It is good water," he repeated many times.

But it was this patch of the forest we wanted, and no other, because of the view down the valley and this living stream. We were not thinking of the handy water-supply at all, but of its tinkling falls, its mossy banks, its pools and runs and hidden courses under hemlock boughs and fallen logs.

When my ax was sharpened Mr. Seifferth walked with us to the woods.

"Of course," he said, "you will not cut anything that shades the brook."

"No."

"They're often dried up that way."

"Yes; I know that much."

"This is a splendid timber-lot," he said, gazing at our corner with admiration and regret. "My gracious! I don't see why I sold it."

"Because," said Nancy, "you wanted to be good to us."

"Ain'd it?" he replied, a little wistfully, but yielding in the end to Nancy's graceful view of it.

I stood just outside the timber, leaning on my ax, eager to begin, but hesitating. There could be no more beautiful forest anywhere. The trees on these mountain-sides are exceedingly tall, and straight and graceful, because of their great numbers. The soil seems capable of nurturing every sprout to its fruition as a tree. Long ago, the gigantic hemlocks and pines that once flourished here were felled and stripped by the tanners, and the hardwood sleeping in their shade opened their green leaves in the clearings; but so thickly did they spring, and so tenacious was their hold on life, that in their lusty crowding they stretched to enormous heights, reaching for the sun. Their branches form a canopy, supported by clean-cut trunks, from forty to sixty feet high, their symmetry unbroken by a twig. Such hemlocks as were too small for the tanners have since matured and filled with their somber forms the spaces between the hardwood. The undergrowth is a tangled motley of young maple, beech, ash, birch, balsam, spruce, and hemlock.

I learned all this from Mr. Seifferth as we stood on the borderland. Before we could enter our forest, we were compelled to cut a path with the ax or force our way through resisting branches.

I experienced a feeling of impiety as I approached my task, as a pygmy ought to feel who contemplates the destruction of helpless majesty. I approached the first small tree of the undergrowth, however, and examined it coolly. I laid my coat upon the grass. I felt the edge of my ax and cut my thumb.

"It's sharp," I said.

Mr. Seifferth smiled and left us, descending the hill slowly, his arms behind his back.

"Now, girls," I said, "take your hatchets, and keep clear of me. One never knows what may happen with an ax."

I cannot tell how many times I struck and missed that day. Twice I know my ax went hurtling through the underbrush. We cut no mature trees that afternoon, but cleared the undergrowth in a wide swath some thirty feet beyond the forest-line. Those were happy hours that we cut and slashed. The irregular whack-whacking of the girls' hatchets was interrupted only when they dragged forth their prey. I caught momentary glimpses of their struggling forms through the intervening brush. There were scratches on their flushed faces; their hair was in disorder.

A little before sunset we stopped to view the clearing we had made.

"Our dooryard," murmured Nancy.

"Yes," said I; "we might build the house just back of us."

In the morning, after breakfast, the girls went with me to turn the grindstone. It was not long, however, before Mr. Seifferth, hearing the sounds of our labor, came out to us. He took the ax and glanced at the edge.

"You must have been working in a quarry," he said, laughing loudly out of sheer surprise. "How did you do it?"

"I hit some stones, I guess."

"Well, you mustn't do that. If you cut in the woods you must look out for them. You couldn't keep an ax no time that way. You would be no good."

For over an hour I turned the crank, and the sweat poured from me. He bore heavily upon the ax, for the nicks were deep.

"They must all be ground away," he said; "for even a little dull spot will spoil the force of a blow."

I did not care to repeat that performance on the crank, and when we reached our forest my mind was on my business. I checked a first impulse to throw the ax upon the ground, and stood it carefully against a tree. Since then I have learned that even this proceeding is unsafe, and that to leave an ax in security you must bury its edge in a stump or a piece of timber.

"And now," said Nancy, "where is the house to be? I would like it close to the brook."

"With a window overlooking it."

"A casement window."

"A very wide, low window, something like the usual frame put in sidewise."

"With diamond frames."

"They are hard to look out of."

"But they are so pretty, especially in the woods."

"We might have each window in four parts (I did not then know the word 'sash' to use it correctly), the two at the ends stationary and of large panes, and the two center sections, fixed to swing open, filled with diamond panes."

"Lovely!" said Nancy, with her usual enthusiasm in a temporary approval of what she in no way understands.

"And now," I said, "let's all walk backward slowly through the trees, until the view down the valley is just as we want it."

This we did, and to a chance observer we might have been taken for members of some mysterious religious sect at their rites. We kept our gaze fixed upon the distance, and wandered backward, now to the right, now to the left, until we came together on a spot from which all the bold outline of Hunter Mountain, and a portion of the valley beyond, with its intersecting range, could be seen. The forest on either side of our clearing hid the rest of the world. We stood upon a slight knoll, close by the brook, gazed critically through our leafy window and colonnade of lofty trees, and found an increasing delight in this tantalizing glimpse down the valley.

The enormous trunk of a fallen hemlock lay along the bank of the brook, and here I sat while I made rough pencil sketches of our ideas for a house. The girls, one on each side, bent over my knee and chirruped their impossible suggestions. Out of all our dreams, however, a plan was drawn, and we sat in wistful contemplation of this peaceful abode among the trees, its dormered roof, its overhanging eaves, its wide, low windows, its shingled sides, its huge stone chimney at the end.

We were aroused from this sylvan reverie by the blast of a horn, rendered musical by the distance. It was Libbie calling us to dinner. As we came out upon the clearing, and the whole valley was disclosed, Nancy exclaimed:

"Look! See that touch of red over there."

She held her arm outstretched, and Elizabeth and I, following its direction, saw in the depths of green, midway up the opposite slope of the valley, a tiny patch of flame. We gazed upon this prophet of beauty as do the pure in faith upon the forms of the saints.

"The autumn spectacle has begun," I said.

"We must hurry on," said Nancy, "and get back."

We found Mr. and Mrs. Seifferth in the kitchen, and consulted them. We explained our plan for a cottage. They listened critically, asked plain questions, and finally decided that it would do.

"Whom do you think I had better get?"

"Well, how are you going to have it done—by contract or by day's labor?"

"I haven't thought about it. What do you think is best?"

"Well, of course that all depends. You might get better work and build it cheaper by the day's work; that is, if you know anything about such things."

"I don't."

Mrs. Seifferth leaned back in her chair, and laughed, her good-natured way of saying, "God help you, then!"

Thus by force of necessity I began to learn something of the folk about me. I was not simply an isolated being seeking my own pleasure, as I had fancied. I was one among others. Coming from the city, I was yet one of a community in which men were dependent upon each other. I sought service from them. Presently I was to learn that I also had some service to offer.

"There's Charley Burns," said Mr. Seifferth. "He's a good carpenter."

"Yes, Charley Burns," said Mrs. Seifferth, "would be all right if it's a contract job, but if it's done by the day he's pretty slow."

"Brice, over here," said Mr. Seifferth, "could build your chimney for you."

"There's Jimmie Dale, down here," I ventured. "He's learned the carpenter's trade."

"Oh, there's carpenters enough," said Mrs. Seifferth, "but they all have their little ways. I mind the time they were putting the addition on this house for us." She laughed at the recollection, and continued as only those can who enjoy the humor of their troubles past. "They were working on the roof—four stories up, you mind—with a stairway of ladders to go up and down, and not a team could pass along the road but Charley Burns hailed it. He climbed down that ladder twenty times a day to talk with his acquaintances."

"Yes, yes," said Mr. Seifferth, with a genial laugh, "and me a-paying for it."

"Where shall I find Mr. Burns and Mr. Brice?"

"I heard Charley was building a barn for Martin."

"He lives right down here, about a mile. They can tell you."

"And Brice?"

"He lives right next to Jack Dale's."

"Where is that?"

"Why, right down here—it's the third house. There is Andrew Dale—the first house back from the road, on the hill; then Jack Dale; then Brice."

A few moments later we were walking down the road, on our first pilgrimage of business. The plan for our house was in my pocket; and as we came in view of our corner of the forest, far up on the hillside, and saw the dark recess of our clearing, I experienced emotions at once exquisite and melancholy.

We passed the first house, a plain, unpainted, weather-beaten building, exposed to the sun and the elements, in the center of a large field, its bleak aspect modified, however, by the sheltering forest that inclosed it and rose back of it in ascending undulations of green.

The second house was close to the road, in a hollow. It was a low building with a wide porch, almost hidden among the shrubs and trees. We passed these places with indifference. Even the names of their owners were forgotten. It seems strange to me now that this could be so, that I could have ever looked upon these habitations with a stranger's casual eye.

Fortunately we found Mr. Brice at home. He was at the dinner-table, in his shirt-sleeves. At first glance I saw a surly-looking man, short, thick-set, unsociable. His face was spare and weather-beaten. His round head was covered with iron-gray hair, closely cropped, and a heavy, drooping, reddish mustache gave a sandy appearance to his countenance.

"Is this Mr. Brice?"

"Yes," he answered in a gruff voice, scarcely looking up.

"I have bought a piece of ground of Mr. Seifferth, and am thinking of putting up a cottage."

"Whereabouts?" he asked, with some show of interest; and when I told him he looked at me squarely, with attentive, calm eyes.

"You've got far enough from the road," he commented, and turned his attention again to his plate.

In spite of the heavy mustache, I caught a glimpse of a droll smile, which, on the instant, made me feel at home and comfortable with him. Perhaps, I thought, this man is not surly, after all.

"I want a chimney."

"Stone?"

"I think so. I want a fireplace on the first floor that will take four-foot logs, and a smaller one on the second floor. How much will you build it for?"

"I'll have to do some figuring." He ate in silence for a moment, then asked: "Want it lined with brick?"

"Do I?"

"Yes."

There was another silence. Mrs. Brice refilled her husband's coffee-cup, and meeting Nancy's eyes, smiled pleasantly. I think they made some effort at conversation, but it was at that time forced and meaningless.

"What kind of stone?"

"I thought we could use the stone on the place."

"You can. There's plenty of it."

The spirit of that droll smile again passed through his mustache.

"I want a rough chimney, all sorts and sizes of stone, put in as they come."

"You'd better not do it by contract," he said, looking up from his plate. "I'd rather you'd hire me by the day. You can get just what you want then."

"About what will it cost?"

"Well, it will take about two barrels of cement—Rosendale will do for that; or do you want Portland?"

"Which is the best?"

"Portland is the dearest, and for cellars, or where it's damp, a good deal the best; but for chimneys I could never see the use of paying for it."

"How much is it a barrel?"

"I think it's three dollars. Rosendale is a dollar and a half."

"Well, you do as you think best."

"It will take ten barrels of sand. Mrs. Gaffey has a sand-bank, and Tom Seifferth, I guess, would draw it. It would take a man and a team three or four days to get the stones—perhaps longer. It would depend on how handy they were. I suppose I could build it in two weeks—that would be five dollars a day for me and my helper. Then there is the brick. Well, I should think about five hundred of brick would do it. We'd have to get that down the mountains. Well, I wouldn't want to contract it for less than one hundred and twenty-five dollars. But it might be cheaper for you to do it by the day. It couldn't be any more, anyhow."

"I know nothing at all about it," I said.

"It's hard for me to make an estimate," he continued. "I would rather work by the day on a job like that. I don't want to make any more out of you than my wages, and I don't want less. But if I contracted it, I would rather estimate too high than too low."

"All right. We will do it by the day. When can you begin?"

"Well, you have caught me just right. I finished a long job this morning. That's why I get a warm dinner to-day."

For the third time the ghost of a smile came and faded, and I felt sure he was not surly.

We were walking eastward to the head of the mountain, and the valley, rising and broadening before us, seen in the bright sunlight through a misty autumn atmosphere, formed a picture of radiance and repose. But for me there was much that was unfamiliar in the scene. The hand of a mason had, for the first time, been laid upon my dreams. I had introduced him to my bower, and he had brought with him ten barrels of sand, five hundred of brick, tons upon tons of stone, saying: "I must have a place for these." He had thrown his mortar-box among my ferns.

We may gaze in idleness upon a phantom house among the trees; but, before it covers us, we must consider what cement to buy—whether Rosendale or Portland.

We found Charley Burns at work upon a barn in a meadow, some two miles up the road.

"How much," I asked, "will it cost to build a house like that?"

He looked at my plan, and gave it back to me.

"That depends, of course, on how you build it."

"Yes?"

"On the kind of material you use, and the finishing inside. Them's queer-shaped windows you've got there, and the doors are not regular. All such things add to the cost. Stock doors and windows are a great deal cheaper."

"I want it shingled on the outside."

"Yes; that's all right. It makes a tight job. How about the inside?"

"We will leave that unfinished, I guess. It's only for the summer. If we ever want it for winter use, we can seal it afterward."

"What will you use for sheathing, then—shiplap?"

"What's that?"

"You don't know?"

"I know what a two by four is, and a shingle, and a lath, but that's all."

"Well, it's pretty hard to figure on a house unless you know what kind of material goes into it."

He took my plan again and looked at it, shaking his head hopelessly. I felt sorry for him.

"You will probably be busy on this barn for a while, anyhow," I said.

"About two weeks longer, I guess."

"Well, I couldn't wait. The house must be finished in three weeks at the most."

He did not seem to regret the loss of the job, but showed me through the barn, talked enthusiastically of sidings, sheathings, flooring, of the uses of pine and spruce and hemlock; and as I was leaving him, bewildered by these mysteries, he suggested that I should see Mr. Goslee, a carpenter in Tannersville.

"If he can't do it himself," he assured me cheerily, "he can tell you who can."

We were now outside the barn, in the warm sunlight, facing the long, low range of mountains that inclosed the valley to the south. The meadow that surrounded us, the stone wall skirting it, the trees by the wall, an orchard, a pretty house in the shade of giant maples, were before my eyes, but they were vaguely seen. Shiplap or flooring for sheathing—which? Will hemlock shingles do, or is it cheaper in the end to pay the price of pine?

"You are a wise man, Mr. Burns," I said, "to stay here in the mountains. In the city there are no such scenes as this to work in."

"I would like the city first-rate," he said, "if it wasn't for the labor-unions. It's them that keeps me here. Of course, if you don't get any one before I am through with this barn, I would like to build for you."

"All right," I said as we left him.

I have often thought of this carpenter, standing as we saw him last, his canvas apron full of nails, a hammer in his hand, a friendly smile upon his lips, a little anxiety in his eyes; for he possessed so much of the knowledge I desired, and yet how little revenue it had rendered him! Acquainted with the traits of every stick he handled, grown old in this timbered valley, his scenes of labor always inviting, and, at times, fantastic in their beauty—his knowledge and his environment meant little more to him than the wages they produced.

Competition and contention give a certain zest to life, which, I am told by practical men, is all that normal maturity can grasp of the vision of happiness that youth pursues. I know that most of my acquaintances have accepted this as a rational conclusion. Placed as I was then, with a house to build, they would have waded aggressively into the problems of material, worrying conscientiously over a choice of things, and priding themselves somewhat upon their shrewd bargaining with lumber-dealers, carpenters, and masons.

For me, success in life means the preservation of a tranquil mind. Delight is a luxury to spur ambition on, but tranquillity is that necessary competence no man should be without.

I wished I knew what material to select, so that I might talk intelligently with those who labored with me. Such knowledge would, as well, have given me a more intimate acquaintance with my house. But, ignorant as I was, what could I hope for in these three weeks but anxiety and great trouble if I undertook the solutions of the problems this house involved? Shrewdness I might exhibit by suspicion, and I might, perhaps, save fifty dollars by a watchful eye and the concentration of all my faculties to that end.

As I realized this, while walking back to Seifferth's, I cast these problems from me, determined that I would put into wood and stone only so much of my dreams as would preserve them.

I laid this reasoning before the girls, and they agreed with me.

In the morning we walked to Tannersville. We went early, paying that much tribute to business; but we took the path over the hills, loitering when we wished to, walking briskly when this pleased us, and, in the warm hollows, lying prone upon the grass in indolent forgetfulness.

We found Mr. Goslee at a bench in the workshop of the lumber-yard. A plane in his aristocratic hands, long and sinewy, was caressing the edge of a board, throwing a cascade of savory curls upon the floor. I recognized in him one of our distinctly American types. He was tall and angular, nervous and cautious, alert and gentle. He smiled with pleasure when I told him of my errand, took my plan, and nodded approvingly as he glanced it over.

"Now," I said, "I don't know anything about material. I would like to have a pretty shingled cottage, with wide eaves, big dormer-windows, unfinished inside, but with hardwood floors, built as cheaply as it can be built honestly and well."

"I know just what you want," he said.

"Could you make a guess as to the cost?"

"I think so." He figured on the planed surface of a board and said:

"Somewhere between three and five hundred dollars. I think you could get what you want for that; but, of course, you could spend as many thousands if you cared to."

"You are the man for me," I said. "Now, when can you begin?"

"As soon as you have the foundation laid I will be there."

And in his comprehending, pleasant eyes I saw our clearing in the woods, the bordering brook, the distant view, the house half hidden by the fir-trees. Across the valley there rose before me the great purple flanks of the mountains. I heard in fancy the drumming of the partridge among the evergreens which were behind the house, rising toward the crests of Round Top and High Peak. I could imagine the beds of lush ferns along the brook, and scent the perfume distilled by the summer sun from the raspberries in the clearing. I pictured a return to nature, a life simple, wholesome, elemental. To me at the moment nature was all. That other human beings, my brethren, had already made their homes in these vast mountain spaces was something of which I, a dweller in the cities seeking a primitive Eden, had no thought. I forgot them in a selfish reverie. But I was yet to find that the conquest of nature is not all—that humanity has its claim in the mountains as on the city streets.

CHAPTER IV

Strange Voices In The Woods

HE three weeks during which we were building passed in a succession of radiant, warm fall days and frosty nights. Every morning additional touches of color appeared in the foliage of the valley and the mountain-sides. At first we were able to note this increase, counting the solitary trees, far and near, which overnight had exchanged their hues of green for gold or crimson. By the end of the week, however, we no longer counted. It is impossible to say just when the reckoning was lost.

Here was a magician's show. The branches above my head, the bushes I brushed against, eluded me. All the majestic landscape within my view, the forest in which I stood, the ferns at my feet, assumed innumerable shades and tints, distinct and brilliant, softly blending and glaringly defined; but though I watched the transformation hour by hour, I never caught a leaf in the act of changing—I saw nothing but miraculous effects. My roving eye saw only green above me. A crimson leaf fell at my feet. I looked again, and beheld a bough of crimson. Was it concealed before, or had it changed before my eyes by imperceptible transitions?

Nor was the sense of unreality disturbed by the sounds of our labor. Every morning Mr. Brice came out of the woods into our clearing, accompanied by his helper, a genial, silent giant named Will Dolan. A moment later there was a sound of hissing and bubbling in the mortar-box, and the steam from slacking lime rose over the shrubs that screened it. Then came the sharp blow of a mason's hammer on the stone, and the patter of chips falling among the leaves.

Voices sound melodious in the forest, and something exceedingly musical issued from Mr. Brice's throat as he spoke in the husky guttural peculiar to him. For days at a time he would labor, speaking only at intervals to his helper, saying, "Mud" or "That one."

"Mud" called for more mortar, and by "That one" he would indicate to Dolan some particular stone he wanted from the heap beneath him on the ground.

I sat upon a log and watched these men, marveling at the freedom of their voiceless intercourse. Dolan carried up mud and stones and laid them on the boards across the scaffolding. It was seldom necessary for Brice to ask for either. What he wanted, as the chimney rose in lines, made constantly irregular by the material of every size and shape, Will Dolan had placed beside him, so that the cobble or the flat stone or the jagged piece at hand was the one to fit. There was always a big stone ready for each corner of the outer wall, and little ones to pack in around the flues.

So long as I talked with Dolan in such a way that he could answer, "Yes, yes," the range of our converse was unlimited, and never have I found a man of readier sympathies. He needed no other form of speech, for by this phrase he could indorse the profoundest philosophy, the tenderest sentiment, the most subtle of surmises. And if he could not agree, he could maintain an unobtrusive silence difficult to quarrel with.

And every morning Mr. Goslee drove up the hillside and turned his horse to graze. He had chosen for his helper Jimmie Dale, who had lately learned the trade and who lived in the valley about a mile from us. Jimmie, like most of the Dales, was a strapping lad. There was something singularly pleasing in the contrast of his large proportions and the ingenuous, confiding expression of his countenance. His eyes were of a baby-blue, round, encircled by long black lashes. His forehead was white, high, and broad, his cheeks round and rosy. A heavy, silken brown mustache did not quite conceal the full lips, nor the dimples when he smiled.

His voice was rich and manly. When he was not singing or talking, he whistled tunefully. This pleasant voice, accompanied by a ragtime rhythm of saws and hammers, was no disturbance in this lonely forest.

Under a clump of tall maples in our door-yard I built three rustic chairs and a rustic couch, covering this last with a mattress of balsam boughs.

"I think," said Mr. Goslee, "we will need a little more tin for the dormer-windows."

"Mud," said Mr. Brice.

I stood by Dolan at the mortar-box.

"That is the end to the lime," I said. "It might be called to its death, and yet you see it is only changed to mortar."

"Yess, yess," said Dolan.

"Hear that partridge drum!" said Jimmie, suspending his hammer. When it fell again he resumed an interrupted bar of "Dixie."

Of course there was never a moment when the leaves were silent. An occasional gust passed through them, and then the tall trees swayed and the lofty branches creaked.

All this time Nancy was busy with the brook, clearing its brink of litter and removing unsightly dams of twigs and decaying leaves. She worked with a toy set of tools—a spade, a rake, and a hoe. For two weeks she spent her days in the shade and dampness, toiling with intense delight.

Then for two days she kept her bed, and passed the remainder of the week upon the couch of balsams.

When our time was up the little house was not completed, but the shell was there, a perfect outer form; and we left it there among the trees, our little house in the woods, our shrine, our symbol of hope, a patient, alluring embodiment of our dreams.

For three years this house remained unvisited. Two summers were spent upon our island in the Sound, a luxury bestowed upon us by a siren.

The winters found us in New York, where we lived in such a simple way that, out of an income very moderate for New York, we saved seven thousand dollars in three years. We bought clothes and food and lodging, and took our pleasures from the grab-bag.

During these three years, all the seemingly insurmountable obstacles that made a life together on our mountain farm impossible were smoothed away.

Last winter Nancy's business prosperity was at its height. Her profits were increasing month by month. At that time, also, Fortune, as she is usually conceived, seemed suddenly to have taken note of me. In three years we had lived on nothing to save seven thousand dollars, and now in twelve months more we could have saved as much and lived more extravagantly as well. Our love, however, for the soil and the forest and the open fields was real.

During these three years also we had lost Elizabeth, and so, when the first of April came, the date we had fixed upon, Nancy and I gladly abandoned our prosperity and returned to our mountain home alone.

CHAPTER V

Runaways From Fortune

TANNERSVILLE, a little town in a hollow surrounded by mountains, is the very heart of the Catskills. For two or three months in the summer it is in close touch with all the world—only a few hours from New York and seemingly as closely allied to it as is New Rochelle or Yonkers.

The broad platform of the station, the streets of the village, the roads of the region round about, are thronged with active idlers in gay attire. A few weeks of hubbub, and again the long repose.

From December until June direct railroad communication between Tannersville and the world ceases. The mountains again belong to those who dwell in them. Although these regions have been inhabited for more than one hundred years, foxes and partridges—these creatures that love the silence—still abound, and when beech-nuts are plentiful the snows of the forest are sometimes trampled by bears. For seven or eight months Tannersville is forgotten. There are no trains, and only such mail service as the stage affords.

At nine o'clock in the morning of an April day our panting engine stopped at Plaaterkill Junction, and Nancy, Bob, and I stood upon the platform of a little station in the woods, six miles from Seifferth's and our house in the Plaaterkill. On either side of us rose the precipitous sides of the gap called Stony Clove, the narrow gateway between the mountains and the plains.

For many years Nancy and I had been escaping, for longer or shorter periods, into the country, but only as truants heretofore. Twice we had passed through this gap together, bearing with us the knowledge of our swift return. We had built a house, three years before, down in the valley now opening before us, vaguely hoping that at some distant time, perhaps when we were old, we might have it for a home. Now, on this April morning, as we walked along the railroad track out of the Clove, all that we had hoped for had come to pass, and with half of life still left to us. In my pocket was seven thousand dollars in bonds and stocks. The almost finished house, with its surrounding land, was paid for. A year before we had added seven acres to our original purchase.

With a cow or two, some chickens, an orchard, and a garden, together with three hundred dollars of interest, it seemed to us that we might pass the remainder of our days in simple comfort. We were, at last, entirely free. The strident voices of the city could not reach us through this mountain wall. There was only the wind among the trees.

We left the track and took the valley road, reaching Gaffey's Corner by a long, gradual ascent, and found ourselves at last in the Plaaterkill.

Bob, released from his long confinement in the train, racing over the fields in pursuit of the birds, dancing and barking along the road before us with the unrestrained joy of a dog, gave expression to our own impulses as we walked briskly to our mountain home.

Days upon the hillside, long rambles through the woods, hour after hour of quiet reading, pleasant labor in the garden, a little writing now and then for my conscience's sake, years of peace, simplicity, and content, an old age of repose, and a final resting-place together in our own earth, among the balsams—this was the present and the future we conceived.

For many the road we traveled and the scene around us would have been desolate and lonely. During the walk of six miles we met no one. The houses near the road, passed at long intervals, were, to all appearances, cheerless abodes, small, and most of them unpainted. We gazed over all this vast wilderness of somber evergreens and naked hardwood, seeing only a remote house or two, each in the center of its little clearing on a mountain slope.

Had I been a stranger, rid of the world I knew, entering this valley in search of a home, the evidences of its somber life might have depressed me. I would, at least, have looked with greater interest upon the habitations of my neighbors, and more wistfully, perhaps, at the faces peering from the windows, at the people standing in the doors.

Nancy and I, however, were walking side by side, so close that our hands in swinging touched. This, anywhere, would have been enough for us. It is only the hungry who look about them with a restless or a greedy eye. A warm sun tempered the chill spring wind, and it was only cool, sweet, and invigorating.

Registered dogs must have a distinctive name. The one I chose for Bob was Bob Golightly. During the time of his captivity in New York thousands of people have paused, in the eager morning rush from the Brooklyn Bridge to business, to watch him pose and leap and run in the grassy inclosures of the City Hall Park. If any of these read this book, they will know the dog I mean and the reason for his name.

Bob is a pure Scotch collie of the tawny hue. His thick, silken hair is of a shiny reddish-yellow underneath his body, deepening to a dark brown where it parts upon his back. He has an exceedingly wide, snow-white collar, white breast and legs, and a white star upon his forehead. His ears are edged with black, and little black horns of hair, like the points of the Turkish half-moon, encircle the white of his breast. When in repose, or trotting tranquilly on his way, his heavy tail, hanging gracefully, just escapes the ground, its curving tip snow-white. His nose is long, delicate, and pointed.

When I first received him from his mother's breast, he was a sensitive, affectionate, unselfish creature who would leave his saucer of milk for a caress. I have taught him the meaning of the words I most frequently use, and have never deceived him. He was almost two years old at this time, and, so far as he knew, there was nothing in the world but friendliness and sincerity. He was bold, joyous, confiding, and eager.

We passed a flock of sheep grazing upon a hillside, and Bob, who had been chasing birds in the adjoining field, came upon them unexpectedly. He stopped, his head and one forepaw uplifted, and gazed at them for one tense moment. Then he trotted daintily in their direction. I called to him, and he instantly wheeled and returned, standing before me, his clear, brilliant eyes full of inquiry. His are the sort of eyes that one may talk to. There is no anticipation there. He listens.

"Bob," I said, "those are sheep. See!" And as I pointed to the field, he turned his head to look. "Those are sheep—sheep, my boy. You must leave them alone."

He looked at me intently, and trotted on ahead, looking frequently toward the sheep, and uttering an occasional plaintive note, an expression of wonder and desire, for he was a willing child of Nature, stirred now mysteriously by her promptings.

This flock called to him as did the fields and forests to me. I had seen a garden, and I wished to be busy with the soil. There was only this difference in our knowledge: I knew that I would soon be standing on my own domain, but Bob could only feel, without knowing, what these emotions meant, nor how to satisfy the instincts that produced them. His life was in my keeping, and he did not know that I had a cow in mind for him.

In one of the fields of the lowlands along the river we saw a man, a boy, and a team of oxen turning under the stubble of last year's oats.

"The first thing we must do," I said to Nancy, "is to have some plowing done."

On a hill surrounded by the forest are a small wooden church and burying-ground. At the foot of the hill beyond was an old house, without porches or ornament, very old and very much weather-beaten, deformed by the heavings of the frost. There were two enormous stone chimneys, one exposed for its entire length at the end, and one rising from the roof in the center. These seemed to be supported by the building, which they, in turn, supported.

Bob, a little way ahead, was suddenly assaulted by three dogs, two huge hounds and a mean-eyed shepherd, who rushed yelping from the gate and rolled him in the ditch. Bob, as nimble as a chipmunk, whisked from under the heap. I rushed to his assistance, howling savagely. Bob stood facing them, stiff and alert, but with more of surprise than anger in his eyes. My belligerent shouts and motions excited strong, new emotions in his breast. He quivered and yelped in anxiety, for joyous and friendly as he was, he could not in a moment grasp the significance of this assault, nor the part he should play in it.

At my noisy rush the dogs drew back, snarling, by the roadside. I saw a young woman's face at the window of the house, and a young man, opening the door, stepped slowly out to the door-step and stood there motionless. I turned savagely toward him. My barbarous and combative instincts, aroused so suddenly, were, however, checked in time, and we walked on in silence.

Bob came to me, looking into my eyes anxiously and whimpering with excitement and distress.

"You are a good boy," I said. "Never fight if you can help it, but never run. You will get along with such creatures as these if you are watchful, bold, and brave. It was all right, Bob. Now, run along."

He understood, at least, that I was satisfied with him, and the incident was at once forgotten.

We reached Seifferth's at noon, and over our salt pork, potatoes, cake, and tea we talked eagerly of our plans.

We thought these plans were well defined, and that, simple as they were, they might be encompassed with a thousand dollars. Two or three hundred dollars, at the most, would make the cottage comfortable, even for the winter. I expected to make rustic chairs, beds, and tables. The range, cooking-utensils, dishes, and other such furniture as we needed would cost, perhaps, one hundred dollars. We had thought some of putting up a summer-kitchen at the end of the house. There would be, of course, a small stable for the cow and a chicken-house, such as I could build myself. All this, with the cost of the chickens and the cow, would require somewhere between seven hundred and a thousand dollars. This would leave us six thousand at four and a half per cent—three hundred dollars a year.

For us who did not require ten dollars' worth of meat a year, this income, besides our own milk, butter, eggs, and vegetables, was luxurious.

As we contemplated our tranquil future, I said to Nancy: "We must not be deceived by this prospect of ease. We will be obliged to labor, even if we do not need to. A man must be doing something that he thinks is important. We must work a little to be happy."

"I would like to do nothing," said Nancy, "for at least a month."

"A year of idleness would do you good; but within two days, at the most, you will be at something will all your might."

"What makes you think so?" she exclaimed, smiling up at me.

"Such is your nature, and your habits have confirmed it."

"Well," she said, "I will promise you that for a month I will do nothing."

"It will be two or three weeks before we can move into the house to live, and these you can spend on the hillside."

"It's delicious," said Nancy, with a happy sigh.

After dinner we took the old road up to our beloved woodland, and gazed in silence at the little house concealed within our clearing. Three years of weather had stained it with hues in harmony with the forest that sheltered it. There was a gap of more than three inches between the roof and the chimney. Somewhere at the foundation of this massive pile of stone, the microscopic workmen of the frost had entered, heaving it as easily as you could move a pin.

Slowly we walked through our sacred grove, made sacred by the communion of the saints—affection, memory, and hope. Solemnly we unlocked the door and swung it open.

A house that has been used and abandoned acquires an air of desolation after long neglect; but for us there was no reproach in our unfinished, vacant chambers.

The sunlight, falling freely through the bare branches overhead, preceded us, and we stood in the center of the room, in its light. The gray stone of the chimney and the yawning fireplace looked cold, but we could readily anticipate the roaring fires that would soon be warming them. We found our tools in one corner, but the old clothes we had used and left here were scattered in bits and remnants, torn and eaten by chipmunks, porcupines, and skunks that entered through the spaces between the two-by-fours along the edge of the floor.

We heard a rumble as of distant thunder, as affrighted birds fluttered from their nests in our chimney-flues.

Just outside the door, in the center of our clearing, was an enormous pile of brush, an unsightly litter, and so obtrusive that the eye could not pass it to the view beyond. As I stood in the doorway, Nancy walked briskly to it, and with the unconsciousness of habitual activity, laid her hand upon the tangled mass, pulling at a branch.

"We can burn this in the fireplace," she said.

The branch did not move, and she dropped it; but there was a look of business in her eye as she turned away, saying: "I will get at that in the morning."

"And your month of idleness?" I asked.

She smiled.

"There is your balsam couch," I continued; "and there your hillside and sunshine."

"Oh, I don't feel so tired now," she said. "I am happy. Really, I don't think I could be quiet with so many pleasant things to do. That brush-pile will be good for me."

Under other circumstances, perhaps, we might have spent that afternoon around our clearing, along the brook, noisy from the recent rains, or lying on the hillside; for it was our custom to take as we went the present's due proportion of the pleasures we anticipated; but now that this would be our home, and the future lay unlimited before us, we were willing to spend three weeks preparing for the happiness to come. We were willing, even, to hurry and push matters, so that these preparatory days might be quickly over with.

It was in this spirit that we went to Tannersville, found Mr. Goslee where we had met him first, ordered the lumber for the floors, the ceiling, and the stairway, and returned satisfied because in the morning the labor would be begun.

That evening, as we sat by the stove in the kitchen, I asked Mr. Seifferth if he knew where there was a cow for sale.

"Not around here," he said. "Every one has one or two—just what they need. A cow around here anybody wanted to get rid of you wouldn't want to buy, I guess."

"Well, how can I get one, then?"

"Oh," he said, "you will have to look around and inquire, of course. Over there in Jewett, or over Windham way, they have dairies, and you can get a cow there 'most any time if you will pay for it."

"Well, what's a good cow worth?"

"Well, that depends, of course, on how good she is, how much the man wants for her, and how much you are willing to pay. What kind of a cow do you want?"

"I want a gentle cow—one that gives rich milk, and plenty of it."

He threw back his head and laughed.

"'Most any one would like to have that kind," he said; "but they are hard to find here. There used to be good cattle in this country in the old days when they first brought the Durhams here; but for a long time now they have been mixing them with Jerseys and Alderneys, and all kinds of fancy breeds, until you cannot find a real good cow that will stand this climate anywhere. Well," he added, after a moment's pause, "there's Jack Dale's cow, and she's a good one; but you could not buy her for less than a hundred dollars. But she is old now—and, then, no cow is worth that much."

"What's a good cow worth—about how much?"

"Well, there ain't no cow in these mountains worth more than forty dollars, and thirty dollars would be enough for what you would be likely to get."

"How much milk ought a real good cow to give?"

"Well, now, that depends upon the breed. If a cow gives rich milk, she won't give much."

"How much do your cows give?"

"Sometimes more, sometimes less—depends upon the time of year it is. I have four cows that have just come in—one gives eight quarts to a mess, and another four; and so it goes."

"Sixteen quarts a day—I should think that would be very good."

"Yes, of course, there are some that give ten and twelve quarts to a mess; but I don't know of any around here that will do it, unless it's Jack Dale's, and of course that's only in June or July, when the pasture is best."

"Does a cow need much pasture?"

"It takes a good bit of land to keep a cow."

This made me pause a moment to reflect.

"I don't suppose my woods," I said, "would make good pasture."

"No," he answered; "it would have to be cleared off for that."

"I suppose you turn your cows upon that hillside across the brook from us?"

"Yes, I have three pastures for them; and when one gets poor, I turn them into another."

"I will need a fence, then, if I have a cow, or keep my cow fastened to a stake?"

"Well," he said, "she will have to have more grass than you have got. You might let her run with mine."

All this made me thoughtful. I had seen a picture of our corner in the woods, the forest gone, and I turned in horror from it. A cow imprisoned to a stake, or feeding on my neighbor's meadow, was not a pleasant prospect, either.

A little later, when the moon was up, Nancy and I went out upon the road and walked to the bridge to view our distant boundary. Between the road and our forest-line was an open, grassy hillside of some twenty acres, dotted with small balsams. Its surface was littered with stones, with here and there a great boulder; but, for all this, the grass grew luxuriously, and there were broad patches of unbroken sod. Many times I had looked upon this field with desires I scarcely recognized, but now I listened to their voices thoughtfully.

"Nancy," I said, "we ought to have that hillside."

"Do you know," she said, "I think so too."

"This is our home now, and we want room enough in which to live. With that amount of land we could make our living, if we had to, with our own hands. We would feel secure. Now, it might cost two thousand dollars, and it might cost less. Stocks and bonds are not always secure, and the revenue they supply is a lifeless thing. The price of that land would bring us ninety dollars a year, at the most, in interest. I would rather earn that much in some other way for the pleasure of possessing it."

"Yes," said Nancy, "this is our home, and I think we would be happier with our money here."

Before we went to bed, the land was ours for fifteen hundred dollars. I have been told we paid too much, and it is true that you can buy a farm of one hundred acres in this region, with more or less decrepit buildings on it, for a smaller sum. There are places around us on these mountain-sides that can be bought for seven dollars an acre that would have suited us had we chanced upon them first. But Mr. Seifferth loves his land; he does not need to sell. This place of ours was his richest pasture, his finest timber. It abutted for a long distance upon the valley road. It was bounded at its base by one of the largest mountain streams. It held the spring from which he drank. He delighted in its beauty and its view.

Strange anomaly! It was through sentiment that he held it dear, and through sentiment that he sold it.

He took the good price, more than half regretting it—but he took it, for he wished us well.

I was content with the purchase, for to me there was something more than a mere bargain, good or bad.

So far in my life I had achieved happiness without land or money, and I did not wish to lose it now in exchange for these.

CHAPTER VI

A Man On His Domain

E no longer approached our home by way of Seifferth's Lane; for now, the moment we left the highway and crawled through the bars, we stood upon our own land.

A man may lead a brilliant and a useful life dwelling in apartments, drawing his income from the activities of civilization; but whatever he may achieve, there is something lacking until he sees himself surrounded by land enough to support him.

A man and a tree belong to the same family. The one stays at home. The other may seek his fortune where he will; but if he be a man of sentiment, the soil will forever be to him like the memory of a tender mother to her son. He will be homesick if he stays too long away. Civilization is restless, for it is still an adventurer, seeking wealth and honor in foreign parts, nor will it find contentment until it brings its treasures home.

Society has created hothouses, but the old gentleman, in his box at the opera, forgets his winter boutonniére, lost in the elementary emotions of his youth, when he went wooing with a garden rose.

The most powerful emotions of life, though vague, are those which precede ambition. First, there is the voice of our mother, who speaks to us of God, a dandelion, and the stars. We wonder, and make portentous resolves. Then ambition leads us to the counting-house, where our aspirations dwindle to intrigue.

Through all the ages Nature is pleading with her children for a civilization planted in the soil and cultivated in faithful obedience to her laws, that she may produce fruit, sound, delicious, wholesome, sufficient for them all. When man has yielded to Nature's voice, the brotherhood of man still makes its claim.

For Nancy and me, this final purchase changed our vague feelings of uncertainty, which, though unrecognized, were still associated with our venture, into a sense of complete security. So long as this green hillside lay between us and the road, separated from us only by the width of a brook, we must have fenced our cow in from its tempting pasturage, and borrowed a good deal of our own delight from our neighbor's field. We could have done this cheerfully, with an easy conscience, if we had been unable to buy it; but to wish for it, and need it, and deny ourselves, hugging a bond to our bosom, would have placed us at once among those cowardly misers who pose as cautious men.

Now we could stand in our dooryard and gaze over the valley with a contented eye, coveting no more of it, for we could use no more.

Our way now seemed very simple. There would be three weeks of labor on the house, and we would live in it. We had only to find a cow and some chickens; to have a little plowing done; to plant some seeds and watch them grow. We would have milk, butter, eggs, and vegetables for a little pleasant labor.

We had a thousand books that we might read together in the long leisure of the days.

On Monday the first load of lumber came up the old road, through the lane, across the creek. The horses plunged down and scrambled up its steep banks, jolting over the stones, straining up the rough, uneven hillside. This reminded me that I must make a roadway of my own.

Mr. Goslee came, bringing with him an apprentice for a helper. I was now to discover the difference between the fall, when the rush of business was over, and the spring, when it was just begun.

Through the week Mr. Goslee seemed anxious and distraught. The apprentice, who could not drive a nail without denting the wood with abortive blows, constantly hampered and vexed him. They hung the windows, partly laid down the floors, and sealed a portion of the interior. In all of this I lent a hand, eager to have the business done.

Nancy spent the days dragging at the brush-pile, bringing it, branch by branch, and burning it in the fireplace. When the roaring fire could receive no more, she hurried eagerly to the brook, again impeded by the litter of three years. She toiled with an almost feverish intensity. All her poetic instincts and finer qualities, so long repressed, had found a sudden liberty. She reveled in the nature of her surroundings and her tasks; but here, in this ideal spot, she had brought with her the habits formed in commercial enterprise, so that sentimental delight took the form of restlessness and activity.

All day she tugged and dragged at that brush-heap, as if it were a rush order in her copying-office, promised in the morning, which she must stay up all night to do.

In nature there is constant activity and perpetual repose, and we are safe only as we acquire this mysterious balance.

The week was passed in straining effort and impatience. It was for us like those which, in endless succession, constitute the lives of most people.

No one pursues happiness, for it is beside us always, and it is its shadow that we pursue. We possess it when we take hold of it, look into its eyes, walk with it hand in hand.

Saturday afternoon, when Mr. Goslee was packing up his tools, he looked at me for a moment in smiling apology, and said:

"I cannot be here next week. I will have to leave you for a while."

"Why, how is that?" I exclaimed.

"Well," he said, "we have an awful lot of work in the parks, preparing for the summer people, you know. I have been disappointed in getting men, and have got more to do than I can possibly attend to."

"But you promised to get us in shape here," said Nancy, gazing at us blankly. "We aren't much better off than we were."

"I know," said Mr. Goslee, shrugging his shoulders and bending his troubled glance to the ground. "I hate to disappoint you, but it can't be helped. I've got too much at stake."

"Well," I said, "when will you be back again?"

"Within ten days, or two weeks at the most," he said. "I can come then and finish the job for you."

"Can we get anyone else?"

He smiled and shook his head.

"I don't think so. Even I can't get men enough. You see, all the work around here comes in a rush. We must do everything in a few months."

We watched him drive away in silence. Nancy was standing by the remnants of her brush-heap, her face, which had been growing strained and pinched recently from excessive labor, now became overcast with the shades of disappointment and anger.

For some moments I stood frowning in the doorway, and then, casting these disturbers from me, I turned to Nancy.

"Well," I said, "what of it?"

Her little form had suddenly lost its expression of alertness. She stood in a listless attitude, weary through and through.

"I didn't think Mr. Goslee would be capable of such a thing."

"Well," I said, "he can't help it."

"He could have told us what to expect, in the first place. He came here to finish the job, and he should have done so."

"That's true enough, but what is that to us? When we were in the city we thought that it would be enough just to get up here. Think how many days we have been happy with no house at all!"

"I know; but I am so anxious to get our things unpacked, to move in, and to be settled here."

"Think what it will be, to sleep among these trees, spend our days in this quiet forest, to look out upon it every morning for years and years to come."

"Yes; I suppose, since we are here for good, we might endure the few weeks of delay."

"Nancy," I said, "come inside a moment. You talk of unpacking and settling here. Have you noticed this room with any reference to that?"

"Why, what do you mean?"

"Well, it's all windows and doors, and in no place is there more than two feet of wall between them, except in that corner, where the stairs were to be; but if the stairs go there, where can we put the piano, unless it backs up against the window; and there is no place at all for a china-closet or a cupboard."

"Why," said Nancy, looking around eagerly, as one who wishes instantly to refute a statement disagreeable if true—"why, why," and then in final helplessness, "why, sure enough!"

"Well, now," I said, "I like this room just as it is. It is a classic. With that huge chimney and fireplace at one end and some heavy rustic furniture, it will be complete."

"Oh, I wouldn't change it," she assured me eagerly.

"Well, then we need another room. We ought to build a combination kitchen and dining-room here at the end—another little house, in fact; and instead of having two bedrooms up-stairs here, we could have a kitchen and another bedroom for you or me, as well as a storeroom."

"Yes," said Nancy; "we certainly need a storeroom. I have thought myself that in this house, as it is, there will be no place to put anything. How much will such a building cost?"

"Well," I said, "judging from this one, "I should say it could easily cost four or five hundred dollars, but we might build it for half of that if we wished to."

"Oh, a very simple affair, I should think, would do."

"Well, it is decided, then. We will have an addition of some sort, anyhow."

When we told the Seifferths of our plan that evening, Mrs. Seifferth said at once: "You will need a cellar."

"Yes; I suppose we ought to have one."

"Of course," she said emphatically; "if you are going to live there in the winter, you must have a cellar."

"How would you keep your potatoes," said Mr. Seifferth, "if you didn't."

"You will have canned fruit, I suppose?"

"Sure enough," I said, glancing with delight at Nancy, "we must have canned fruit."

"Why, I remember now there are any quantity of blackberries and raspberries growing here," she exclaimed; and I saw in her sparkling eyes the vision of those fine fall days when we should be busy picking and preserving them.

Later, when we were alone, I said to her: "The cellar need not cost so much. I can dig that myself. I can be busy doing that while we are waiting for the carpenters to return."

"I wish," she said wistfully, "that we could get our stuff and things moved in there now. Why couldn't we?"

There is certainly no better place to board in all the world than Mr. Seifferth's, and there was no place where we had been happier or felt so much at home; but now, with this nest of our own so close at hand, every day there was like an imprisonment; for to all of us values are not real, but fanciful.

The next morning we drove to Tannersville, and bought the household things we needed to supplement those we had brought with us from the city.

At the end of our house, opposite the fireplace, was a small brick chimney, built to accommodate a stove; for we knew that in extremely cold weather the fireplace alone could not heat our large room.

That afternoon our things were delivered. The range was put in place in one corner. Back of it, one six-foot window overlooked the brook, and in the wall at the side was another, from which the valley could be seen through the tall trees of our dooryard.

We had bought a little supply of provisions. Mrs. Seifferth had given us milk, butter, and eggs.

It was a warm spring afternoon, and a little before sunset, at a table before our open double doors, we had our first supper—oatmeal with cream, toast, eggs, and coffee. That evening our lamp was lighted for the first time in our own home. It was the good, clear light of a student-lamp, but in this long room it created only a luminous center encircled by a pleasant twilight.

With the nightfall, however, we built a fire in the fireplace, and the ceiling, walls, and floor shone in its dancing light. The great forest outside, awakened by the night wind, sang to us a song of welcome. Neither of us had ever before seen such a roaring, crackling, brilliant, pleasant fire in so cavernous a fireplace.

When all the room was well illuminated we went outside, walked to the edge of our forest-line, and turned to look. The little house, with its dormered roof, its wide eaves, its beautiful, broad windows with diamond frames, all glowing with a cheerful light, seemed, in truth, the creation of some tender magic that had befriended us; and this forest from which its glowing windows peeped, one of the enchanted forests of the fables we had always more than half believed.

The Houses

Clearing the woods for the House. (*House in the Woods, 1904*)

Hewing the sills. (*House in the Woods, 1904*)

The boundary pool. (*House in the Woods, 1904*)

The House in winter, with Bob Golightly at the ready. (*House in the Woods, 1904*)

The House in the Woods, from a scrapbook found in the library of the second House. Arthur Henry is pictured with a triad of Scottish collies, although the book references only one—Bob Golightly. However, Mrs. Walter Lowe, daughter of the book's "Elizabeth", recalled an Anna Mallon visit in which a collie was presented as a gift—which her mother, as soon as propriety allowed, bestowed on her neighbors, the Effram Zimbalist family. (*Author's collection*)

The living room of the first House. The rocking chair survived the fire into the present, and is still in use. The Dryden quotation rests on the mantel of the fireplace built of rocks from the brook and site. (*Courtesy of Antoinette Martignoni*)

Bob Golightly driving Jennie and Maggie to pasture. (*House in the Woods*, 1904)

The second House in the Woods, built after the fire, with a Scottish collie—probably not Bob Golightly—enjoying the view. It is this House, virtually unchanged, that survives in the present. (*Author's collection*)

The House of Four Pillars, an historic structure that once served as a station on the Underground Railway. Although literary scholars take issue with the claim, Maude Wood Henry is vehement in her recollection that Dreiser started *Sister Carrie* here. (*Courtesy of Maumee Valley Historical Society*)

The house at Narragansett Pier. Henry died there in 1934, his obituary noting that "he always loved New England … [and] cherished particularly the house at Narragansett." (*Author's collection*)

Dumpling Island, a few hundred yards off the shore of Noank. The "island cabin" is partially shielded by trees. Might the figure peering at us from the island shore be none other than A.H. himself? (*Courtesy of Noank Historical Society*)

The Players

Arthur Henry (top) Maude Wood (bottom) and Theodore Dreiser (right). Undated portraits, most likely taken during Dreiser's brief stint as a stringer for the Toledo *Blade* and lengthier stay with the Henrys at the House of Four Pillars. (*Courtesy of Cornell University Archives*)

Anna Mallon. Handwritten on back of photo: "Anna Mallon Henry 1893. Taken before her marriage to Arthur. Daughter of James Mallon, brevetted General in Civil War at age 26, killed in Va." (*Author's collection*)

Anna Mallon, after her return to the House in the Woods, with two new collie companions. (*Courtesy of Antoinette Martignoni*)

The Meadow Lawn. The boarding farmhouse of Thomas Seifferth and his wife Sydney, where Arthur, "Nancy", and "Elizabeth" began their Catskills adventure. (*Courtesy of Martin J. Farrell*)

Owners of the boardinghouse, Meadow Lawn, Thomas and Sydney Seifferth. (*Author's collection*)

Brigitte "Beezie" Seery, the book's "Elizabeth", with her and George Main's daughter. (*Courtesy of Mrs. Walter Lowe*)

Katie Convery, will-o'-the-wisp mother of the Convery clan, at work in a hayfield. (*House in the Woods, 1904*)

The Converys in the hayfield. (*House in the Woods, 1904*)

Delia Farrell Seifferth, who became Anna Mallon's dearest friend and counselor. (*Author's collection*)

Clare Kummer, prolific playwright and Arthur Henry's third wife, from 1935 ASCAP records. (*Author's collection*)

Recently released from jail with their reputations
intact, members of the cast of *The Night Before* pose
humorlessly with a smiling attorney from ASCAP. The
young ingenue stands with Arthur Henry in the back
row. (*Brooklyn Evening Graphic*, *November 22, 1928;
courtesy of Mrs. Theodore Rinehart*)

The Bohemian Club. Arthur Henry is seated far right, and Brand Whitlock is standing behind the skeleton. (*Chicago Tribune, January 28, 1945; courtesy of the Tribune*)

The Bohemian Club. Arthur Henry is atop the piano at which Brand Whitlock sits. (*Chicago Tribune, January 28, 1928; courtesy of the Tribune*)

CHAPTER VII

What A Stump Revealed

LL of our rooms extended across the entire width of the house, with windows looking into the forest on one side, and out upon the valley on the other.

Through a window at the end of my bedroom I can catch glimpses of our brook between the trees and overhanging shrubs.

That first night I lay a long time listening to the sound of the forest and the running water. I settled myself comfortably in my bed, closed my eyes, vaguely wishing that I might not sleep, but that, through the night, I might enjoy the drowsy ecstasy this lullaby inspired. A moment later I was wide awake, the light of the morning in my room. I heard Nancy singing in the room below, and jumping from the bed, I shouted for my breakfast, and moved from window to window as I dressed.

It was all true, then. We had spent the night upon our possessions. Long years of liberty lay before us, and, to prove it, here was the day. The forest was awake. I swung down through a hole in the floor, removed the box and the chair that served for our stairway, and while Nancy was getting the breakfast took my ax, chopped down a tall, slender maple near the door, cut it into poles, and made a ladder. It was only eight feet long, but so heavy that I could scarcely lift it and put it into place.

I put the ax on the floor beside me while I ate, and when I was through I carried it outside to the end of the house where the addition was to be. The huge stone chimney had required a little room for its building, but the dense line of forest, with its tangle of underbrush, was not more than ten feet away. I had to push my way through this in order to measure off the space for our kitchen. It took me one step beyond an enormous hemlock rotting upon the ground. It required an hour to cut away the brush and pile it in a heap outside my clearing. There were a number of slender beeches and maples, and five large trees—two maples, one beech, a birch about a foot in diameter, and a hemlock nearly two feet.

The hour of cutting and hauling had wearied me, and I stood for a moment, leaning upon my ax, to breathe; but as I glanced about me, it seemed to me that I had done a good deal. Thinking only of the progress I was making, I stepped to the maple nearest me. Imperfect memories of woodsmen I had seen at work, and a little experience three years before, gave me some notion of the way to fell a tree. I knew there should be one slanting stroke and one straight cut in to release the chip; that the ax must be given a free, full-arm swing. I knew that I could not be breathing properly or I would not pant and puff so. My strokes were terribly uneven. The chips did not fly, but clung to the tree until I hacked them off. I had made a jagged hole. By the time it was two thirds through I was exhausted, very red in the face, almost unable to breathe. While I was resting, Nancy, through with her dishes, came out.

"My!" she said, "what a clearing you have made!" Then, glancing eagerly around, she thrust her hands into an old pair of gloves, saying: "I suppose all these stones must be removed. I can be doing that."

Her presence awakened me to a possibility I had not thought of before.

"It will not be safe for you to work around here," I said. "A tree might fall on you."

As I spoke a gust of wind passed us, and the tree began to rock and creak.

"My Lord!" I exclaimed, "it will hit the house."

I stood for a moment looking helplessly at this monster towering some fifty feet above me, and then jumped aside, warned by the violent tearing of its fibers. It was not due to me that the house was not demolished. Fortunately, however, the tree leaned a little to the west, so that it fell crashing to the ground, just escaping the eaves, hitting the house a slanting blow with its branches, but doing no harm.

"That seems to be dangerous," said Nancy, looking anxiously at the remaining trees.

"I didn't cut it right," I said. "I will do these others differently."

"It will be all right," I continued, as she still looked anxious; "for none of these trees lean very much, and of course they must fall in the direction of the deepest cut."

I had been thinking of many pleasant things before, but I saw now that when one is at work in the woods he must first acquire the instincts, the knowledge, the habits of a woodsman before his thoughts are free.

I cut the branches from the fallen tree and chopped it into short lengths. These Nancy helped carry from the clearing. By noon the giants had all been butchered and removed.

Nancy knew how to cook only a very few things. Always, before, when we were away from the city, we had paid for our meals as we found them, taking them as they came. During the two summers we had lived on the island Elizabeth had cooked for us. There, of course, fish were plentiful, the life of a fanciful nature, the labor light and picturesque.

This was our first dinner alone that Nancy had prepared after a hard morning's labor. Thinking little about it—for, of course, her coffee was good, and that, with bread, butter, and an omelet would ordinarily be enough for us—she had prepared these things and placed them on a table, daintily arranged, before the open doors.

"Are there any more eggs?" I asked, when everything was eaten.

"Yes," she answered gleefully. "Do you know that I am hungry, too? There's some oatmeal left from breakfast," she added.

"All these stumps," I said, "must be dug out, and I must have some tools to do it with."

A ride to Tannersville, which in other times had been a pleasant jaunt, now seemed only a necessary interruption. I was annoyed at my lack of strength and endurance. I could have worked no more that day even if I had had the tools.

"I suppose," I said to Mr. Seifferth, as we were harnessing the horse, "I will need a pick and a shovel to grub stumps out with."

"You will need a madax," he replied.

"What's that?"

"Well, it's a kind of a thing you dig and cut roots with. You can get it at Allen's. They will show you what it is."

When I got to Allen's I asked for a madax, and they gave me an implement with one prong like that of a pick, and the other a long, thick, narrow hoe with a sharp beveled edge. I knew that I should need a shovel, so I bought a short-handled one, the only kind I had ever used.

The ride of four miles and back had rested and refreshed me. I forgot my weary limbs and aching muscles, and lifting my eyes from the haunches of the horse, looked over the valley. It was still serene, and beautiful.

In the evening we unpacked some of our things, put the heaps of bags and bundles and boxes into a little better order, got out the piano-lamps with their gorgeous shades, drew our rockers to the fireplace, spread a rug at our feet, and forgot for a little while our unsettled state in these glimpses and promises of comfort.

The next morning we had eggs, oatmeal, and coffee for breakfast, and I went out with my madax, as I supposed, to begin upon the stumps.

I had left word with Mr. Seifferth to tell Mr. Brice, when he saw him pass, that I wanted him to lay the walls of the cellar, and that I should be ready for him soon.

"It will take me, perhaps, four or five days to dig it," I said to Nancy.

The first forenoon I had cleared the ground, and would get the stumps out on the second day, and two more days of just plain digging, I thought, should do it. It was to be only a small hole, sixteen by sixteen, and six feet deep.

We rose early in those days. It was, in fact, a few moments before six o'clock when I stood over one of the maple stumps, looking at it critically. There were five large roots, forming the base of the tree, extending like prongs from it in all directions, visible for a few feet, like ribs, and then disappearing in the ground. It would, of course, be necessary to get the stump free from these roots. In order to do that, I must dig away the soil between them. I was clothed only in my trousers and shirt. Grasping the handle of my madax, a weapon of some weight, I swung it above my head, expecting to bury its blade in the soil. There was a hard, sharp sound. I felt a sudden giddiness; a stinging sensation passed from my palm over my arm and to my shoulder. The pain nauseated me. My arm seemed paralyzed. I had struck a great stone reposing under the roots, and covered with about an inch of forest mold, as unresisting as dry moss.

Nancy, appearing at that moment, saw me doubled in a contortion of distress, hugging my arm, my face twisted. Instantly her eyes grew large with anxiety and alarm. Unconsciously the expression of her face mimicked my own, and these purely sympathetic contortions enraged me, for they expressed a suffering so much greater than the fact.

"Oh!" she exclaimed, "are you hurt?"

"Yes," I roared; "but not as bad as you look!"

The malignancy of my glance was like a blow to her. The invisible daggers of the eye, how they can pierce the affections! In a moment our positions were reversed. The pain had left me, and Nancy was the wounded one.

With Elizabeth, a laugh would have made all right again, but not with Nancy. She would have met an apology or a caress with a wan smile, and would have made a profound effort to forget the incident, but she would have brooded over it. There are fathomless depths in every nature, reaching from the individual to the infinite. When Nancy was at peace there were no barriers of personality or artifice, but from these luminous depths there flowed warm and pure affection unrestrained.

An injury is big or little according to the degree of sensitiveness that receives it. A pinprick in the affections is a sword-thrust to one like Nancy. It stirred emotions that she really was unable to control; but aside from all this sincerity there was the element of the mind, which at such moments separated itself from the soul, becoming a personality of its own, the alert actress, with an imagination and sensibilities, seeing an appealing part to play. Great happiness is possible for such a woman. She can both feel and bestow it, but she cannot find nor keep it for herself. One who would be happy with her must understand her, and be able at such a time to say: "Look at me, Nancy. Here is your soul. I have injured it, but it is my sweetheart, and I would see it smile. Now here is your mind. It is a good actress, we know, but let us give it another part to play. This one is pathetic, and we do not care to weep."

Standing by the stump above my fallen madax, I said to Nancy almost what I have written here. She listened in astonishment. There was no longer any wound. The actress forgot her rule, and we had a happy ending of the drama without its three long acts.

When Nancy is happy she is beautiful, at once ingenuous and mature, like a warm day in autumn that recalls the spring.

She sat near me on a neighboring stump, and I returned to work. I stooped over now, the handle between my legs, picking at the dirt cautiously, removing it from the stone I had hit. I found that it filled the entire space between the two prongs, running under them and some distance beyond. Following its surface away from the tree, through a network of roots, dirt, and stones, I made in an hour's time a hole about two feet deep, somewhat circular, and perhaps four feet across at the top.

All this time I had been stooping. The long, hoe-like blade was constantly becoming fast in the roots. It was impossible ever to strike a telling blow. It was all tug and strain and almost fruitless tussle. The thing had become a conflict, and in the heat of it I had unconsciously increased my exertions, moment by moment, until I could have done no more had I been engaged in a death-struggle with a beast.

"Why don't you rest a little?" said Nancy. "Your face is flaming."

"I want to get the d—d thing out," I said. I tried to stand up straight and found it almost impossible.

"I can understand now," I continued, pressing my hand against the small of my back to ease the aching muscles, "how men become crooked in such work as this."

I had worked an hour, but had not uncovered this first obstruction, and not a root of this first stump was cut.

If I get these out today, I thought, I shall probably be used up, and there are four more of them. Then, after that, there is the hole to dig.

I looked at my job thoughtfully. As I was standing so, Mr. Brice came around the corner of the house.

As he greeted me, I saw the smile beneath his mustache that had first enlightened me concerning him.

"I heard you wanted me," he said.

"Yes; when can you come?"

"Well, that's what I wanted to speak about. If I come at all, I might as well come one time as another. I've got jobs enough on hand to keep me busy every day all summer."

"I hope you can do this for me," I said anxiously.

"Well, I will," he answered. "I can get some one else to wait, I guess. You're not going to dig it yourself, are you?" And this time the smile lighted his quiet blue eyes.

"Well, I thought I would."

"I guess, then," he said, looking at me drolly, "there will be no hurry."

"Well, I'm beginning to think that myself. I don't know as I can dig it."

"I suppose you could," he said, "in time; but you'll find it pretty hard. I can see you're not used to it."

There was something in his eyes as he glanced at the stumps that made me ask:

"How is that?"

"Well," he answered, "if you'd been you wouldn't have chopped down these trees. You can grub 'em ten times as easy with the tops to help you."

"No," I said, with sudden conviction; "it's foolish for me to attempt this. Whom can I get to dig it for me?"

"Oh, I don't know," he said. "There are several good men. I guess, though, they are all busy now." He thought a moment and added: "There's Jack and Andy Dale. I don't think they're working anywhere. Perhaps you could get them."

"Where do they live?"

"Why, Andy Dale is right next to you here, and Jack is next to him."

"Then you must pass them on your way home?"

"Yes; I go by there."

"All right. Will you stop in and tell them to come and do this for me?"

"Well," he said slowly, "I wouldn't like to tell them that. They're kind of peculiar about some things. I wouldn't like to tell them to come and do it. I can say you'd like to see them about some work that they might do."

"All right," I said. "How long do you think it ought to take?"

"Oh, you can't tell that. You don't know what you are going to strike when you begin to dig."

"Well, I would like to have you all ready when it is done."

He took the tool I had been using, stepped into my hole, dug down some six inches until his blows produced a dull, muffled sound, making scarcely any impression on the solid earth.

"This is hard-pan," he said. "Still, it ought not to be so bad after the stumps are out. I guess, probably, by the first of the week it might be done."

"How can we get to that chimney without disturbing it?"

"I see it's moved a little," he said, looking up its length; "but that's not much for three years, and I guess it's settled now. Oh, you ought to be able to get within two feet of it. It rests on the hard-pan, and that won't give."

"I didn't suppose it would be so hard to dig," I said to Nancy when he was gone.

"It must be awful hard."

"Let's have a bath."

She went inside and got our towels, wash-rags, and soap. We followed the rough road down the hillside to the creek that bounded our place. The bed of this stream was of solid rock, worn smooth in places by the water; in others, impeded by piled-up stones, with now and then a solitary boulder. There were ledges at intervals, like steps, forming a steep ascent up the mountain-side. At these places there were miniature waterfalls. It was a long, sinuous tunnel of the forest, roofed by overhanging trees, filled with an illusive, liquid melody.

In one of our explorations we had found two shallow basins, in broad, smooth slabs, extending across the bed of the stream, scooped out by the eddies of centuries. An enormous boulder separated these basins, acting as a screen, affording us two bath-rooms beneath the trees. Nancy had a grassy bank, surrounded by bushes, for a dressing-room, and I a low, broad rock, with a flat surface, warm and dry.

Hard labor, free perspiration, and, afterward, a nipping bath, give one an imperious appetite.

"It is a wonder to me," I said, "that country people don't bathe oftener."

I was no longer lame or weary. We hurried home to eat. We had bread, potatoes, eggs, and coffee. I left the table hungry, although I could eat no more—a circumstance that surprised me, for it was unusual. My courage was renewed.

"These men may not come," I said to Nancy; "and I will get at those stumps again. I feel more like it now."

When I went out, I heard a rustling in the brush, and from the woods there stepped a sturdy-looking man of medium height, thick-set, with a full gray beard, and white hair rather long and scant. He came slowly to where I was among the stumps, and stood before me, his hands in his pockets, looking, not at me, but critically over the clearing I had made.

"You want a cellar dug?" he said.

"Yes; are you Jack Dale?"

"No; I am his brother, Andy."

"Well, here's the place. Can you dig it for me?"

"Well, that's what I came to see about."

I waited a few moments while he was seeing.

"How much will you pay?" he said.

I had asked the Seifferths about this, and they had told me that a dollar and a half a day was the usual price.

"A dollar and a half a day," I said.

He looked more like an old Scotchman than an Irishman. There was a shrewd twinkle in the blue eyes, deep-set beneath bushy brows. There was an indescribable, plaintive minor in his husky voice, but it was pleasant to listen to.

"Well, now," he said, with persuasive dignity, "don't you think it's worth a little more? It will be hard digging here."

"I know," I said, motioning to my hole; "for I've been testing it. What do you think it's worth?"

"Well, I should think a dollar and seventy-five cents would be more like it, now."

"I want to do the fair thing."

We exchanged a smiling glance, and he said:

"Yes; it's better to do that."

"A pleasant feeling is worth something."

"It's a good deal better to have it that way," he replied. "Do you want us to furnish our own tools?"

"I have only these, and I expect to help you."

"The only reason I asked"—looking past me with troubled eyes—"is because my own aren't very good. They're about worn out. Still," he added, with sudden conviction, looking at me frankly, "at that price we ought to furnish the tools." He left me, agreeing to return in the morning with his brother.

A little before seven the next day they came, and by noon there were five jagged holes in my clearing, and five stumps that had been wrenched from them, crushing the bushes on one side.

I had watched the men's labor in amazement.

Jack Dale had been cast in an imposing mold; tall, classically proportioned, he possessed the strength of a horse and the grace of an Indian. Long, dark hair, touched with gray, crowned his fine head. His face was clean shaven. The network of wrinkles, the deep seams in the firm, brown skin, were like an open book. Toil, hardship, and exposure place wrinkles in the face, but it is the spirit of a man that gives them their direction. This dark-hued countenance, with square, protruding chin, large mouth, aquiline nose, broad, low forehead, overhanging brows, and large, deep-set eyes, might readily have been a somber or a tragic thing. If the soul behind it had been cowardly and avaricious, it would have served as a mask for Irving in the tragedy of "The Bells"; but there was something droll about the firm, broad mouth, a gentle humor in the eyes.

He came from the woods with an easy, swinging gait, a crowbar, an ax, a pick, and a shovel held as lightly on his shoulder as I would hold a broom. There was the unconscious scrutiny of a wise man in his eyes when I first looked into them; but a moment later I saw there only the twinkle of a kindly welcome. He thrust out his long right arm, and shook me by the hand.

The first time I spoke to him I called him "Jack," and he seemed to think it natural.

"You see," I said, "I've been busy here."

"Well, I wish you hadn't," said Jack, explosively.

"Brice told me I should have left the trees alone."

"It would have been a good deal easier to get the stumps out."

"Well, well," said Andy, "you can't blame the man for it, being as he didn't know."

"There, you old fool," said Jack, good-naturedly, "I'm not blaming him; but it's the truth."

"Heigho!" he said, swinging his tools to the ground; "but it can't be helped. Nothing could be worse, though, than these beech and maple stumps, unless it is the hemlock; but if we must, we must." So saying, he laid off his coat, and strode to the stone I had partially disclosed.

"We ought to have a madax," he said, "to work among these roots. I have none, and Andy's is no good."

"Well, here's one," I said, holding out my tool.

"That's a grub-hoe. It's no good for work like this. What did you get this thing for?" he said, lifting my shovel from the hole.

"To shovel with."

"It's been some time since I've seen one of these short-handled shovels," he said, poising it in his hand, meditation in his eyes. "They used to make them all that way; but you can do more work with a long-handled shovel, and it's easier on your back."

"Well, now," said Andy, "some likes them that way, so they do."

"Why, yes," said Jack; "some like a muzzle-loading gun, and some would walk to San Francisco before they'd venture on a train. Have you got an ax?" he asked, turning abruptly to the stump.

I gave him mine.

He cut a notch out of each of the two roots, above the stone. His first two blows were terrific, one on each side of the chip, causing it to fly some distance beyond the clearing. His next two were lighter, and his last a quick, sharp cut, completely severing the root without touching the rock it pressed against.

Andy, meanwhile, had been picking the dirt from the roots upon the other side, driving the prong in among the fibrous network and drawing up masses of the soil. Jack severed the huge roots as they were exposed.

"Now," said he, "give me that crowbar." He jabbed it around the stump, meeting everywhere the same sudden, absolute resistance.

"That stone," he said, "runs right through under it. I tell you, it's a big one by the sound."

"If that's so," said Andy, "there can't be no big root underneath."

"Well, we will see," said Jack, "whether there is or not." He jammed the crowbar under the stump, between it and the stone, braced himself, and gave a mighty lift. There was a loud sound of rending, and the stump rolled out bodily, carrying with it a mass of stones and soil, broken roots, and fibers.

"I think, Nancy," I said at noon, "we will have our cellar in a few days now. These men are wonders."

In the afternoon Mr. Seifferth came up, bringing a stranger with him. He was a short, thin man, clothed in a patchwork of garments. His face was cadaverous and gentle, his eyes ingenuous, anxious, and appealing. He held himself daintily, stooped a little when he stood, and when he spoke his head was held sidewise and thrust somewhat forward, like an observant bird's.

"This is Johnson," said Mr. Seifferth. "He is the best judge of cows in the mountains. He can get you a good one if anyone can."

I looked at him quietly for a few moments, and he returned my gaze.

"All right," I said; "I will tell you what I want. I want a cow that will give good, rich milk, anywhere from six to eight quarts to a mess. I want a friendly cow, one that will milk easily—the kind you can be proud of, you understand."

"Yes," he said, looking earnestly at me; "I know just what you want, and I will get her for you."

A few days after this Johnson returned to me, saying that he had found the cow, but that he had no money to buy her. Forty-eight dollars was the price. I gave him this and five dollars for his trouble.

As he was leaving he turned back and said, with a solemn kind of earnestness:

"Now don't you be worried if you don't see me for a few days. I must bring her from a distance, and I want good weather for it. It don't do to be careless with a cow. I will bring her to my place to-morrow if it's a pleasant day, and keep her overnight; but if you don't see me for a few days, don't you be anxious."

I assured him with equal earnestness that I would trust him absolutely. He seemed pleased at this, and went away.

That evening we went down to Mr. Seifferth's to see if one of the boys, with his team, could do my plowing for me.

"We are busy now," he said. "We have to work on the road; but I can get a man for you. Where will you have your garden?"

"I haven't quite decided yet. Somewhere on the hillside, I guess."

"That patch of fallow in the woods beyond the house would be the place for you."

"You ought to start an orchard there," said Mrs. Seifferth.

"Yes; you could plant an orchard there, and cultivate a garden at the same time. It would be good for the trees. I cleared that fallow a long time ago."

For some time there was silence in the kitchen. Mrs. Seifferth was knitting. Mr. Seifferth, the picture of placid old age, still hale, sat in his armchair, his chin upon his breast, lost in reflection.

"We can have plums, can't we?" asked Nancy.

"Yes," said Mrs. Seifferth. "Plums do well up here."

"How long after an apple-tree is planted will it have fruit?"

"Oh! that depends upon the kind."

Mr. Seifferth looked up and, with a fine burst of enthusiasm, said: "My, what a crop of rye I got that year!"

"Mr. Johnson has found me a cow," I said.

"Humph!" said Mrs. Seifferth. "You had better look out for Johnson."

Mr. Seifferth laughed. "Have you seen it yet?" he asked.

"Why, no," I answered in some surprise. "He came to get the money."

"And did you give it to him?" asked Mrs. Seifferth.

"Why, of course!"

"Well, that's the last you'll see of it."

"Oh! he'll bring you some kind of cow if he thinks you'd make it warm for him."

"Why, I thought you recommended him so highly," said Nancy, her eyes big with astonishment.

"I told you that he was the best judge of a cow in the mountains, but you must look pretty sharp when you are dealing with him, though."

"So Jack and Andy Dale are working for you?" said Mrs. Seifferth.

"Yes; they are digging a cellar."

"How much do you pay them a day? I heard you gave them a dollar and seventy-five cents."

"Yes," I said, flushing guiltily beneath her sharp, inquisitorial glance.

She cast a look of severe reproach upon me, but said nothing.

As we walked home, Nancy looked at me eagerly, a little anxious, but more amused.

"Well, what do you think of that?" she said.

"I'm not thinking much yet," I answered. "I'm listening."

The first day's work upon the cellar had removed the top dirt. A square hole was made about two feet deep, scooped out clean, leaving the hard, smooth surface of hard-pan exposed. It was like a stone floor.

All the next forenoon Jack and Andy picked this out by dint of steady pounding, accumulating little piles of small, hard pieces not much larger than gravel. The point of the pick could not have been driven with an engine more than an inch or two.

Hour after hour these men sunk their picks, demolishing the compact soil by sheer force and persistence. Twenty times that day Jack said: "I don't think we will ever get through this." But he would smile grimly at me and renew his blows.

A little before six o'clock, Jack, working in one corner, beginning a new layer, struck his pick into a softer earth.

"There, by h—l!" he cried; "we are done with hard-pan."

"It will go a good deal faster now," said Andy.

"Well, I guess it will," said Jack. "We can do a foot to-morrow for an inch to-day."

"Well," I said, "we have gone a little over two feet and a half in two days. We ought to go three feet and a half deeper in two days more; so you can tell Brice to come on Monday."

The hole was not large enough for three to work in, and so I sat outside. After an hour's work the next day, all the hard-pan was removed. A soft, yielding clay had been uncovered, and they tossed it out in solid shovelfuls. Every time they crossed the hole it was from four to six inches deeper, and they had crossed it three times by the middle of the afternoon. With steady regularity the point of the shovel was placed upon the earth and pushed deep into it by a powerful pressure of the leg. After several hours the clay had been growing softer, so that now, when the shovel was lifted, it tore away more than its own width from the surrounding surface. It became more and more like a soft putty, and I marveled that these men could continue so long to heave these heavy loads and toss them beyond the embankment.

While I was watching them, Nancy came hurriedly around the house.

"Here's Johnson!" she exclaimed. "He's got the cow."

I stood up and saw my man walking quietly through the trees of our dooryard, leading by a rope a beautiful fawn-colored Jersey cow. The rope he held was slack. Her nose was but a few feet behind his back, and when he stopped she looked about her tranquilly.

"Come, Jack," I said, "and tell me what kind of a cow this is."

He climbed out of the hole, exclaiming: "Well, by the lightning, if that ain't Johnson! What are you doing here," he bellowed, "you old reprobate, and what kind of a scarecrow have you got here for a cow?"

"This is a good cow," said Johnson, mildly; and then, looking at me with the anxious ingenuousness that gave a sort of solemnity to his gaze, "Her name is Jennie," he said. "She knows her name."

Jack looked her over carefully, squeezed out a little milk, examined her head and the milk-veins, and said:

"She's pretty thin."

"Well," said Johnson, "she belonged to a widow woman who kept her all winter; but she got too poor to feed her, and she had to sell her."

"How much milk does she give?" I asked.

"Well, she's only been in about two weeks. I milked her this morning, and she gave six quarts. Of course she won't give that much to-night, being in a strange place. See how gentle she is," he said, rubbing her between the horns.

Nancy was opposite me, and I could tell by her face that she was pleased.

"What a dainty creature!" she said.

"She looks to be just what I wanted," I said to Johnson.

"Well," he answered, "I wanted to suit you, and I think I have."

"She looks like a good cow," said Jack.

I turned the cow loose upon the pasture, and sat watching her for a while in supreme content, then somewhat reluctantly returned. As I approached the cellar I heard a loud dispute.

"I tell you she's a farrow cow," said Andy, doggedly.

"Oh, farrow your grandmother!" Jack replied.

"This old croaker here is finding fault with the little bossy," Jack continued, as I joined them. "I say she's as pretty a creature as you can find. I know Johnson is a skinflint, but he seems to have treated you all right."

"Well, you wait and see," said Andy. "You've got a farrow cow."

CHAPTER VIII

The Beginnings Of Wisdom

E had our cow, but we had no pail.

"And we will need some milk-pans," I said to Nancy. "Let's go to Tannersville."

"All right," she said. "We need some more provisions. My! I wish those carpenters would come. We have no place to put anything."

"Nancy," I said, "let's not build a kitchen just for cheapness. We really need a good one. I have in mind a fine, long row of cupboards. We can make such a pretty room—a china-closet, with glass doors, in one corner; the cupboards along the side."

While she was getting ready I went out and said to Jack: "I suppose the cow will need some feed."

"Oh, yes," he said; "there's not enough grass yet for bossy."

"What do you feed her?"

"I give mine middlings."

"Let's stop in to Seifferth's for our dinner," I called to Nancy. "It will save time," I added weakly, although, almost unconsciously to myself, this idea was prompted by the craving for a hearty meal.

We found them just at dinner. As we were starting off to Tannersville, I turned to Nancy with a glowing eye.

"It was the pie," I said. "That's it. It was the pie."

"That dinner did taste good," she said. "I'm hungry all the time up here."

"Well, I've been thinking lately, and I believe that the whole secret of our contentment here now lies with you."

"How is that?" she asked in smiling wonder.

"Good, hearty meals are what we need, and especially the pie."

"Perhaps," she said, "I can learn to make a good pie."

We got our pail, our pans, provisions, and feed, and hurried home again. I realized then that I needed a shed at once for Jennie in case of storm, and it occurred to me that this might be built roughly out of small trees at very little expense.

"As soon as the cellar is dug," I thought, "I will have Jack and Andy build it for me."

"I am going to stop here," said Nancy, "and see Mrs. Seifferth about pies and things. I might just as well learn to cook."

When I reached my own bars I found Jennie there. She must have been looking out for me. She thrust out her nose as I passed her, and followed me up the hill. I was obliged to carry what I could of our purchases, for the rough road we had been so far using would have given too severe a shaking to anything but a heavy wagon.

"I must build me a new road at once," I thought; "and it must be a good one."

Jennie kept so close behind me that I had to take a quick step now and then to avoid her friendly horns.

"But I must build me a cow-shed first."

As I climbed the hill, going diagonally over it from the bars to the house, I looked about me for a good location for a road. The ground on the lower half of the pasture I saw was too soft, for it received some of the overflow of the brook, and was probably full of hidden springs of its own. With these things in mind, I reached the little house among the trees, and was immediately summoned by the voice of Jack.

"Here, boss," he cried from the cellar; "here's something I don't like the looks of."

Climbing over the pile of dirt they had thrown out, I discovered that it was covered with sticky mud and water.

"I guess you've got about as much cellar as you will get," said Andy.

"The more we dig the higher the bottom gets," said Jack. "I've been shoveling mud out of this corner for the last two hours, and I can't gain an inch on it."

They were, in fact, wallowing in a curious substance. It was clay, no doubt, but it acted under their feet as would a large hot-water bag, fat and full: it puffed up under them.

"What's that?" I asked in astonishment.

"I don't know what causes it," said Jack. "I've never seen anything like it before."

"Perhaps it's a spring," I said.

"I'd think it was," said Jack, "but it seems to cover the whole cellar."

"I don't see as we are doing any good paddling around in it," said Andy.

"Well, I don't see how you are going to get it dug," said Jack, "if you don't paddle in it. Your shovel won't work alone."

"We're not getting no deeper, so we ain't."

"You're afraid of getting your feet wet."

"Well, I'm not, either, now; but I don't want to stand in this water for nothing. We ought to have dug the drain first."

They had suggested this before the digging was begun, but I was in such a hurry to have the cellar ready for Mr. Brice that I asked them to let this go until he could get to work.

All the while the men had been talking they had not stopped their labors for a moment. It was almost impossible to drive the shovels in. It was like pushing against rubber. There was a sound of sucking and gurgling. Their conversation was punctuated with grunts, and the repartee made more effective by gasps and false notes, for men lift on the pneumatic principle, and their wind is needed for the machine.

Jack suddenly stood up and leaned on his shovel.

"There's no doubt about that ditch. The drainage from the spring rains may have been stored here, or perhaps there's a spring near by that keeps this wet. We better dig the ditch and give it a chance to dry."

There was no help for it.

Jack took the ax and trimmed out a narrow alley through the woods, down the hill, about one hundred feet. It took them three days to dig the ditch. These were three days of almost titanic effort. Every few feet there was a tree to grub. For the entire distance the top soil was a mass of stubborn roots. There were stones upon stones, and every now and then a huge boulder, which had to be encircled with a hole two or three times as wide as the ditch. To get some of these out by hand required a back like a derrick, the cunning of a fox. One must know that every obstacle has its weak point. One must have the sagacity to find it, the strength and will to take advantage of it. Tool after tool found its way to that ditch—crowbars, sledges, wedges, chains.

"Ram your crowbar in there."

"No; I think this is the spot. There, by h—l, she gives!"

"Hold on now until I get a cobble under there."

"Well, be quick about it!"

"There! she's slipped back again! Wait until I get my bar in."

"Leave your bar alone and attend to that cobblestone."

"I don't think you can start it alone."

There was a grunt and a heave from Jack, and Andy slipped a cobble under.

"Will the old devil split?"

"This looks like a crack," scratching the dirt away with a finger.

A wedge was inserted, and a blow from the sledge broke a small chip.

"That's the end of your crack."

If a boulder was rotten it was broken with a sledge. If it would neither split nor break, it was pried up inch by inch with crowbars, and hoisted on an accumulating base of small stones to the top of the ditch, and rolled to one side of it.

The second morning Jack said to me, "I was talking to Hughie Convery last night, and he says that he once had the same trouble with a cellar. Even if you got yours dug, you couldn't lay a wall on that kind of stone. He says the drain did his no good. He took two big hemlock logs, the length of the walls, and sunk them in the clay. He put two of them side by side, about a foot apart, under each wall. They were as solid as a rock."

Andy shook his head.

"You will never get deep enough in that hole to put them logs in."

"Convery says he's coming up to plow to-morrow, and we'll just get him to superintend that job for us. Hughie's the boy!"

I saw little of Nancy in these days except at meal-time and when she whisked out of the house to the brook for a pail of water. She had placed two kitchen tables side by side in the center of our kitchen and dining-room, parlor, library, and sitting-room. Marvelous odors were wafted to me from the open doors and windows, accompanied by the clatter of dishes and the incredibly swift patter of feet. Things were steaming and stewing and simmering and boiling upon the stove. Now and then I heard the oven door slam to. On the table were a cook-book and dough. Every meal was a new amazement for me. I could scarcely waddle after them. I beheld a heap of puffs upon a platter, with cheeks the hue of a young girl's summer tan, and interiors of cotton-batting.

"They are Mrs. W.'s muffins," exclaimed Nancy, with a proud and joyous dignity.

She looked at me anxiously when the first pie appeared. It was of prunes, one quarter of a pie upon a pretty plate, served with half a cup of cream. It looked delicious. I tasted it, and closed my eyes.

"Do you think you can repeat that?" I asked her. She looked bewitching, pressing her palms upon the table and leaning toward me, flushed and triumphant.

"You will never make a better one than that," I said. "No one could. It's a dream!"

"I'm going to make corn-muffins next," she said; "and look at this." She went to the cot, at the side of the room, that served as our pantry, and lifting a corner of the muslin curtain, revealed a pan overflowing with cookies shaped like drop-cakes.

These cookies are at the present day famous throughout the country-side.

That afternoon I found myself trying to recall something. I thought it was a familiar melody until I suddenly discovered that it was the sound of those quick footsteps, those clattering dishes, the opening and closing of the oven door, trooping through my memory like minnesingers improvising a pleasant song.

"We must have a churn," said Nancy; and, going to another cot, our creamery, she lifted another cloth, and there were six pans of milk covered with thick cream.

There was no difficulty in paying instant tribute to the source of this sweet blessing, for all the time we were at dinner Jennie had been watching us, her head in the open doorway. She was chewing her cud now, and looked at us with large, tranquil eyes, almond-shaped, protruding, a dark-reddish buff.

"We would get more milk," I said, "if Jennie would stay in her pasture. I think we ought to get another cow for her. It's just pure lonesomeness."

It was difficult, in fact, for me to keep her out of the ditch when I was in it. She followed me everywhere like a dog. Now and then I would speak to Bob, and he would take her to the pasture; but when he left her she returned. Then Bob would follow me about, seeking earnestly to catch my eye, looking alternately from me to her.

"Look at him," Jack would say. "Oh, Bob, you rascal! You're a jewel of a dog!" Bob would look at him, wag his tail, and then look anxiously at Jennie and eagerly at me. I could see that this cow of his was maturing him. There was more thought, more gravity, in his sparkling eyes.

The first morning after Jennie came, Jack and Andy found me milking her at seven when they arrived.

"How much does she give?" called Andy. "Now, be honest; tell the truth."

"About five quarts to a mess," I said.

He smiled, and Jack bellowed:

"Why didn't you say seven or eight? We had a bet."

They looked into my pail.

"Well," said Jack, "I call that a good mess of milk for a Jersey cow."

"But," said Andy, "it's nearer four quarts than eight, so it is."

I got up from the box I was using for a stool, my hands aching with the unaccustomed strain.

"Why don't you finish her?" said Jack.

"I guess I've got it about all," I said.

"Why, man, that won't do. You must milk her clean—until the last drop. Leave a gill to-day, you will lack a pint to-morrow."

I sat down again and struggled with the teats.

The next morning, about half an hour after Jack and Andy were in the ditch, I got my pail and went to Jennie, who was waiting for me close at hand.

"Well, by the lightning!" said Jack, "how many times a day do you milk?"

"Why, I haven't milked this morning yet," I said.

"Well, you want to milk at the same hour every day, night and morning."

"I do?"

"If you care anything about your cow, you do; and at this time of the year you can't milk too early after sun-up."

Nancy and I were getting up at five o'clock, sometimes at four. After that I milked before breakfast, between half-past five and six.

Jennie is a friendly creature. Sometimes she turned her head and scraped my ear with her tongue as I milked her. But even the gentlest creatures can acquire bad habits. She constantly moved her position as I milked. Her front legs were motionless. She chewed her cud, and seemed content, often half closing her eyes; but her hind feet were now here, now there. Sometimes she would lift a foot, and I had to be quick to check it with my elbow on the instant, or she would have put it in the pail.

It was desperately hard for me to milk, anyhow. I have since learned by my "Farm Journal" that it is an art that few ever really master, and that many good farmers fail in it all their lives.

During this process morning and evening I felt nothing but my aching fingers; could afford to see nothing but the movements of Jennie's feet. I refrained from kicking her; but my morning song was often loud and disjointed: "Be still there! Keep your feet down! What's the matter with you, anyhow? Wake up, you old fool!"

After a time, however, I got used to working before breakfast; and when my first copy of the "Farm Journal" came, stealing a moment to look into it for information as to the feeding and care of cows, I chanced upon these lines:

When you are angry, don't kick the cow. Kick the milking stool.

When you've got your mess say, "Thank you, bossy."

Pet the cows. They will soon learn to expect a caress, and it pays.

I have found that there is truth in this—sometimes; but there are times when a gentle tone will soothe my Jennie; and when she grows drowsy and contented her body sways, her legs are restless.

However, by making the effort I could be gentle with her. I found that she gave down her milk more readily if I petted her a little and whistled as I milked. I might also finish my task in a more cheerful mood. Sometimes I sang to her.

CHAPTER IX

SINISTER WHISPERS

N the road to Tannersville, half-way between our place and Gaffey's Corner, at the foot of Spooky Bridge hill, there is a rickety group of buildings. On the south side of the road are the stables, built of scraps, ill-shaped, yawning in places, patched in others. Close to the road on the south side is a house in ruins. The rain beats through its broken windows. The barn-yard is littered with broken wheels, axles, rotten rigging, pieces of machinery, scraps of old iron, wagons and bob-sleds.

At one side of the house there are three lonely apple-trees, affording a meager shelter for two or three dilapidated buggies and a sleigh. Scythes, old and new, hang from the branches. The dooryard is swarming with chickens, ducks, geese, pigs, and calves. Sometimes, when a cold north wind is blowing, fifty or a hundred of these animals stand in the sunlight in the shelter of the house, as close to the south wall as may be. When the door opens, a chicken or a pig sometimes slips in. If there are not too many already there, it may remain.

"Who are these people in Spooky Hollow?" I asked.

"The Converys."

"I wonder why they don't replace the window-panes."

"Oh, they live like pigs. She goes about half naked. Whatever you do, don't ever go inside."

"Why not?"

The answer was whispered.

I uttered an exclamation of disgust.

"What can you expect? They are filthy. People say they're not honest. Mrs. Convery was arrested once for stealing a cloak. She sells butter and eggs in the parks. Perhaps she begs. Anyhow, people give her things. They say her house is filled with bundles of clothing she has accepted and thrown in a corner. She has never even untied them. She goes about in rags to get more sympathy."

This was all I had previously heard about the Converys, and so when Jack said, "Hughie's the boy," my interest was awakened.

I was inclined to be surprised that Mr. Seifferth had selected so shiftless a person to do my plowing for me; but there was something in Jack's voice that put me on my guard against judgment. I prepared to watch and listen. I had brought unconsciously some of the narrow prejudices of the town, but I was becoming aware of new issues. I found myself loving the men of the mountains who helped the building of my home. Was my part to be only that of a grudging employer and thereafter a hermit, self-absorbed? Vague questionings as to the meaning of the natural life came and went, and the answers were swiftly taking form.

Every one came early that morning. The ditch was almost to the cellar, and Jack and Andy were anxious to get the drain at work. They appeared at half-past six, and at the same moment I heard the noise of a wagon jolting up the hill. A boy was driving. There was no seat in the wagon. He braced himself back upon the lines. Behind him stood a tall man, bolt upright, a huge hand resting upon each shoulder of the boy. They stopped among the trees of the dooryard.

"Hello, Hughie!" called Jack. "Come over here."

I heard the sound of reverberation as from a deep-toned bell. The man was speaking, his whole face illuminated by a smile.

"Well, well, Jackal, are you tunneling the mountain? What are you trying to do to the man's place, anyhow?"

He walked over to the cellar and looked into it.

"What do you think of that mud-hole?" asked Jack.

He was an angular giant, as tall as Jack, with long arms, long legs, wide hips, narrow shoulders, a lean, firm body, shoulders humped with muscles, a long, thin neck with an Adam's apple, a head like that of Millet's "Man with the Hoe." Millet depicted darkness. The countenance of Hughie was like the dawn.

His retreating forehead was smooth and white. His brows suggested intellect. His cheeks were rosy. The soft brown eyes revealed a shrewd, gentle dreamer. It was a smiling countenance, even in repose.

"Well, now, Jackal," he said, "this is not so bad. It looks bad, but it can be fixed, as I told you, with hemlock logs."

"But we can't go deep enough to put them in," said Andy.

"Oh, I think you can. Just dig a trench wide enough for them, and dig the rest out afterward."

"With this ditch to drain it," suggested Jack, "a few days of dry weather ought to help us some."

"All right," I said; "leave it for a few days, and we will build a shed for Jennie."

"I suppose, then, from to-day," said Jack, "we will get carpenter's wages."

"It's just a case of extra honors."

"Well, I am used to that," said Jack. "I have grown old and poor on honors." He smiled, and picked up his ax. "Well, how are you going to have it built—log-cabin style?"

"No," I said; "I thought we would stand the timber upright." I laid my hand upon a hemlock about three inches in diameter. "If we build it that way we can use trees of this size, for they won't have to be notched, as they would in the log-cabin style."

"There is something in that," said Jack; "but I will tell you this much, spruce and hemlock don't last long exposed to the weather. They're all right covered up or underground. We had better make the sills, plates, and rafters of spruce and hemlock, and use hardwood for the walls."

"You will be able to crawl through the holes between them," said Andy.

"Why, I should think," I said, "we could get enough straight timber to make a tight job."

"These trees look straight," said Andy, "until you come to stand them up side by side."

"A little hewing will fix that all right, Andrew," said Hughie.

"I only want it for a summer shed. In the winter it can be lined."

"Well, boss," said Jack, "pick out the spot. We can't stand here and build it."

"I thought I'd have it here in line with the house, and about forty feet from the end of the kitchen when it's built, and sometime I can connect the house and the barn with a woodshed and a storeroom, or a wagon-house when I come to get a horse."

"That's the way they build their places down East," said Jack, "and it's a good idea, too."

"You will find that handy," said Hughie, "if you spend the winter here. Boy, boy, we have snows in these mountains. I have seen it after a storm when you had to get out in the morning and hunt for your barn with a compass and shovel."

"I suppose," said Jack, "we might as well begin right here, and make a clearing forty feet."

"You are going to plow that fallow in the woods back here?" asked Hughie.

"Yes. I don't know how you are going to get to it with your wagon, though."

"Well, I do," said Hughie. "There's an old wood road that runs along the creek. The Seifferths made it when they cleared the fallow. I was by along there last fall, and I noticed that it hadn't been much overgrown. Come, Will," he said, calling to his boy, "turn about and get the wagon out of here. Be careful of the trees."

"Yes, yes," said Will; "I will look out for them."

"Go easy, now, for easy does it."

Will went ahead and cramped and backed, turned in between two trees a little way, then cramped and backed again, talking to the horses persuasively as he guided them with steady reins. "Get up a little there, now. Back, Fan. Back, Maje. Easy, Major. Easy does it."

When the team was out of the dooryard and facing down the hill, we climbed into the wagon, drove down to the creek, and turning abruptly on its bank, clambered up a stony roadway through the forest that hemmed it close. We were obliged to dodge the overhanging branches. In places the horses waded to their bellies through underbrush. I dropped to the bottom of the wagon, and hung to the edge to keep from being jostled out.

"I will have to make a roadway from the barn to the garden," I thought; "this is too rough and roundabout a way."

We issued from the leafy tunnel at one corner of the fallow. It was an ancient clearing of about an acre—a sunny, south hillside, covered with thick masses of brake, fern, raspberry and blackberry bushes, flowering weeds, and here and there a little patch of grass. There were a few clumps of balsams, and a number of solitary, good-sized hemlocks. At the time of the original clearing none of the stumps had been removed. These were everywhere.

"It's a good thing," said Hughie, as he looked over the hillside, "that I have got this heavy plow. Boy, boy, but it's a grand instrument for a country like this." He ran his hand over the heavy iron beam as he would have caressed a horse. "I was almost two years," he said, smiling down upon me, "trying to get that plow."

"Would you exchange it for an automobile?" I asked.

"Well, now, I might," he answered, with a mellow laugh, "if they would give me another one to boot. This is a fine warm spot for a garden," he added, as they took the plow out and transferred the team from the wagon to its beam.

"Which shall we do," asked Will, "plow crosswise, or up and down?"

"An old farmer like you," said Hughie, "to ask me that!"

Will grinned and said: "Well, I suppose we had best go crosswise."

"Yes, yes," said Hughie. He turned to me and added, as he hauled the plow into position: "This is a regular side-hill, Syracuse plow, you see, and you can flop the shovel from one side to another, going back and forth, turning the furrows all downhill. You see, that gives the horses a steady pull all the time, one they can get used to."

At that moment a loud halloa came to us through the forest. It was Jack's voice, calling upon the boss. Following the sound, I broke my way through the woods between the garden and the house, crossed a brook running between deep banks, splashed through a hole filled with water-cresses, denoting a spring, and, some fifty feet beyond, came suddenly out upon the clearing around the house. I was surprised at the short distance. The garden was not more than two hundred feet away on a straight line. It had always seemed a remote and lonely place before. Its direction had been vague—a patch of warmth, of fragrance, of sunlight, hidden somewhere in the vast, unknown forest that surrounded me.

"Now," I thought, "it only needs a straight road to bring it to our door."

"Here, bossie," said Jack, "Andy and I are in an argument. I say we might as well use the timber we are grubbing out for the walls of the barn. Even these big beeches and maples will work all right if we split them. Andy says they won't split so they can be used."

"They'd make good corkscrews," said Andy. "Of course you might get one now and then with a straight grain, but look at that one, now."

"What's the difference?" said Jack. "We've got to hew the crooks out, anyhow. It's easy enough to get a split log out of wind. Ain't that so, boss?"

"What do I know about it?"

"You can't cut it," said Andy, "so the edges won't stick out. It'd be a rough-looking wall built that way."

"Well, I don't mind that. The rougher it is, the better."

"There, Andy, you see," said Jack, "you aren't up on this rustic work."

"Well," said Andy, "I've got a number of real crooked sticks on my place I can spare if you'd like them. I like to be accommodatin' to my neighbors when I can."

"And here's another thing," said Jack. "We were wondering how you wanted the ridge-pole hung. Here's a tall, straight tree with a crotch in the top of it that would do for one end, and I know another one to match, about one hundred feet, back here in the woods. I saw it yesterday as I came through that way."

A few moments after they were at work again, Will appeared grinning, his face covered with sweat.

"I came for a crowbar," he said. "I suppose it's down by the ditch."

"And you'd better take the sledge and the wedges along," said Jack.

I took my ax and went to work on the underbrush, while Jack and Andy grubbed the trees with grunts and heaves and arguments. Now and then I heard, off in the forest, the voices of Hughie and Will. It was, for the most part, a low murmur, for they spoke gently and easily to their team, but now and then there came an explosive "Whoa!"

Again Will appeared, still grinning, still sweaty, his clothes now plastered with dirt.

"Have you got any chains here?" he said.

"Why don't you bring your own tools?" asked Jack, good-naturedly.

"We will to-morrow," he replied; "but it's a good deal worse that we thought it'd be. Mr. Seifferth said it'd been plowed before, but it don't act like it."

"Well, it never was," said Jack. "He had some rye in there about a hundred years ago, but it was only raked in."

"Pa says he wishes you'd come over if you can. We ain't got once across yet."

I found the plow out of the furrow, the horses standing with their heads down, breathing hard. Hughie, at the end of his crowbar, was prying at a boulder, shoving a stone under it with his foot as he gained a quarter of an inch. He stood up when he saw me, the sweat dropping from his nose.

"Boy! boy!" he said, his face radiant and smiling, "but this is what makes the water come. Here, now, Willie, slip your chain under there when I heave. Be careful of your hands; you don't want to lose them yet."

I added my weight to his, and we heaved up an inch; the chain was under.

"There!" said Hughie. "Now, get your Maje and Fanny hitched to this, and we will see what we can do."

Will took the reins, and Hughie put the crowbar under.

"Now, Maje," he said, "you want to do your best, for I'm helping you here."

"Get up, Maje; get up, Fan," called Will, letting the reins fall upon the haunches.

"Don't do that," said Hughie. "Let them take their time. They don't want to find their load too quick. Let them get kind of used to it. Go easy, now, for easy does it."

The horses found their load; the chain creaked; they held it taut, felt for a little firmer hold for the feet, and leaned steadily forward. Hughie, at that moment, seeing the boulder move, gave a mighty lift. The horses felt the movement, and suddenly laid down to it. The muscles stood out upon their legs, and the boulder was torn from its bed.

"I suppose you want all these out," said Hughie.

"It will make hard plowing."

"Well," said he, "it's about the worst I ever saw; but still, it's not so bad. We can do it easy enough if the plow holds out. Of course it will be slower than I thought; but still, these stones have no business in a garden."

"We will take them out," I said. "They would always be in the way."

"Yes," he answered, throwing the plow into the furrow again, "this new forest land makes the best soil there is, but you've got to conquer it. If you don't conquer it, it's always a-resisting you. Boy! boy! the acres I've conquered."

CHAPTER X

My Gray-Haired Neighbor

I T took two weeks to plow that little patch, to haul the stones off, and to harrow it.

The second day I put Jack to work with Hughie, and Will to help Andy with the barn. The fourth day we all went over there.

One portion of the field was covered with a dense growth of brakes. Here sod piled up in heaps between the plowshare and the beam, so that it was necessary to stop and back and lift the plow free every few steps. There were patches of hard clay and gravel, where, in order to keep the plow in, Will stood upon the beam as he drove. Twice he lost his balance and was thrown headlong. He rose grinning, still clinging to the reins.

I learned to stand upon the beam and to guide the plow. During the last ten days this part of the work—the easiest part—was left to Will and me. Jack and Hughie and Andy got the stumps and boulders out, with occasional assistance from the team.

The trees we uprooted and the old stumps we grubbed out we piled in heaps upon the plowed land and burned them.

"There is no better manure than wood-ashes," said Hughie.

"I don't think much of these hemlock ashes," said Jack. "These hardwood stumps are all right."

"Well, I don't know as there is much good in hemlock. I know the manure you get nowadays from the stables in town is no good since they've got to using sawdust for bedding."

"I suppose I'll have to get some manure," I said.

"Well, I don't know where you will get it, then," answered Jack; "that is, not enough for the whole patch, anyhow."

"What are you going to plant?" asked Hughie.

"Well," I said, "I want one row of plum- and cherry-trees and one row of apple-trees to begin with this spring. By another year I'll know better what varieties I'll want to complete the orchard. I thought I would put most of the piece into potatoes, working over one corner more carefully for a little truck-garden."

"Well, you'd better leave your garden truck alone," said Andy.

"Why is that?"

"Well, it don't pay. Potatoes do pretty well up here, and peas are all right, but that's about all you can raise."

"Why not sweet corn?"

"The frost kills it. It gives it a clip at both ends. We are likely to have regular black frost here in the middle of June, and again about the middle of September. If by any chance it escapes the frost, just the minute a corn-leaf shows the crows take it, and what the crows leave the chipmunks get."

"No," said Jack, "you aren't likely to get much sweet corn. Still, if you like, there's no harm in chancing a little. Oh, me! oh, my! how I used to glory in sweet corn before my teeth were gone!"

These things were not said as smoothly as I have written them. They were uttered brokenly between the lifts. A sentence was frequently suspended while the speaker heaved upon a stone or wrenched away a stubborn root.

Imagine to yourself Jack, this graceful, huge, muscular old man, whacking with an ax, prying with a crowbar, swinging a sledge in tremendous blows, lifting enormous weights with his long, sinewy arms, serene, determined, and invincible as he accounted for his missing teeth.

"Two or three of them," he said, ramming his crowbar under the prongs of a stump, "are," (a long heave, during which the words were muffled)—"in the woods around here—somewhere. One—I suppose, is in the dunghill—back—of the barn. Another one was thrown out of old Steve's blacksmith shop down in West Saugerties—ground into dust, and blown into Mrs. Babbitt's front yard. It made good fertilizer for her posies. Generally when I'm around home and the toothache gets too bad, I find me a waxed end, slip a noose over its old neck, find me a good stiff maple limb as high as I can reach, pull it down, make my waxed end fast to the end of it, and let go. That's the last of the tooth. Swish goes the limb. I have seen the waxed end wound around it as tight as a bobbin, but the tooth was whipped off into the woods somewhere. One day, though, I thought I would try another method. It was a big molar in the upper jaw. The limb works all right with the lower teeth, but it isn't so good a dentist with the upper ones. So I took a heavy weight from a pair of steelyards, and went out to the barn, my waxed end hanging from my jaw, climbed into the lumber-wagon, put a sheepskin on the edge of the box, and put my chin on it. I tied the steelyard weight to the other end of the waxed string, and set it on the edge of the box close to me. When all was ready, I tipped it off with my finger, and it went crashing to the floor, old Mr. Molar with it. One day, though, I got caught down in West Saugerties. My, how that tooth did ache! I was almost drunk with the pain of it. I knew old Steve had a pair of forceps. Old Steve is a terrible Republican, and I generally drop in there, anyhow, when I am in town, to have an argument. I like to get the best of the old devil. He is a nice, good-natured fellow as you ever saw. Well, that day I laid down on the floor. He got his forceps out and put his knee on my chest. 'Is that the tooth?' he asked. 'Yes,' says I; 'by h—l, don't be feeling of it, but get it out.' He took a good hold, and gave a little pull. 'Are you sure this is the one?' he asked. I couldn't speak with my mouth full of pincers and with the pain of it. 'Now, Jack,' he says, 'promise me you will vote a straight Republican ticket next fall, and I will pull it out. I know you can't speak,' he said, 'but wink, and I'll pull it out.' Well, sir, it pained so that I had to wink, but I guess he knew what that meant. There must have been murder in my eye, for he jumped through the open window, forceps, tooth, and all, and before I could catch him, he was hidden in the hotel on the corner."

It suddenly occurred to me that in this paradise of ours there were no dentists, and more than ever I appreciated the spirit and the ingenuity of the man who could extract humor out of situations so uncomfortable and grim.

"If I were you," said Andy, "I would not try to plant potatoes here for the first year, anyhow. I'd sow it to rye, and let that pulverize the soil for you."

"Why, there's nothing better," said Hughie, "than new land for potatoes."

"That's all right, but it's too much work to get them in and cultivate them."

"No, no; there's nothing easier. Just lay your potatoes on the ground and throw the sod over them. That is covering enough, with a handful of dirt and a little boughten pulverizer dropped in with the potato."

"Yes," said Jack, "and when you come to dig them in the fall, you just lift the sod off, and you will find a hatful of potatoes to the hill."

The trees came before we were ready to plant them, and we put them in the bed of the brook that ran by the garden, covering them over with hemlock boughs.

"They will be all the better for that," said Andy. "The roots will sprout there in the dampness."

"We ought to have a little manure to put in the holes when we plant them," said Jack, "and you ought to have some for your garden patch; and I don't see but I'll have to give you a load."

A few days after that he said to me:

"I was talking to a fruit-grower down in the mountains last night about your trees, and he said it was better not to use any manure now, especially in this new soil. He said to cultivate the ground around them well, and late in the fall to put the manure on as a top dressing."

"I will tell you another thing," said Andy. "In the winter, after the first big snow, you want to come out here and tramp down around all the trees. If you don't the little mice and the chipmunks will nibble the bark off. They can work right along all winter if the snow is deep and thick and loose."

"The little rascals!" said Jack. "It keeps them warm; but they won't come out in the open on top of the snow if it's packed."

Every day, as we were tearing up the ground, the future of this garden patch was being revealed to me. It was past the middle of May now, and time to plant the early peas and the sweet corn. I must wait for the full of the moon in June to put my potatoes in, and about a week later it would be safe to plant my beans.

As we were turning the last furrow, near the edge of the woods, on the upper side of the garden, Jack cast a pleased look of triumph over the hillside.

"That's the way," he said, "I like to see work done. If the farmers in these mountains would handle their fields that way, they would get more out of them."

These two weeks had been passed in almost unendurable toil for me. My hands were cracked and bleeding. For several days I had been too tired at night to bathe, and there had not been a moment in the day when I could do so without taking somebody from his labor. I had expected to have a day's plowing done, and this was the end of the second week, with three men, a boy, and a team, besides my own exhausting toil; and for two days Nancy had piled the little stones in heaps. We had hauled tons upon tons of stones and boulders, and piled them in a great heap in a hollow, where we expected to cross the brook with our road to the house. As it was, some of the stones were still left, and a number of enormous rocks, which must be blasted.

"I don't wonder," I said as I followed Jack's glance, "that they don't do it, though. Take a field like this, and for one man alone it would mean ten years of labor, and almost impossible then."

"Yes, yes," said Hughie, "land like this just laughs at a man unless he's fitted to conquer it."

The next morning Jack came early, and we got the trees planted along the western border of the garden, where they would be most sheltered and get the most sunlight. As we were almost through, Hughie and Will arrived, and were putting the team to the stone-boat when Andy appeared.

"Have you noticed that chimney?" he asked.

"No," I said, looking at him quickly. "What of it?"

"Well, you had better drop things here and get all hands to work. The chimney leans a good three inches more than it did when we left it, and I see this morning that the bank under it shows signs of caving in."

In spite of the dry weather, we had not got much benefit from the drain. The cellar bottom was still soft. Upon Andy's warning, we all hurried over there. There was certainly no time for delay. Either the cellar must be dug and walled up at once with heavy stone, or it must be abandoned and filled in again with dirt. The chimney was, without doubt, in danger of toppling over.

I looked at this massive structure of stone, and it seemed to menace me. If it fell, it would carry a portion of the house with it. There was a long crack in the dirt wall on which it rested, which had appeared there since I passed by in the morning. The stones of the chimney were firmly held together by the mortar, and the method of construction their uneven shapes had made necessary. It was one huge, solid mass, and because of its imposing bulk, its rugged and artistic proportions, aside from the cheer and comfort of its cavernous fireplaces, had been in every way the central feature of the house. We were proud of it. Now it threatened me with ruin. A few inches more, and no power we could bring to bear could prevent its fall. I looked at it with staring eyes, hearing in imagination the rending timbers, the deafening crash, and seeing the whole house torn apart and twisted.

"Will," said Hughie, "bring the team here. We will get these hemlock logs ready as soon as the trenches are dug."

"I was in hopes," said Andy, "that you would let me off, for I'm not feeling real good."

"Well, he won't," said Jack. "You'd be feeling all right if you didn't have this cellar to dig. Now, you get in there, or I will throw you in."

"Well, you won't throw me in," said Andy. "If he'd wanted me to stay, I'd have stayed, anyhow, and I wouldn't ask to be let off now with things as they are; but I don't feel well, and I would like to rest up for a day."

By this time they were in the cellar, and Andy was throwing the first shovel of dirt out as he spoke. When he made a hole, the water ran in it. It was almost impossible to work in the soft, sticky substance. It sank down with them, making little hollows where they stood, into which the water ran, covering their feet. In order to avoid this, Andy kept moving about, digging now here, now there, in the limits of the trench they were making. Wherever he stood, however, the water followed him. At the end of two hours he was still slipping and splashing in the slop. By this time Jack was standing on dry ground. Andy looked behind him, stood up suddenly, and asked him to change places with him.

"You are where it's dry," he said. "You've given me the worst of it."

"Well, I won't," said Jack.

"Well, you needn't think," said Andy, "I'm going to have all this water to myself. You can come here and work in it for a while."

"Do you see that hole in the corner there?" said Jack. "Well, I stood right there and dug, standing in the mud half-way up my boots, until I got it deep enough to drain this corner. If you'd done that, you'd be on dry land now."

"Well," said Andy, "let's dig a trench here through this ridge between us."

"And let your water down in on me? Well, I guess not. That's what I left that ridge for."

"Well, I will dig it away, so I will."

"Well, you won't," said Jack, making a line behind him with his shovel. "This is half-way across, and you will stop right there. I will attend to this half myself, and you can attend to yours."

"Well," said Andy, "I have no time to quarrel with you." He cast an anxious glance at the chimney and returned to work, redoubling his efforts.

It was a dangerous place, directly beneath the chimney. I stood upon the bank all day, watching the chimney closely, ready to warn them at the first sign of disaster. A little before noon, Jack stood up and looked at me.

"We're not going to get this ready for Brice in time for him to build the wall to-day. Now, it would be a good deal worse to take this dirt out along this side and leave it unsupported overnight. I think we had better stop where we are and go at another side; then get here early in the morning, and have Brice on hand, all ready to lay the wall the moment we get the logs in."

Without waiting for a reply, they went to work upon another trench at the opposite side of the cellar. These men had become my counselors, my instructors, telling me what to do, and how to do it. No one any longer called me boss, but Jack sometimes in affection called me "bossie."

Now and then, off in the forest, we heard the crash of a falling hemlock, and by nightfall eight huge hemlock logs, sixteen feet long, had been dragged to the cellar wall.

"Now," said Andy, slowly, as he climbed out of the cellar and stood upon his shovel, "if I'm not here in the morning you will know it's because I couldn't."

Those who had given me my information concerning the Converys had also given me to understand that Andrew Dale was not very fond of work. "Of course," they said, "he will do an honest day's work while he's at it, but the trouble is to get him at it."

While we had been at work upon the garden, I learned that Mr. Seifferth had secured the wire and was about to build a party-fence between our place and his. He was proceeding to do this without reminding me of my duty in the matter, but, of course, one half of such a fence was for me to build. So I paid my share of the expenses, and sent Jack for a day to help Fred Seifferth build it.

At that time Andy had said to me: "I suppose you and I might need some kind of a better fence than the one we have got. It's just a poor brush fence now, and I am afraid my cattle and sheep will be coming over here."

We talked the matter over, and I agreed to buy the wire and he to build the fence. When I told the Seifferths of this, they laughed at me, saying that I had better keep my wire under cover until Andy wanted it, or it would rust away.

"I have been wanting him to help me at that fence for years and years," said Mr. Seifferth, "but I could never get him at it."

All these things had, of course, influenced the opinion I was unconsciously forming of my neighbor. I was still a stranger in this community where I had come to live, and I possessed only the personal observation of a few weeks against the accumulated gossip of a lifetime. In my daily association with Andy, I was beginning to love him. Honest, pessimistic, sensitive, kind, and testy, you must either misunderstand or love him, that is, if you are not cynical, selfish, or indifferent.

But that evening, as we stood by the unfinished cellar, I was influenced more by what had been said to me than by my own instincts, so, without looking at my gray-haired neighbor, sweaty, red-faced, breathing heavily, besplattered with mud and water, I said:

"I hope you will stay by this until the chimney is safe."

"You can rely on it that I will, if I am able; but, of course, if I can't get up or can't work, there is no use of my coming. I don't feel good lately."

At six the next morning Jack and Andy were again at work in the trench along the wall by the chimney. Without waiting for my breakfast, I renewed my watch. The crack in the wall of dirt had widened overnight, and the chimney leaned at least an inch farther from the house. At half-past six Hughie and Will drove up, and hitching on to the stone-boat, cut a road through the forest at the back of the house, to a spot where the dry bed of an ancient watercourse offered a mass of exposed flat stones. These they hauled out for the cellar walls. At seven Mr. Brice appeared, and went with Hughie and Will to bring down the larger stones to lay on the logs at the bottom.

Without a word, Jack and Andy struggled with the sticky clay, appearing so soft, resisting like rubber, holding the shovel fast when forced at last to admit it. For every two inches removed, an inch oozed into the trench again. The bottom continually puffed up. The crack in the wall widened. A huge block of earth at one corner slid into the cellar. This, for a moment, looked like the end. It was almost noon, and these two men had done more than a full day's work. By sheer exertion they had outstripped the clay oozing from the sides and puffing up from the bottom. The trench was dug. The hemlock logs were resting on the crest of the dirt-pile, rolled there by Hughie, Brice, and Will. Skids, made of four-inch maple-trees, rested on the bottom of the cellar. The men above stood ready to roll the logs down them. The land-slide fell directly in front of Andy, filling his corner just as he was about to leave the trench. His face was purple with the morning's exertion. Without a word, he bent again to his work, throwing the dirt out with dogged haste. He stood with his legs apart, so that Jack, behind, could thrust his shovel between. When the trench was cleared, he went to the opposite wall and leaned against it, wiping his face with his sleeve. His lips and chin were covered with blood, from a hemorrhage of the nose.

"I guess," he said, "I will go home now. I don't feel real good to-day."

By working overtime, the logs were placed in position before dark, and the wall, entirely composed of huge, flat stones, was completed along the one side of the cellar. The chimney was saved. Ten days later the cellar was finished. Three springs gushed from the bottom. We pounded the clay full of broken stones, spread four inches of gravel over these, and laid broad slabs over all, filling the cracks with cement.

This was the little job I had undertaken more than a month before, expecting in my ignorance to do it in four days at the most.

Andy did not leave his bed for several days. He was feeble all summer. Early in the fall, as soon as he was able to do anything, he built our party-fence. I had bought the wire, and I would gladly have built the fence, in spite of his protests, if I could have found the time. But every day had been occupied.

CHAPTER XI

An Eden With Toil

OIL, toil, toil. Everything to be done, and to be done first. We found an hour, now and then, to run over to the garden and plant a row of seeds. By the full of the moon in June, our potatoes were all in. There was no rain for nearly two months—an unprecedented drought. Every evening, at sundown, Nancy and I carried water from the garden brook for the trees, the rows of peas and beans, the beds of turnips, beets, spinach, and lettuce, the hills of cucumbers, squash, and sweet corn.

It was sometimes eight o'clock before we could have our supper. We were often too tired to eat. Of course if we could summon the courage to bathe, we felt better; but without the habit of years to help us, the effort would not have been made. We no longer wondered at the failure of country people in this. The farmer who religiously gets into the wash-tub once a week is a punctilious man.

In the latter part of May we got another cow through Johnson, and I named her Maggie.

There were at this time two young girls working at Seifferth's, preparing the house for the boarding season, beginning on the 15th of June. Their names were Maggie and Jennie. Jennie was a demure, self-possessed little maid, and it so happened that my Jennie was as near like her as a cow could be. She was orderly, selfish, and pretty. Maggie was a cousin to Libbie, and was of a similar disposition. She was younger, however, better formed, and better looking. But she was a bustling, eager, hard-working girl, and she was bristling with joyous vitality. Life for her possessed a masculine form. She loved life. If a boy came near her, she expected to be tickled, and she giggled and dodged beforehand. I have never seen her with a lover, but evening after evening I have met her upon the road, towing the demure Jennie. Were there boys at a distance behind? She walked slowly, casting frequent quick glances over her shoulder. If they overtook them, she drew Jennie to the roadside and let them pass. When they were some distance ahead, she walked on more rapidly, no longer looking behind. Night after night I have seen her sitting on the porch, muffled in a fascinator, bright-eyed, expectant, motionless in the long silence. Once I saw her jump suddenly from her seat and run behind the house to hide. She had heard the sound of a horse. An old man passed in a buggy. She was coquetting with illusions.

Now, my new cow lacked the imagination for this, and she had also missed the moral influence of insinuations and whispers that well-taught young girls receive. Natural instincts were strong in her, and she obeyed them impetuously. She was, in fact, more like Libbie; but still, at the root of the matter, the name was justified, and I called her Maggie, since Jennie was already there.

Maggie was a good milker. She gave from sixteen to eighteen quarts a day. We churned three or four times a week, and made from six to nine pounds of butter at a churning. We discovered that butter-making required a grim endurance of weariness and pain. One must also know everything, and apply his knowledge systematically and with patience.

Do you salt your cows regularly?

Is the milk kept at the right temperature?

Here is a pan I overlooked. It is covered with mold.

There are white specks in the butter. The cream was too warm.

The butter is bitter. The cream was too ripe.

It is not enough to keep a cow—you must keep her clean, feed her enough and not too much, supply her with a correctly balanced ration, or waste your feed.

One morning Hughie, on his way to us, heard a familiar sound in a strange place. He recognized Maggie's bell, and climbing the fence, found her in one of Mr. Seifferth's fields, grazing near his cattle. She had been wounded. Another cow had hooked her. He drove her home, and rubbed turpentine, kerosene-oil, and melted butter on the wound. For over an hour he worked at the teats, freeing the bag from the cakes of blood and milk. She would let no one else do this, but she stood quietly for him. His voice was deep and musical. He talked to her softly, like a lover.

After this he came early in the morning in order to milk and attend to her, and when his day's work was over he remained to do this, as a matter of course.

During all this time we had been living in our unfinished house, one half of our things unpacked and in the way.

When Nancy was not skimming milk, or working over her butter, or baking, or washing, she was lugging water from the brook or gathering wood to burn. It seemed impossible to get a day to cut any. The roof was not yet on the cow-shed. I had no chicken-house. Mr. Goslee had failed us entirely, but we had arranged with a rival contractor, who had agreed to send us two men. They would soon be here, and I must have a road ready at once by which to get the lumber up, for the old road was now cut off by a party-fence.

"What do you do with your skim-milk?" asked Mrs. Seifferth one day.

"We make pot-cheese of some of it; but, of course, most of it we throw away."

"You ought not to do that," she said. "You should have a pig. You get a young pig now, and in the fall you can butcher it for your winter's meat."

Mr. Seifferth offered to get me one when he got his own. I found that no one raised pigs for sale in the mountains, but that everyone bought one or two in the spring, to fatten, and that it was hard to get them. A pig four weeks old, as soon as it could be weaned, was worth three dollars.

The route for the road I finally selected led directly from the house down the hill, through a little patch of woods, made a graceful turn, and followed the bank of the creek to the main valley road. The distance was about an eighth of a mile. There were knolls to be leveled off and hollows to be filled up, sluices and bridges to be built, trees to be grubbed out, boulders to be broken, and stones without number to be removed. A ditch must be dug on either side, most of its length, to take the water off after every rain, for this entire hillside was subject to a deluge. We dragged the logs from the forest for sluices and bridges, removed the worst of the stones that impeded, and grubbed out what trees were necessary in order that a load of lumber might get through.

Will, Hughie, the team, Jack, and I toiled against time, and kept the first load waiting fifteen minutes for the completion of the bridge. It made a rough journey up the hill, and I could see that more than a month of labor would be required before a buggy could pass comfortably over it.

A little later the carpenters arrived. While I was talking over the work with them, Mr. Seifferth drove up, bringing our pig and his own. I called to Jack and Hughie. It was necessary for them to drop everything and build a pig-pen out of logs. I had agreed to keep both pigs for a while, as they would do better together, and I had the milk to spare.

"They must have nothing but sweet milk for a week or two," said Mr. Seifferth. "After that you should put a little middlings in, and then you can begin to feed them sour milk—a little at a time, at first, with the sweet skim milk."

When the pen was finished, Hughie went back to help Will with the road, and Jack and I remained to put the roof on the cow-shed, using the rough boards brought in the first load.

The carpenters had already put the sills upon the cellar walls, and the sounds of their labor were like music to us.

"We will need a ladder," said Jack.

I brought from the house the one I had made, and put the carpenters to work upon the stairs. When I gave the ladder to Jack, he threw it upon the ground and picked up his axe.

"I'm not going to lug that load all around this barn," he said. "What did you want to build it of maple poles for? They're too heavy. You want a couple of small balsams."

He stepped into the thicket, and gave two or three blows with his ax, and came back with the trees upon his shoulder. The ladder he made I could handle easily with one hand.

"The real way to make one," he said, "is to take a nice, straight spruce-tree, rip it in two, and bore holes for your rungs. Some day, when we get time, we will make one for you."

Jack got upon the roof, and I handed the boards up to him; but the third one he threw upon the ground, saying, "Find me a better one. There's a knot-hole in that."

"Oh, go on, Jack," I said, "and use it. We have no time to be so particular."

"Well, I won't," he said. "This board goes right over bossy, and I'm not going to have the rain trickling down on her through that knot-hole."

I got him his good board, for I had learned by this time to let Jack have his way.

At noon Nancy brought out a pan of milk to feed the pigs for the first time. They were pure white and very clean. Their eyes were bright and intelligent.

"I always thought," said Nancy, "that pigs were so dirty. These are pretty creatures. I wonder if we can't keep them clean."

"Well, you can," said Jack, who was leaning over the pen; "that is, if you will throw dry leaves in here now and then. It isn't the pig's fault that it gets filthy. It will keep itself clean if it can."

But we had no time to watch them. I went into the house for my dinner. Nancy picked up two empty pails and hurried to the brook for water. As she came lugging these in, I noticed the drawn and weary look on her face. It seemed to me that she was growing thin.

"Nancy," I said, "we ought to have water piped into the house."

"Can we do that?" she asked eagerly.

"I don't see why not. We could sink a half-barrel up in the brook back of the house, lay pipes to the kitchen, and use the cellar drain for an outlet. We could attach a boiler to the range and have hot and cold water to a sink."

"Oh, what a relief that would be!" she said. "Let's have it, then."

We had been here almost three months, and had not opened a book, nor taken a ramble, nor passed a day upon the hillside, nor slept in the sunny hollows. Every hour seemed to add to the turmoil of our peaceful retreat. We were weary.

"Of course," I said, "we have found a hundred things to do that we didn't anticipate; but when we are once through with our building, when the roads are done, and the first work of getting a place like this in shape is over, everything then will be as we expected it to be."

"Yes," said Nancy, but I could see that she was making the same effort to repress unwelcome feelings of disappointment and impatience that I was making.

It was time now to get our chickens, if we were to have any, before their molting season began. No one in our neighborhood had any for sale, and Mr. Seifferth offered to take me, with his team, through the country in search of them, for he wanted some, too.

Jack and I built a long, low chicken-house, hastily, out of timber and rough boards, and the next morning Mr. Seifferth and I started on our search. We drove some thirty miles through the East Kill valley, through Jewett and Windham, and around by Hunter. Nowhere was there a hen for sale.

In Hunter we found a dealer in poultry. He had some fifty chickens and roosters, of all varieties, he had picked up the fall before. He held these at sixteen cents a pound, live weight. This was more than Mr. Seifferth cared to pay. He took five of them, however, and I took forty-five.

"You can buy your eggs of me this summer," I said, "and, perhaps, when you want chickens for the table, I can spare you some."

"Yes, yes," said he, genially; "we will buy all your eggs. My gracious, what a lot we use! There's a good market for fresh eggs here in the summer-time."

It was after dark when we got home and put our chickens in their coop. All the next day the place resounded with their cackling. We found nineteen eggs in the nests.

Nancy fed the pigs three times a day. She always called to them as she left the house, telling them she was coming. They learned to distinguish her voice. They had made a little nest for themselves in one corner of the pen, where, curled up together, they slept most of the day; but whenever they heard her voice or saw her pass, they would jump up and run squealing to the side of the pen nearest her. The squealing pigs and the cackling hens were pleasant sounds to us. The second day, however, there were fewer eggs, and on the fourth day there were only three. By the end of the week I was certain that there was something the matter with the chickens. Their combs looked pale and sickly, and they stood moping in the sunlight. They were covered with lice. In the evening, when they went to roost, we caught them one by one and sprinkled insect-powder on them. Still, this did not cure them all. I mixed sulphur in their feed. I learned that it was not good to feed them corn in warm weather; that corn served only to heat their blood. I fed them oats. Once a day I mixed them up soft feed, sometimes boiling potatoes and middlings together. They were evidently not picking up grit enough. I mixed sand and gravel in their soft food. Gradually their combs became brighter, and they began to lay again. Through the summer they laid from eighteen to two dozen eggs a day; but it was necessary to watch them constantly, to hunt for the nests they had hidden, to regulate their diet.

The kitchen was built with a bedroom over it, and we were able to put the house in better order; but we still found that we needed a storeroom and a milk-room. If we were to keep our kitchen and dining-room pleasant and clean and comfortable, we also needed a place where I could mix up my feed and where the work of the farm could be attended to.

Since we had brought water into the house, it occurred to us that it would only require a little more to have a laundry, a bath-room, and a toilet, so that most of the hardships and inconveniences of country life could be avoided.

In sealing and finishing off the original house, and building the kitchen and dining-room, the lumber bills had amounted to large sums. They, with the carpenters' work, had so far cost us about seven or eight hundred dollars. I thought we could build an addition cheaper; so Hughie, Jack, and I took our axes and went to work upon it. We could build it almost entirely with these tools out of timber. We selected hemlocks for the sills and the plates, and small, straight spruce for the rafters, peeling the bark off to keep the worms from working during the winter. We searched through the forest for straight beech- and maple-trees, from four inches to six inches in diameter, to be cut up into eight-foot lengths and split. These were for the sides.

"Now," said Hughie, as the trees were felled and lay scattered through the forest, "it would be a good idea, before we cut this timber up, to have Tom and Sammy come with the little oxen and drag it all out close to the house. It would be cheaper than to work at it, scattered as it is, and carry it piece by piece on our shoulders."

In this way I became acquainted with two more members of the Convery family.

Tom was fourteen, Sam ten. Each owned a team of oxen, which they had trained themselves, using them the winter before to haul out Christmas trees from the sides of High Peak—a task that few men would be willing to undertake.

In the morning Tom and Sammy came with Sammy's team, the little oxen. The boys, with axes on their shoulders, went smilingly into the forest to begin their task, without a word of direction. I took a little time to watch them. They did not ask where the logs lay, but found them.

Tom was a tall, slender lad, gentle and smiling. Sam was short, thick-set, and sturdy. His motions were quick. His cheeks were blooming and red, his eyes bright.

"Now, Tom," he would say, "we will hitch on to the butt of this one, and snake it out between that beech and hemlock."

It might be necessary to fell a tree or cut a road through the underbrush, or to hitch on one end of a log, drawing it a little in one direction before hitching on to the other, to pull it out. Whatever the circumstance required, Sam saw at a glance, and the two boys accomplished it under his direction.

When the chain was around the end of the log, Tom stepped to the head of the oxen, tapping them gently with a long branch from which the leaves had not been stripped.

"Come, Harry," he would say, his voice like a pleasant murmur, scarcely audible. "Gee there, Jerry."

Sam walked beside the log, carrying a handspike made of a small balsam-tree he had chopped and peeled. If the front end of the log caught against a root or a stone, he would lift it up with his handspike. In making quick turns he would swing the rear end around, saying now and then to Tom, "Easy, Tom, for easy does it."

As the logs were hauled to the house, they were put neatly in a little pile in a clearing close by the new building.

Jack and Hughie took them one at a time, and placed them across two logs in notches that held them fast. Jack drove his ax in directly above the heart. Hughie struck in an exact line a little ahead of Jack's ax. Then Jack struck again in the crack, widening it, and so to the end of the log. In this way they kept the split fairly straight, even if the grain wound around. In such cases the two halves were constantly held together by interlocking fibers, but these were chopped in two as they proceeded. Of course, in spite of these precautions, the halves were often somewhat winding, and it was necessary to hew them out of wind.

The first day the sills were hewed and put into position on stone piers. The second day the logs were split for the side walls. On the third day the plates were raised on corner poles, the ridge-pole hung, the rafters cut and peeled and put into position. It took three days more to erect the walls, for in each case the edges of the timber must be hewed and fitted, and hewed again until they came close together their entire length. When all this had been done, we had the frame of a building. The side walls served also for sheathing and clapboards or shingles. They were strong and ornamental, but they were not warm. In spite of all our efforts, you could easily see through them, and in many places you could put your fingers in the cracks. This portion of the building cost sixteen dollars. We turned it over to the carpenters to seal inside, to lay the floors, and put the roof on. One corner of this building we partitioned off for a bath-room and toilet; another corner for a milk-room. One side we devoted to a laundry, stationary tubs, and a sink for the work of the farm.

The plumber spent two weeks with us. It cost us about two hundred dollars for our hot and cold water, two sinks, our bath and toilet, and stationary tubs.

To have always this winding forest brook before our eyes, to hear always its tinkling waterfalls and merry runs, to be able to dip our drink from its pools in the cool shade—these were the things imagination saw when we chose our location for a nest. But it is difficult to drag pailful after pailful for the every-day uses of a farm and house from even the most picturesque of pools, and to remain serenely receptive of beauty.

We passed, however, in the community for people of ordinary common sense in building close by a brook that never went dry.

"It is a great thing to have water," they said to us.

In the midst of our labors, we were interrupted by a storm. Not a drop of rain had fallen for nearly two months. It now fell for three days in torrents. The valley was filled with its slanting downpour. The mountains were concealed. It made a great noise among the leaves of the forest. Strange sounds reached us from far and near. The savage voice of Roaring Kill came from across the valley. Our own creek at the foot of the hill surged madly down the mountain, foaming and leaping among the rocks. The brook by our house swelled to a torrent. Dry watercourses were overflowing, and hidden springs gushed forth. The water beat against the house, swept the dooryard, flooded the cellar, and ran through the barn. In the morning, when I waded out to feed the pigs, I found them standing up to their bellies in a rushing flood. I was obliged hastily to get boards and build a platform some two feet from the ground, and lift them on it.

The roadway that we had been building served now as a grand waterway. The overflow from the brook and the torrents gushing from unexpected sources found their way here, and went plunging down it, washing away the dirt, making cuts and gullies. I now discovered a number of places, unnoticed during the dry weather, where sluices must be built, or the road would be almost destroyed after every storm. It was also evident that the rise back of the house must be cut and graded from it, with a ditch at the foot of the grade, sufficient to carry a turbulent stream around the buildings and some distance from them. Here was work for another month, at least.

After this there were occasional rains, just enough to keep the ground wet. Whenever we went out and in, we dragged in mud.

I do not know how many times a day Nancy wiped up the floor, but she kept it clean.

I knew that in the fall and winter and spring it would be necessary to go often to the barn. We must have a woodshed sometime, and now that the laundry was built, there was just space enough left for one. Of course we expected to have a horse, and with the horse a buggy and a cutter, for one can count upon a long winter and several months of sleighing up here. The shed we had erected of timber, I discovered, would not do for a barn. It was not large enough. It could not be made warm enough, and it would not last very long. The upright pieces, serving as a wall, were spiked on to the sills, and these spikes, the carpenters assured me, would soon rust off.

"It would not pay you," they said, "to line such a building and put floors in it. You would have to build a new building in a few years, and you might better build one now." While it stood, however, it would do for a wagon-shed. We, therefore, gave orders for a woodshed and a barn.

It had been so difficult to get any pigs in the spring that I determined to raise them. Of the pigs Mr. Seifferth had brought me, one was a boar, the other was a sow. He took the boar as soon as they required more milk than I had for them both.

One of his sows, in July, produced a litter, and I bought four of them, two boars to fatten for my own winter's supply, and two sows to keep, with the one I already had, for purposes of breeding. I wished these pigs also for another purpose. My hillside pasture was only partly productive. It was sod-bound. There were stones everywhere. Weeds, briers, brakes, and ferns abounded. I longed to see this hillside of a rich and uniform green, luxuriant in clover and orchard-grass. It would require a fortune or a lifetime to accomplish this, cultivating it as we had subdued my garden patch.

"Turn a drove of pigs in there," said Jack, one day, "and they'll do the work for nothing. They grow fat on these brake-roots, and it's the only way to kill them. They will root up a stone a man couldn't get out with a crowbar."

In my "Farm Journal" I saw advertisements of hog-fencing, and I sent for enough to make four pens. As the pigs cultivated a patch of ground and laid it bare, the fencing could be moved to other pasturage.

When the little pigs were four weeks old, Mr. Seifferth told me I must come and get mine.

"But," I said, "I haven't enough sweet milk for them all."

"Oh, that don't matter," he replied; "give then sour milk."

"Why, I thought that wouldn't do for a while yet."

"Oh, yes," he answered genially; "you can give them sour milk at once. Why, they do better on it."

Most of the quarrels and lifelong feuds in this community have sprung from things no more important than this trifling inconsistency. I took the pigs, and found that, by increasing the bulk of my sweet milk with warm water, the little pigs did very well, for they had good pasture this time of year. The moment they were rolled from the bags upon the ground, they went to rooting busily.

Our row of buildings, including the barn, was one hundred and sixteen feet long. It was the first week in October when they were finished outside and in.

The nights were now growing very cold. The days were, for the most part, warm. Once there was a flurry of snow. The winter was approaching. It was necessary to have a warm place for the pigs and a warm house for the chickens. The one Jack and I had hastily constructed had proved a poor shelter, except in the balmiest of weather. It was neither dry nor warm. We built a combination pig-and-chicken house. On one side of the partition were the chicken-coops. The walls were slanting, with windows the entire length. On the other side were the pig-pens, roofed over, and the loft above served the chickens for a roosting-place. This building was sheathed, papered, and shingled. The buildings were all finished on the 23d of October, almost seven months from the day we had alighted on the platform of the little station in the woods, our eager faces turned toward dreamland.

Only three hundred dollars of our seven thousand remained. We had spent our money, and we were glad. The road to the garden was finished, and we had carried over it fifty bushels of potatoes, storing them in the cellar. We kept enough for ourselves, and sold the rest for twelve dollars. We had got one dish of greens from our beets. The turnips had not appeared. We picked twelve ears of sweet corn before the frost killed it. We could have had an unlimited supply of peas and beans if we had had the time to plant them in succession.

I spent a portion of a day attempting to hoe a row of potatoes, and gave up the task. I could do nothing against those stubborn clumps of weeds, the heavy sods, and the roots and stones that still remained. Jack and Hughie and Will and Sam went through thirty rows in a little less than two days, digging cheerfully, sweating profusely, passing steadily from hill to hill, hour after hour, until the job was done.

The hill back of the house was graded, and a wide ditch dug, leading around the barn. The long road down the hill was graded, and protected with ditches and culverts.

During the summer I had said to Jack that I wished some way might be found by which we could have water in the house all winter, without the enormous expense such a luxury implied. This would require a reservoir of sufficient depth, so that if it froze on the surface, there would still be free water underneath.

A reservoir is an expensive thing. This region is filled with costly dams abandoned, for they would not hold.

Jack thought the matter over, and matured a plan. He found a place in the brook, near its source, where two enormous trees stood opposite each other, about twenty feet apart, the brook between. Here, with the help of Hughie and Andy, he built me a perfect reservoir, costing only the labor of these three men for two days, and three dollars for two long iron bolts three quarters of an inch in diameter. They dug a trench to hard-pan between the two trees. Into this they rolled a hemlock log, twenty feet long, its ends firmly embedded among the roots of the opposite trees. They hewed the top of the log to a flat surface, chopped a groove through the center from end to end, and filled the groove with cement. This log curved outward as it lay. Jack found another tree

about the same size, a little over two feet through, with an almost identical curve. This was hauled to the dam by Sammy's oxen, hewed flat upon its under side, and grooved. The two bolts, one at each end, had been run through holes bored in the first log, and now extended above it, ready to pass through the second. Blocks of timber were placed upon the log to the top of the bolts, and long skids extended from these to the ground. The second log was bored and rolled up these skids until the holes were just above the bolts. The skids were carefully removed, and the huge log slid down the bolts upon the first one, crushing the cement as it fell and filling every crevice. The water trickling under the dam was now to be stopped up. Limbs were cut from the near-by hemlocks, and their furry twigs separated with a knife and piled in heaps. These were pounded under the bottom log as you would pound calking into a crevice. It is a singular fact that these hemlock twigs will stop water where nothing else will.

Since its completion this dam has never leaked, and it has been tried by the freshets of this stormy fall.

It would have been an enormous task to have dug a ditch through the forest deep enough to bury iron pipes below the frost. It would have been necessary also to make a wide circuit, in order to avoid the twistings of the brook.

Sam and Will and Hughie cut two hundred feet of six-inch hemlock logs. I got them bored in Tannersville, and through these we get our water now. They were laid in the bed of the brook, or upon ground covered only with brush and leaves.

CHAPTER XII

Judgment

HROUGH all these months the Converys had come singing or whistling to their work. No task was difficult. There was no obstacle that could not be overcome. They always came a little early, and seemed loath to go at night.

While they were working for me, Mrs. Convery and Katie, a girl of fifteen, little Hughie, seven, and John L., three, attended to the stock, planted and cultivated several acres of garden truck, worked in the fields, built more than a mile of fence, mended the rest, planted and hoed three large fields of potatoes, and several times a week carried their produce to market. Before and after the day's work with me, Hughie and the boys had plowed their fields and sowed them, working by moonlight or in the light of the stars when the nights were clear.

Sammy dug my potatoes, and brought them in bags, two bushels at a time, upon his back, from the garden to the house.

One evening, after the rest were gone, I was surprised to see him, with his load, coming from the garden at sundown.

"They are all done," he said cheerily. "My, that was a fine crop of potatoes over there!"

"I know," I answered; "but why didn't you wait until morning?"

"Well, I wanted to get them done. I thought maybe you wouldn't need me in the morning."

"Oh, I will need you, for there's plenty to be done here yet."

"Yes, yes," he said. "There's always something to do around a place like this."

That evening he returned, bringing a pail of raspberries little John and Hughie had picked for us.

"Why didn't you wait until the morning," asked Nancy, "and save that long walk over?"

"I didn't mind the walk. They were having a great time when I got home. The pigs had all got out. Oh, my gosh, I guess there must have been a hundred of them, little and big. They were in the woods and in the oat-field and scattered all over the flats. My gosh, we had great fun chasing the little devils and getting 'em back in again."

"Well, did you get them all?"

"Yes, yes. Oh, they had to come."

"Well, I should think you'd be tired," said Nancy. "Aren't you, now?"

"Not yet," he answered, as if willing to admit he might be sometime, if he lived to do enough.

In September the Converys left us for a while. The haying season had begun. Whatever they might say of Hughie by lamplight in the evenings of the spring, in September he was certainly in great demand. Mr. Seifferth summoned him to cut his hay on shares. For almost a month I didn't see him, but I heard of him, now here, now there; now on this farm, now on that, cutting the hay of the country-side. Hay is a precious article in these parts, and cannot be dawdled over. A man who loses his hay loses everything. At this season of the year the weather is uncertain. Hay cut to-day should be got in to-morrow. If it is caught too frequently in the showers of this season, it will spoil. In such an emergency a man like Hughie has his points.

While he was gone Jack missed him sorely. These two men worked together like a piston and a driving-wheel.

One night Nancy and I walked over to Spooky Hollow. We found Katie, little Hughie, and John sitting on a pile of logs by the roadside. The others had not come home.

"Did Mrs. Convery go too?" asked Nancy.

"Oh, yes; ma goes with them when they are haying."

"Why, what can she do?"

"Why, she can run a rake as good as any of 'em."

"I guess she can," said little Hughie. "She can rake more hay than a man can, any day."

"It must be eight o'clock," I said. "What time do they come home?"

"Oh, my," said Katie, "you can't tell that. They're working over there by the Fabian House. It's been a good day for drying, and they mightn't come home for a long time yet."

"Why, that's more than half-way to Hunter," I said. "It must be four miles away."

"Yes, yes; it's all of that."

Little John sat at the end of the log, looking upward, motionless. He was three years old, but he seemed the only aged member of the family. His head was large, his countenance grave and wistful. He spoke now in a thin, piping, plaintive voice.

"It's a nice night," he said, as if speaking to himself.

No one answered.

And after a while he piped again, still gazing upward: "The stars are all out."

Little Hughie, a child in tatters, tall for his age, angular, a face the miniature of his father's, his body always in motion, his face contorted with smiles and grimaces, pressed now against my knee, and, peering up at me, said:

"What, in h—l, are the stars, anyhow? I never could make 'em out."

Katie laughed at this speech, but instantly rebuked it.

"You better not let pa hear you swear that way."

"Well, he ain't here," said Hughie, laughing gleefully.

"Why aren't you off with the others in the hay-field?" I asked.

"Because I have to work around here."

"And what do you do?"

"He rolls this thing around all day," said Katie, motioning with her foot to a cart-wheel in the dooryard.

"Yes," said Hughie, "I have to work at that."

"I wanted him to get me some wood to-day, and he told me he was too busy working that thing around."

"Why," I said, in some surprise, "it can't be that you are lazy?"

"Yes," he said, laughing like an imp of cheerfulness, "I'm lazy, so I am. I tell Katie she must do her work, and I'll do mine. She wants me to help her with the dishes and bring in wood, and that's no work for a man."

"I should think Katie had her hands full if she does all the housework."

"Oh, that ain't all she does. She milks the cows, and hoes in the garden, and feeds the pigs."

"And you don't help her?"

"Why, no, of course. She must do her work, and I'll do mine."

"Well, John," I said, "what do you think of it? Is Hughie lazy?"

"He surely is," came the piping, plaintive answer.

"And what do you do, John?"

"Well, I feed the chickens and help Katie all I can."

"Yes, yes," said Katie; "he's a good deal handier than Hughie is."

"Don't you do a thing all day?" asked Nancy.

"Not much," said Hughie. "I take the milk and eggs over to the park night and morning. [The park was nearly two miles away.] Then I bring the wood up to the house and throw it by the door. I won't take it in, for that's Katie's work. She must do her work, and I'll do mine."

"Where do you get this wood?" I asked.

"Why, off there, in the clearing, where it's cut and piled."

"Where's that?"

"Why, it's beyond them woods over across that field beyond."

"How much do you bring a day?"

"Oh, four or five wagon-loads—as much as I can haul in that little wagon there."

"He cleans the stables out," said Katie.

"Yes; I clean the stables out. Sometimes I forget it, though, and then there's h—l to pay. The other night I had gone to bed when pa came home, and I hadn't cleaned them out. So he made me get up and go out there in my shirt and do the job. I was playing with this wheel here, and I forgot."

This chastisement seemed to be a huge joke with him. He chuckled and laughed as he was telling it, and Katie laughed with him.

"Is that all you do?"

"Well, of course I have to sleep and eat a good deal. I can eat as much as any of 'em. I can eat a whole loaf when Katie first bakes the bread."

Little Hughie was seven years old. Every day he carried perhaps a quarter of a cord of wood from a distant clearing across the fields from the house; he cleaned out the stables after fourteen cows and two horses and two teams of oxen; he walked from six to eight miles a day, carrying milk and eggs to market. This, with other jobs, no doubt, overlooked, were the light labors of the lazy member of this family. There was a lilt in his voice and a sparkle in his eye as he spoke of the care-free, merry life he led.

Suddenly we heard some one whistling a tune.

"There they come," said Katie. "That's Sammy whistling."

A little later we saw shadowy forms approaching down the road, and heard their muffled footsteps in the dust.

"Why, where's the team?" I asked.

"Oh, Will or Tom has taken that over to Tannersville to get the swill from the Blythewood and the Fairmount."

They were close before they saw us. Hughie and Mrs. Convery walked hand in hand. She was a shapely little woman, reaching to the top button of his vest. Her feet were bare. She wore a short petticoat. Her waist was open at the throat. She wore no hat or bonnet, but on her gray hair was a cloth of gay colors, made something like a turban. On this apparel rested her reputation for half-nakedness.

When Hughie saw us he stopped abruptly, put his hands upon his hips, and, throwing his head back, looked down upon me as his custom was.

"Well, well," he said, "I thought you must be lost."

"You're the one that's lost. When are you coming back home again? Jack and I can't get along up there without you."

"I know you can't, and I'm anxious to get through this haying. We are 'most done now. Boy! boy! what work we did to-day!"

His eyes, beneath their half-closed lashes, became suddenly luminous. "We broke the axle of the wagon with the last load to-night. I tell you, you should have seen that load."

We heard the sound of horses close at hand.

"Why, there's Will and the team," said Katie.

"Yes, yes," said Hughie. "We broke the wagon down."

Will emerged from the darkness, smiling, and joined the smiling group. He passed on, and, without comment, hitched the team to an empty wagon in the barn-yard, clambered up in the box, and drove off to Tannersville for the swill. They were under contract with the hotels to remove the garbage, and it was a task to be attended to. It was ten o'clock. They had been at work since daylight.

The rest of the family went in to supper. We followed them. The room we entered was poorly lighted by a lamp without a chimney and without a base, held in position by a coffee-cup that supported it. The wick smoked. It stood in the center of the table, covered with a soiled cloth. The food was heaped in milk-pans and on cracked platters. The dingy walls were hung with old garments. Wooden chairs were the only furniture. The littered floors were bare. A half-opened door revealed a stairway heaped with boots and pants, coats and dress-skirts. A sick chicken was under the stove. A pig was sleeping in one corner.

What excuse did these people make for such a room?

They did not mention it. They were unconscious of its disorder. In Hughie's luminous eyes were visions of the hay-fields. The chicken under the stove for Mrs. Convery was a poor invalid. The pig in the corner was one of her "purty dears." Every animal in the place would run to her when it saw her coming. The chickens would fly to her shoulder. The calves trotted at her heels, putting their noses into her hand.

A few moments there, and I was also unconscious of the room. It was in semi-darkness. Through the smoky atmosphere, in the fitful light of the wick, I could see these glowing faces about the table, and they were enough for me. If I could afford it, I would place them in surroundings neat and comfortable, but from them I ask no more.

CHAPTER XIII

A STUDY IN OPTIMISM

OB was racing over the fields in pursuit of the crows. He, too, has preserved his illusions. I was told that I must not permit him to do this any longer, or he would not be reliable. Even Jack thought, at first, that he was too old to become a good cow-dog. So long as Jennie was alone, he had no opportunity, for she was always following me about, and was at the house before milking time. After Maggie came, she remained in the pasture.

The first evening they were late, I said to Bob:

"Now, Bob, we will go after the cows."

He looked quickly into my face, listened a moment, and started on ahead in the direction of the bell. He remained quiet in front of me, however, stepping daintily, expectant, but not sure. When we came in sight of the cows, he looked back at me.

"You must go around behind them," I said. He followed me in a wide circle, glancing constantly from the cows to me, whimpering in his eagerness. I repeated several times: "You must go around behind them."

The cows saw us coming. They looked up and waited, watching our maneuver calmly. When we were behind them, I said:

"Speak!"

Bob barked, looking into my face.

"No. Speak at them." I pointed. "Go up to the cows and speak to them. Go on!"

He leaped forward, racing swiftly toward them.

"Bob!" I called. "Go easy, boy, for easy does it."

The cows had wheeled at his approach, galloped a short distance, and turned to look at us. Bob stood where he was, his bright eyes questioning me.

"Now go up to them easy and speak." He trotted up to them and barked. Maggie lowered her head and made a lunge at him.

"Take her!" I called. He landed between her horns. She wheeled about.

"Back!" I shouted. "Get behind!" Quivering, barking, very much excited, he still obeyed me instantly. He began to understand. It was uphill, and the cows did not trot far. Before we reached the barn they were walking and Bob was trotting crisscross behind them.

Jack saw us coming, and exclaimed:

"Well, by the lightning, I never saw anything like that. Bob could teach school."

In less than two weeks I paid no more attention to the cows. Bob took care of them. He always did the chores with me. While I was mixing the feed, he kept the chickens from the pail, moving in a circle around me. I mixed in the sand just outside the barn, then carried the pail to a spot near the coop, where I scattered it, Bob trotting ahead and the chickens fluttering around us. Once I slipped back unnoticed. Bob, having seen me start, went briskly on, and the whole drove followed him. When they arrived they seemed surprised. I had never deceived Bob before, and he did not suspect me. He stood calmly in the midst of the noisy horde, his head erect, waiting for me to come.

One of the things that I had learned during these months of actual possession in dreamland was that the blessing of fresh eggs required something more than gathering them. The first nests that I constructed were put together hastily, separated by partitions formed of boards that in some cases were not quite large enough, but left an open space of about two inches between the nests.

The hens were late in setting, but the first week in June some eight or ten of them began to cluck and keep their nests. There were not enough eggs for all of them at once. I put fourteen marked eggs under each of the first two. A few days later I found four marked eggs under one of the other hens, and only ten under one of those I had set. This bit of legerdemain amazed me, for while all the nests were in a row, three empty compartments separated these two nests. I replaced the four, in spite of the protests of the anxious creature who had stolen them. During the afternoon, on one of the occasions when I was peeping into the coop, I saw this hen at work. She was in the compartment next to the hen provided for. Her neck was extended through the space behind the partition. She was thrusting her head under the setting hen, and with her bill adroitly extracting an egg. When this was in the compartment where she stood, she pushed it across and through the space behind the opposite partition. Hopping out of this compartment and into the next, she repeated her performance until the egg was in her own nest.

This fault in my construction caused me endless trouble until all the hens had been supplied. After this I was obliged to pay frequent visits to the coop. Every day or so the setting hens left their nests to drink and wallow in the earth, securing for their feathers the moisture necessary in the process of hatching. When they returned, they did not always go to their own nests. I frequently found one setting abandoned, while two hens were together covering another. There were enough nests for all the hens. Those that were laying, however, seemed determined to use only those that were occupied by these prospective mothers, who seemed equally determined against harboring their neighbors' young. In the battles that ensued many eggs were broken.

After many days of anxiety and disaster, I solved this problem by fitting punctured doors into the nests, opening them late in the afternoon, when the hours for laying were over, and closing them at night. I learned, of course, the peculiarities of these setting hens. Some of them required no watching. They left their nests regularly, attended to their wants briskly, and returned again before the eggs were cold. Others had to be caught and carried back, for they seemed deficient in Nature's instinctive reckoning of time. These hens, whenever they left their nests, did so with a loud noise, and at first, upon their outcries, I was obliged to drop whatever I was doing, and run hastily to the coop to see if it were one of my delinquents. After a time, however, I learned to distinguish between them. These wild clamors, coming to me from a distance, became as distinctive and familiar as the voices of my friends.

One of these hens was a particular nuisance. She has her type in every species. She was a trouble to herself, to me, and to all the world. Somewhere between three and four in the afternoon, the peace of the place would be disturbed by her explosive outburst. She flew from her nest with wild shrieks, a great flapping of wings, discordant squawks, and choking sounds. Alighting on the ground, she would spread her wings, ruffle her feathers, and run as if stark mad, stumbling over her neighbors basking in the sunlight, and scattering those gathered in companionable groups picking insects from the grass. This hen, left to herself, would spend an hour or so running from one spot to another, seeming never to find the right place at which either to drink, to feed, or to moisten her feathers. The innumerable broils that she inspired served also to consume the time. At the first sound of her alarm, either Nancy or I would seize a saucer of food, kept always ready, and a pan of water, and run out to her. When these were placed before her, Bob, who never failed to answer these summons also, kept the other hens away while she ate and drank. We allowed her fifteen minutes after this to gather what moisture she could, and then drove her back, fussing and scolding, to her nest.

I set twelve hens in all, and it seemed a pity that we must be deprived of the eggs from all these throughout the summer, while they were running with their broods.

I heard of a man who avoided this by giving the chickens, as they were hatched, to one hen, who cared for them all.

I constructed a little yard of chicken wire, and put the first brood hatched, with their mother, into it. Two days later I carried the second brood in a basket, and tucked them through the meshes. The old hen, hearing their peeping in the grass, ran over to inspect them, ruffling her feathers and uttering cries of menace. The little strangers, unafraid, ran peeping up to her, disarming her resentment with their bold and innocent assurance. She gave them a disturbed peck or two, and allowed them to mingle with her own brood. The mother I had robbed I took, for precaution's sake, into the cow-shed, and kept her under a box for two days. The moment she was released, she began to look for her lost children, clucking anxiously. She peered behind the barrels in the shed, went outside and around it, ran to the coop, hopped up to her nest and down again, to renew her search outside. A little later, I saw her hurry to the yard I had inclosed. As she stood by the wire fence, her energetic clucking caused a commotion among the little brood inside. Eight wee chicks scurried through the grass, hopped through the meshes of the fence, and joined her. She had hatched out nine. I let this mother have her brood in peace.

Bob was very much interested in the arrival of the little broods. While they were growing up, he remained in the dooryard, often alone, following the movements of the various families in their busy quest for worms and insects. Perhaps he guessed the many dangers to them lurking in the forest world. He was, at least, either watching over them or curiously interested in them for reasons of his own. I know that my neighbors were surprised that no harm came to these families from hawks or rats or weasels, and this may have been because the marauders of the air and of the thickets knew of Bob's presence there.

When the five pigs were in the pasture, I carried five pails of feed and water to the pens night and morning. The troughs were close to the wire fence, and Bob could just thrust his slender head through the meshes. When I lifted the pail over to pour the feed into the trough, the pigs would crowd forward, their stout noses threatening the pail. Then Bob would reach in and take them gently by the ears. When they jumped back, I got the feed in.

When the last pail was empty, Bob, without a word from me, raced off after the cows. He went like an arrow until he reached them, then when they started home, he walked slowly behind. They might stop at the brook to drink, but they must not feed.

One morning in October, about four months after Maggie's wedding, Bob was gone a long time after the cows. He could not hear the bell, and had to circle the place for them. At last I heard him barking in the distance, somewhere at the foot of the pasture-lot. There was an unusual note in his voice. It did not sound to me as if he were barking at the cows. I went to the crest of the hill and saw him on the edge of the woods by the road. He was barking towards the house and calling me. I hurried down. Maggie was standing under the trees, in trouble. She had given birth to her calf too soon. Bob, seeing that something was wrong, had not disturbed her, but had summoned me.

"That's too bad," said Jack; "and yet it might be worse. It's a good thing she was not dry. You will have milk all winter now, and in the spring you can drive her again."

"What's the cause of it, Jack?"

"She may have lain upon a stone, or some of our summer friends, the boarders, may have found her in the way and hit her with something. It couldn't be from harsh driving, for Bob don't drive them harsh."

One stormy morning, about two weeks after this, I saw Jennie by the barn when I got up, and, taking the pails, I went out, as I supposed, to milk.

"How soon," asked Nancy, "shall I have breakfast?"

"In forty minutes. I will only milk."

It was almost noon when I returned, drenched by the rain, bespattered with mud. We had spent the morning searching the country-side for Maggie and endeavoring to get her home. Through the same valley, first revealed to me in the moonlight, across my neighbor's meadows, where once Nancy, Elizabeth, and I had journeyed to our bath and slept in the sunlight, I followed my Maggie cow.

Those impulses which in most men lead to irritation and anger, and make of life a series of contentions and hardships, are strong in me. When I saw the hole in my fence that Maggie had made, and realized that I must search for her in the rain indefinitely, with other pressing things to do, these impulses took possession of me, and I might have spent the morning cursing this creature who provides my butter, milk, and cream.

I made two journeys to Seifferth's distant pasture, and the second time I found Maggie by the bars, calling lustily. I heard an answering bellow a little way up the mountain-side.

Ordinarily, when Maggie sees me, she watches my approach with complacent eyes, and holds her head toward me, that I may rub it between the horns. Now, when she saw me, she made a vain plunge at the bars, turned abruptly, and dashed headlong through the underbrush, her tail stiff and defiant. Bob rushed in front of her, and she trampled him. I shouted and gesticulated. We outwitted and outran her, headed her off in all directions except the one toward home, and got her at last through the hole in the fence she had made. I mended it behind her, and drove her to the barn, where she remained two days, until the instincts of unrest were stilled. When this was accomplished, I could enjoy my breakfast at this tardy hour.

Poetical environments preserve their poetry. If it is lost for us, we lose it because we desecrate our habitations by the lives we live in them. I have never known a cynic who could give a clear account of his lost illusions. They had faded and were gone. Somewhere the pleasant paths that seemed leading to a genial world had disappeared, and he had come instead upon the quagmires. I know that in the years between that first summer in the mountains when I dreamed of cows grazing peacefully upon the hillside, and these later days of care and labor, there have been innumerable occasions when, through fear or greed, through anger, vanity, or resentment, I might easily have lost my way.

And how difficult it is to maintain always that impersonal point of view with which a friendly spirit may exist—to maintain it day by day and hour by hour; not to be taken by surprise!

Yesterday I viewed my neighbor with impersonal perceptions.

"He has his faults, but who has not? Let us be kind."

To-day he is a thief.

He has cheated me.

The summer passed, and Jennie continued to be indifferent to the bellowing in a distant pasture.

"It seems to me," I said to Jack one day, "that Jennie is getting too fat. Perhaps she eats too much grass or finds something that bloats her."

"I'd rather see a cow too fat than too thin."

"But she has never been on a tear."

"The old rip Johnson! Perhaps he lied to us. Andy might have been right, after all."

She gave less milk now than formerly, but then the pasture was not so young, and that might account for it.

Without consulting anyone, I began to dry her up.

On the morning of Election Day, Bob brought Maggie to the barn alone. "Where's Jennie?"

He looked at me as if to say:

"I hunted, but I could not find her."

"Go and look for her, then."

He ran off through the woods. I heard his voice, now here, now there, but he was barking on a venture, hoping she might reveal herself by a movement in the brush.

Suddenly the note changed. It was deep and authoritative. Then silence. Then he called for me. I was already on the way, for I had my suspicions.

I found Jennie in a warm grassy hollow beyond the garden, near the creek, hidden by a circle of trees and bushes. A fine buff-colored calf lay at her feet.

This was a holiday. The next morning I told Jack the news. He was grubbing trees to widen the road through the strip of woods at the foot of the hill.

"You have a right now," he said, "to kick Johnson."

"It's a fine calf, Jack."

"And it's the fall of the year, too."

"I'll have milk and fresh butter all winter."

"Yes, and you'll have to milk all winter. Up before daylight in the cold. The lying old devil, he sold you a farrow cow for a new milch-cow. I wouldn't think so much of it if you hadn't treated him so well."

"Jennie is one of the best cows I ever saw. They are both fine cows. From the 9th of May to the 15th of September we made 343$\frac{1}{2}$ pounds of butter and sold 210$\frac{1}{2}$ pounds. We had all the cream and milk we wanted, and there was all the milk fed to the pigs besides. Those cows have paid for their purchase-price and their feed in less than six months. Of course Maggie's misfortune may count against her for a while, but Jennie is better now than when I got her."

"I know she's a good cow, but why didn't he tell you she was farrow?"

"Because I would not have accepted her. He knew that she was nearer what I wanted than anything he could find. He looked very shrewdly into my eye, and took the chance. He was right."

All this time Jack was grubbing steadily.

"Yes," he said [whack], "any one who burns Johnson for a fool" [whack, whack] "will have wise ashes to sell." He stood up to wipe the sweat from his eye and added amiably:

"I've always liked Johnson, for I think there's more good than harm in him."

CHAPTER XIV

OUR LITTLE WORLD

O one could have better neighbors than mine—the Dales, the Brices, the Seifferths, the Farrells, the Converys. They have watched over this place as though it were their own, making no apologies for their advice, giving it directly and peremptorily, but always in the kindly spirit that has made it all inexpressibly pleasant. And yet these people are not any too friendly among themselves.

All Platte Clove is throbbing with a warm-hearted, rugged, generous life. Its society is restrained. About the only rendezvous along the road is Jack's small kitchen. Here every one is welcome. He is loved throughout the mountains. The most cynical must speak well of him.

This restraint in social life, this half-estrangement, is due partly to petty quarrels over trivial things, which the least consideration and tact and mutual desire would have made as nothing. Here, as elsewhere, there is too little reasoning together. There is stubbornness and pride; selfish, one-sided judgments; things said upon an impulse, and held to; grievances nursed in secret; insinuations and whispers.

But in this particular community there is a more formidable cause. Its normal life is too violently disturbed. Every year the natives are submerged beneath a flood of summer transients. Here is an opportunity for pillage. At its best it is a powerful interest, foreign to the place. There are those who, all the year around, lie in waiting, like beasts of prey, living to themselves in the winter-time, preparing for the summer, when they can come forth to feed upon the boarder. There are others who have prospered through this opportunity honestly, by good management and legitimate enterprise; but it has divided all the community, so that we have here in miniature our little world. Here are the producers, and here the shrewd baron, grown rich in the trade.

In contrast to Jack's low cottage under the trees, Andy's bleak house, and the ruin of the Convery's, is the huge white dwelling where the Seifferths live. Theirs is the finest farm in the valley, trim, fertile, and imposing.

This should be the center of our social life. Mrs. Seifferth is an able woman. For years she has borne her crippled state without complaining, and in the circle where her interests lie she is friendly, wise, and generous. And Mr. Seifferth is a genial, friendly man. But the interests of the natives are not theirs. The year for them revolves around the summer-time. The boarders are the world. They have missed the profounder happiness such natures might attain in their eagerness to gain and to accumulate. They pride themselves upon their shrewdness, a pitiful substitute for contentment. They like to buy cheap and sell dear.

Many years ago, when they were just farmers like the rest of their neighbors, before the summer people came, when they toiled in the soil, produced like products, suffered and prospered with them, their place was a rendezvous. There were better times in the valley then, and they helped to make them so.

Now Mrs. Seifferth is indignant at Andy Dale because he asks as much for his mountain lamb as does the butcher. If the Converys would sell their butter, eggs, and poultry to her cheap, she would look kindly on them, for she has a tolerant mind.

For several weeks this summer she cast unfriendly glances upon Nancy and me because, while she was offering us eighteen cents a dozen, we sold our eggs elsewhere for twenty-five.

Mr. Seifferth and Jack have had warm words over fences and dogs, but still they hold each other in esteem. Each in his own way is an important man in the community. Jack is poor, but, at the age of sixty, he is still the best man at a day's labor in the mountains. It would be hard to find his master with an ax. At the age of sixty he can cut up as much stove-wood from standing timber in a day as any man in these regions. He knows and loves the timber.

He was in his day one of the best men in the quarries, for stone is not just stone to him—it is a thing to be studied and to be reasoned with.

He speaks of his cow as though she were a woman, and she is the best in the mountains. His horse, past thirty, will still carry half a ton of hay from his swamp, uphill, to the barn, trotting where the way is level. He does not own a whip.

His pig always weighs the most in the fall. He gets from four to ten eggs a day, almost the year round, from his ten hens. They are noble specimens of the white Leghorn.

He has the best cider in the valley, made from his own apples. It is like apple champagne.

He has toiled incessantly, broken his ribs on two occasions, his collar-bone on another. He is as gentle as he is strong. He possesses a broad, just judgment and a grand form of wit—sometimes exceedingly subtle, at others bald and blunt.

Such a man commands respect anywhere.

It is easier to find fault with Andy, if one wishes to. You can say no evil of him, but you can criticize.

He is a pessimist. He spends hours toiling through the undergrowth of the timber-land, far up the mountain-side, for his cattle, in all kinds of weather, day after day, because he can never find the time and strength to make his fences. His cows are no good to him. They are farrow cows, because, inasmuch as his neighbor's bull was frequently among them a year ago last spring, he thought surely they must have caught, and did not drive them to the bull. He has no orchard. He has never painted his house. He is five years younger than his brother Jack, but looks older. For thirty years he has dwelt upon his place, and still every year he is bothered with stone-heaps when he cuts his hay. His hens, of many sorts and kinds, give him no eggs.

"I don't know what's the matter," he said; "they don't lay at all, or lay out, and the childer can't seem to find the nests."

There was a very fair crop of elderberries this year, but when we offered to employ his children to pick them for us, he advised us to wait until some other year when the crop might be better.

He asks eighteen cents a pound for the hind quarters and sixteen cents for the shoulders of his lambs.

These are his crimes.

He is proud and supersensitive.

He is honest to an extreme.

In all that concerns me and my affairs, he shows the most intelligent and careful interest. He takes great pains to be square and honest in all his dealings. He has a stone-quarry, but he would not sell me any stone until I had tramped way up there, on a useless errand of investigation, to see if the slabs would suit me. He shook his head over every stone, assuring me that it was very likely not to do.

I wanted him to have the money not only for the stone, but for hauling it as well. I had to use great persuasion to secure him this benefit. His horse was off somewhere in the brush; his wagon needed mending; he was not feeling well enough, and it was quite a climb up my hillside road; but, finally, he undertook the job, and did it well. Then it required an hour or more to fix the price. He insisted that between neighbors the market price should not rule; that these stones were worthless to him, and I should pay him only what I thought they might be worth to me.

There is no service he will not perform for his friend. He drove three miles through the cold to get a boar for my sows.

One rainy day in the fall, he brought Jennie to my door.

"I saw her going by," he explained. "I feared she might hurt herself if she got into Jack's apples. Sweet apples are all right, but sour ones dries them up."

Late one night there was a rap on the door. It was Andy.

"Do you want to save the life of two hens?"

"Come in."

"No. I've been to Tannersville and must get home. As I was going by, I saw two hens on the fence by the road. Are they yours?"

"Way down there?"

I went down with him, carrying a lantern to blind their eyes. They were mine.

"The foxes might have caught them," he said.

He will do more for another than for himself, work more willingly for friendship than for pay.

He is, in fact, the nearest approach to Rip Van Winkle I have found. Dear old Rip, whose improvidence has brought fortune to the thrifty here!

What a joyous, whole-souled, happy valley the Plaaterkill might be! How insidiously the element of discord slips in!

I said to myself: "I do not like the attitude of the Seifferths toward their neighbors. If they buy anything of me, they must pay the highest price for it."

Eggs almost caused a rupture. But we talked the matter over, and no lasting harm was done.

On the 25th of December the world is supposed to celebrate the birth of Christ. There is praying, singing, dancing, fighting. There are family gatherings, especial matinees, balls, services, and carousals. There is tenderness and spite, generosity, vanity, straining formality, and greed.

From the dark forests on these lonely mountain-sides over one hundred thousand Christmas trees are taken to New York. They are chopped down, tied into bundles, carted away, and sold. They are haggled over and trucked about. They are trimmed with tinsel and illuminated. They are seldom used here.

"You have some fine Christmas trees on your place," said Mr. Seifferth. "I have not cut them for several years. I will buy them if you want to sell."

"How much?"

"Well, they're worth two cents apiece standing. That's the usual price."

"All right," I said, for this was early in the spring. Later, after my resolution had been formed, Frank Dale offered me two cents and a half. I told the Seifferths it was three. But what can you expect from a money-changer in the temple?

Before the business was over, I told more lies than one.

Frank and Will Gillespie cut the trees. They left stumps about two feet high. While they were at work Mr. Seifferth came up to see.

"You should make them cut close to the ground," he said. "Your land will be full of stumps."

I spoke to the boys about this.

"No one could afford to do that," said Frank. "Look at the way these lower branches spread. It would cost more in time than the trees are worth to trim them. The tree is no good to us below the first perfect ring of branches. We can cut it there without trimming, with a single cut of the ax. It would take ten times as long the other way, and on a thousand trees that would cost more than we could get for them."

"Mr. Seifferth says he always cuts his that way."

"Well, he don't. No one wants them cut that way except Andy Dale, and he can't get anyone to cut them."

The next morning Jack was helping to tie bundles, and he joined in the discussion.

"I can take you now and show you the stumps all over Seifferth's place where he has cut them. If you don't want any more Christmas trees, it's all right to cut them to the ground, and you'll get no more. But nobody will buy your trees and clear your pastures for you."

When I spoke to Mr. Seifferth of this, he said: "You will get more new trees, and better ones, if you cut the old ones to the ground."

"What does he mean by telling you that?" said Jack. "He must want to keep you out of the business, for he surely knows better."

"But look at all these little balsams six inches and a foot high. Wouldn't they do better with the old trees cut to the ground? In some places these stumps, with their spreading branches, crowd them."

"Yes, but new trees will spring from these stumps. And if you cut away all the old trees, the little ones won't come up. They spring from the living roots of those stumps. Cut them close to the ground, and you kill the roots."

"Well," said Mr. Seifferth, when I told him finally why I allowed the stumps to stand, "people have different notions."

Every year Mr. Seifferth takes a car-load or two to the city and sells them there.

Just before he left, he said to me:

"If you have any interest in those trees of yours, and want to sell them yourself, you could make some money. You can use my stand."

I thanked him, and was ashamed.

"Hereafter," I said to Nancy, "I will be content with 'most any price from the Seifferths. They have done a hundred generous things for us."

In the Seifferths' household there are, besides the old people, Fred and Tom, and Tom's wife, Delia. Delia is a daughter of the Farrells. One of her sisters, Nettie, is a trained nurse. Another is a teacher of the modern school. They were educated in New York.

These young women cling to their mountain home because they love it. They are familiar with Broadway, but they prefer this valley road.

They make pretty calicoes to work in. They have tailor-made gowns for occasions, and dresses trimmed with lace. They could pass unnoticed through the Waldorf.

Are you polite and formal? They can be smiling and gracious, saying, "Do you think so?" and "Really?"

Do you want to play snowball? They will do that, too.

Are you hungry? They can cook.

When Tom and Delia were married, the old people forgot their fences.

Why all this whispering? People talk among themselves. Why not out loud?

Now, Nancy and Delia are often together. What do they say?

Once I overheard this:

"No one can be nicer when she wants to be."

"She has been like a good mother to me."

CHAPTER XV

THE AWAKENING

FTER the drought there were two months of heavy rains. The house became damp, the dripping trees monotonous and melancholy. There was too much gloom. A deep and mysterious forest behind us was well, but it crowded us too close, and we needed a clearer view down the valley.

Two hundred of our magnificent trees were doomed.

"Here is your winter's wood," said Jack, as he felled them. "You must have a chopping-bee."

At once certain desires crystallized. Here was at least one first answer, however small, to a question which had followed me. I had returned to nature. I had built the House in the Woods. I knew the joys and the hardships of secluded country living, but what of those who lived there before me, whose hands had been outstretched to me in loyal welcome? The country had brought a new balm to my life. What could I bring to theirs? Here I was, facing a responsibility undreamed of at first. I knew the narrowness, the suspicions and jealousies which are bred of isolated life. It might be only a little that I could do, but if the House in the Woods could serve as a common meeting-place for pleasure and not toil, it should be so, and I thought of something which would pave the way.

A little later I said to Jack:

"How would a chopping-bee and a house-warming in the evening do? Do you think they'd come?"

"Why wouldn't they?"

"We would like to have the Plaaterkill turn out."

"You can expect a crowd, then."

I glanced over these timbered solitudes, and asked:

"From where?"

"From hither and yon. They are in there among the trees."

"A house-warming?" said Mrs. Seifferth. "You will have to be careful about your invitations."

"It's open for the country-side. I don't know my neighbors."

"Well, well," she said, "I will give you no more advice. Go to ruin in your own way."

We named the 26th of October as the date of the bee and house-warming. There was no public announcement. I simply told Jack, Hughie, Andy, and the Seifferths, and engaged Gene Ballou, one of our carpenters, to play the fiddle, and his wife to accompany him.

The last week was a whirlwind of labor.

Our seven months of accumulating tasks came to a climax. Five carpenters were finishing the buildings. Mace Tompkins and Frank Dale, the two who had been with us since Goslee left, seemed now like members of our family. Every morning, as they drove up, Bob went bounding to meet them; and Nancy from the kitchen door, and I from wherever I might be, stopped our work for a moment, to shout this tuneful greeting:

> "And hear their voices, ringing
> In merry childish glee,
> Proclaim the joyous welcome,
> Welcome home!"

Frank, a giant like his father Jack, youthful, handsome, and straightforward, was an able workman and a cheerful man. Mace, one of the best and quickest carpenters in the mountains, was noisy and impetuous. He came from a vigorous Methodist family. He sang hymns and swore and cracked jokes. While putting on shingles or studding the double doors with nails, he sang:

> "I am so glad that our Father in heaven
> Tells of his love in the Book he has given."

He sang in a high voice and very fast, beating time with his hammer on the nails. It was impossible to resist him. Once Nancy seized her dish-pan and marched around the house beating it with a ladle. Jack and I joined the parade, pounding our shovels with ax-handles.

Pleasant as these companions were, however, it was necessary that they get through and go. So Mace brought two more men, and by working hard himself, and singing fast and loud, he pushed matters to a completion on the Friday before the house-warming, October 23.

During this week the dam was finished. Andy dug the last ditch around the end of the barn. Jack felled the trees. Will banked the house, for the heralds of winter were piping through the mountains. Hughie, Tom, and Sam, with the little oxen, trimmed the fallen trees and dragged them into skid-piles, ready for the bee.

As the time approached, there were murmurs in the air. We became mysteriously conscious of those dwellings hidden in the forest. People were coming. How many, we did not know. Teamsters, unknown to us, along the road, hailed us as we passed.

"I will be there Monday."

"The old woman wants to know if she's to come in the afternoon or evening."

"My daughter came up from the city for the house-warming."

"What will I bring—an ax or a saw?"

"Do you want a team, or are the logs piled up?"

Nancy said: "There may be fifty or a hundred. There might be more."

"Yes," said Jack, "in the evening the crowd will come, but fifteen or twenty men make a big chopping-bee."

We intended to provide a dinner and supper for the men, and refreshments in the evening. We bought a whole lamb from Andy, and four big hams, weighing together fifty pounds; baked five large pans of beans, two hundred and thirty-three cookies, twenty-five pies, and forty loaves of bread, and boiled a bushel of potatoes. This, with coffee, tea, preserves, pickles, and sweet cider, were the rations.

Nancy did most of the baking alone, and it was on this occasion that her fame was spread.

When it came time to the actual preparations, Mrs. Seifferth thought only of a successful issue. She helped Nancy with her plans, gently and kindly, giving her of her treasures of experience. She loaned us pots and dishes, and told me to bring all the meat down there Monday morning, and they would cook it in their range, and make the kettle of gravy.

There had been two weeks of fine fall weather, clear, crisp, and bracing. Sunday night the temperature fell thirty degrees. On Monday morning a north wind was blowing. Masses of cold gray clouds scurried across the valley, whirling in eddies, trailing through the trees of the mountain-sides. On my way to the pig-pens, I saw Hunter Mountain through a mist. On my return, it

was obscured. A storm was coming up the valley. A gray curtain hanging between the ranges approached swiftly, concealing everything. The Farrells' house, on a distant knoll, and the buildings of the Seifferths in the hollow, disappeared. The forest around me, swaying and creaking, was suddenly thrown into violent commotion. I saw the snowflakes. They were sweeping up my hillside. They struck my face. The forest received them. The sound, as they fell through the network of twigs and into the thick green boughs of the firs, was like a profound sigh.

"No chopping-bee to-day," I said to Nancy.

"It's too bad," she answered ruefully. "My cookies won't be so good to-morrow."

Then Andy came, an ax upon his shoulder. There were ghostly figures behind him, and Hughie, Will, and Tom stepped out of the maze of snow. I heard sounds back of the house. Two men were at work at one of the skid-piles, moving a long cross-cut saw through a log. Three others came from the direction of the garden. They were Ed Gillespie and two of his boys, Will and Morris, towering six inches above him.

By nine o'clock twenty-three men were at work. These were the Burnses, Mike and Patsy and Pete and Hughie and Owney, old Pat and old Pete; there were the Dales and the Seifferths, the Dibbells, Farrells, Gillespies, Dolans, Brices, Converys; there were Parker, Lindsay, and Johnson.

"Here, you cow-jockey," called Jack, "come here."

"I came to boss the job."

He was dragged to one end of a saw, and kept there until dark.

"There," said Jack, "you can now say you have done one day's work in your lifetime, and I'll support your statement."

Mrs. Jack Dale, Miss Brown, a neighbor from the mountain opposite, Nettie Farrell, and Winnie Gillespie helped Nancy serve the dinner. Delia sent up the lamb, roasted to a turn, and carved.

Nancy wore a new calico dress, and a red paper rose in her thick, dark hair. Her blue eyes were eager, her face flushed. She whisked from the stove to the pantry, to the table, to the stove, to the pantry.

She has smiled at me across a table at Delmonico's, but I never saw her so happy or so beautiful at a dinner as on that day.

The boys ate heartily and praised the fare. They wondered at the way she had taken hold up here.

By four o'clock they had cut over thirty cords of wood. The snow was four inches deep.

They left us quietly, as they came, going home to do their chores and dress for the evening.

The storm and the cold increased.

At half-past six the Converys returned, bringing Mrs. Convery and Katie. "I came early," said Hughie, "to look after the teams."

In the light from the windows I could see the snow falling athwart the near-by trees, the sentinels of our dooryard. Beyond these the world was black.

There was a blur of light. It was a lantern. For an hour these blurs crept up our roadway and became bright, revealing strange forms, casting fantastic shadows. The guests arrived. There were more than a hundred. They came in surreys, buckboards, buggies, and on foot. The Gillespies had climbed up the mountain-side through the forest and returned. People came from near Onteora, beyond Tannersville, from Stony Clove, and from the head of the mountain.

The snow was shaken from a fascinator or a hood. A cloak was removed, and behold, a pretty girl in a dainty evening dress!

The boys were stalwart, amiable, straightforward, and gentle. I think it was because Jack was so completely at home that every one else became so the moment they entered. At eight o'clock Ida Ballou opened the piano, and Gene drew his fiddle-bow.

"Choose your partners for the dance."

Mike Burns took Nancy, and I chose Lizzie Shevlin. I learned later that she lived in the old house with the two chimneys in the hollow by the church.

Give me the country dances.

> "All hands round.
> Take your lady by the hand,
> And lead her down the center:
> Ladies to right,
> Gents to left,
> And balance on the corner.
> Swing the girl behind you.
> Alamon left.
> Promenade all."

Those are the calls for one. It is hard to choose between that and "Pop goes the Weasel," and "Chase the Squirrel," and

"Bow so neatly,
Kiss so sweetly."

In any one of these you can forget the chores.

It was four o'clock in the morning when the last lantern went swinging down the hill.

"Well," said Hughie as he left me, "there is a big difference here since the day I first drove up. You might say now that this place is tamed."

CHAPTER XVI

A Light On The Mountain

A T night, through the naked trees that rise before my bedroom window, I can see a solitary light against the dark background of the mountains across the valley. There was a time when this distant, lonely light—the only one visible in all the surrounding wilderness—awakened a multitude of weird imaginings. My first impression of it, like that of the surreptitious whistle to which Libbie responded, the isolated family of the Gillespies encountered on the trail to High Peak, and the bleak dwellings along the valley road, awakened those conceptions that romance fosters. This light, however, can no longer tempt my fancy to adventurous flights, for I know that it shines from the window of little Miss Brown, a quiet, unassuming maid past forty, who is probably sitting in her rocker by it, inserting a gourd in the heel of a stocking she is about to darn. Jack speaks of her as "the nicest old maid that ever lived." I, for one, would unhesitatingly condemn any community that produced and maintained one like her.

It is not difficult to give a significant glimpse of her nature. She is gentle and unobtrusive—a busy, thrifty, noiseless housewife. Living in the city, she might be mistaken for a timid person; and yet, to live alone with her old mother on this mountain-side is the crowning joy of her life.

One night, as she was sitting by the table, sewing, she heard a noise outside, unlike the familiar sounds of the forest, and, looking up, she saw the bearded face of a man pressed against the window. His brows were scowling, his voice rough and peremptory, as he said: "I want a place to sleep to-night."

"Won't you please go to the next house?" she answered innocently, "for my mother and I are all alone."

If her ingenuous eyes expressed anxiety, it was because she could not shelter him. The man looked at her for a moment, grumbled, and went away.

The Plaaterkill, however, cannot be blamed for her single state. It is true she has been known here for some fifteen years, but only in the summer heretofore. Every season she came with a number of friends and relatives, to act as housekeeper in a little cooperative establishment on the mountain-side, where they could take their vacation from school and office economically.

There are great depths of sentiment in these affectionate and domestic natures, which, unsatisfied and unexpressed, make them wretched in the midst of life's activities. The noises and the passions, the ambitions and misfortunes of a city distress them, for they have not the eye of the philosopher, that sees beauty in a tempest, serenity in the center of the strife. Give them, however, a beautiful solitude for a dwelling, and they will see around them expressions only of the sentiments they feel. For them there is nothing but a joyous melody in the twittering and singing of birds, for here, again, lacking the eye of the philosopher, they do not see the passions within these feathered breasts.

After fifteen wistful years, Miss Brown has realized a great ambition, and has settled down to spend her summers and her winters here.

Whatever timidity Miss Brown possesses does not come from fear of injury or offense to herself from others. If she seems timid, it is because her whole soul shrinks with exquisite sensitiveness from the possibility of intruding herself upon others. This fear, and the affectionate nature that prompts it, gives to her delicate countenance a wistful and anxious expression. There is something refreshing in the egotism of a strong and generous nature which responds promptly and heartily to a request for service; but when Nancy asked Miss Brown to help her at our chopping-bee, this little lady, with an almost appealing glance, asked hesitatingly, "May I?"

She came not for the excitement of the occasion, and her face was not aglow with youthful anticipations of the dance, but she was all a-flutter with suppressed delight, caused by the wonderful hope that she was wanted and could really be of use. She bestirred herself about the tables, made invisible by her self-forgetfulness, serving the men as they ate; beamed over the dish-pan, unconscious of the pretty, plump arms her rolled-up sleeves revealed; and when all the work was done she slipped, unnoticed, into a corner of the room, where, hour after hour, she watched the exuberant dancers, her eyes and cheeks aglow.

During the evening I said to her, "You ought to have a chopping-bee, Miss Brown."

"Mr. Dibbell said that, too," she answered eagerly. This eagerness made her flush, and her eyes a moment afterward were filled with apology and helplessness.

"Well, why don't you, then?"

"Why—I—" she said hesitatingly, "I don't know why they should come. You see, we have no men in our household to attend their chopping-bees; and then," she continued, leaning toward me, and whispering in a childish kind of awe, "they say, too, that they always expect something to drink, and, of course, you know I couldn't offer them anything but tea or coffee, and I don't suppose they would be satisfied with that."

There was such an evident struggle revealed in her eyes between puritanical principles and a wish to judge no one, that I laughed outright; so, when the music ceased and the set was over, I took advantage of the pause to announce a bee at Miss Brown's on Tuesday of the following week.

"Now, boys," I said, "Miss Brown has hesitated to give this bee because certain gossips have said you love strong drink and must have it at a bee. She can only give you coffee. Will you come?"

The room was filled with shouts of "Yes, yes." "You bet we will come." "Sure, we'll give Miss Brown a bee." "Why, sure we will." "Don't you mind the drink, Miss Brown."

When the tumult had subsided, I made a pretense of whispering to Miss Brown, and then, jumping on a table, informed them all that the one who could cut the most wood might hope to win her hand. Miss Brown cast a look of terror at me and upon the noisy claimants, and, with a cry of almost tearful confusion, bowed her face upon her knees. For a few moments the uproar was terrific. There were loud protestations from twenty youthful giants.

"Will there be any time limit?" shouted one.

"Does the day begin at twelve or one?"

"I will be there with my lantern."

The quick wit of these alert mountaineers was busy at once with schemes. Two of them, prompted by the same idea, pushed their way from different portions of the room to where Jack towered above his neighbors, laughing uproariously—Jack, that master with an ax, a woodman's hero for forty years.

"I want you to help me," said Hughie Burns, seizing him by the arm. "This is the chance of my life."

"Now, Jack, you must help me win Miss Brown."

"Hold on there, Jack," shouted Will Dale: "I will make a higher bid."

"She's mine, boys; she's mine," called a voice above the clamor, and Ray Bunt appeared upon the floor, bringing Miss Brown with him, supporting her with his strong left arm. "I'll win her sure, and I'm going to dance with her now to begin with."

"Why, I'm old enough to be your mother," said Miss Brown.

"Well, I've always wanted a wife just like my mother," roared this crude gallant.

"Choose your partners for the dance," called Gene Ballou, and in a twinkling the set was formed. From this until morning, to her astonishment and delight, Miss Brown no sooner sought her corner than she was summoned to the floor again.

It was ten below zero on the day of her bee, for this unparalleled winter was under way. More than two feet of snow was on the ground. Through the snow, in spite of this intense cold, twenty-two men, with saws and axes on their shoulders, came from a radius of three miles, a little after daybreak, and, without even knocking at the door, forced their way through the drifts into the forest back of Miss Brown's, and chopped down, dragged out, sawed, split, and piled into long neat rows her winter's wood.

Mr. Dibbell came with his team, although it was a busy time with him. Not once all day did any one stop to warm himself. They entered the house only to eat their dinner, heartily and fast. By nightfall they had cut eighteen cords of wood from standing timber.

These chopping-bees are the social events of the mountains. They are, in these parts, what the Horse Show, the opera, banquets at Sherry's, are in New York. This particular bee at Miss Brown's might be likened to the Charity Ball.

It has been many years since I envied the wealthy inhabitants of cities, since the show of dress and ornament, the splendor of private palaces, the pursuit of pleasure in a dress-suit has tempted me; but the ready laughter, the crude jokes, the mellow voices of these my neighbors here, who find their recreation in a day of friendly toil, fill me with admiring awe and a profound faith in the future of the world.

For a number of years the winters have been very quiet in Platte Clove. The generation that once gave it life has grown old and more or less estranged by childish feuds, and the households it still dominates are not so readily opened to the impetuous assaults of youth.

We were a new family in the valley, and we fortunately escaped the influence of its warring elements, and the forces within and without us that make for discord and decay. The House in the Woods was built in a friendly spirit, and when it was finished and thrown open, all the friendliness of the region made a frank response. The people were surprised at their own numbers, and at the exuberant good feeling that prevailed. A luxuriant new generation of pretty, blooming girls and stalwart young men were suddenly revealed. Of course they had all known one another well, and some of them had occasionally met at a public dance in one of the halls in Tannersville or Hunter; but they had never found themselves all together in a neighbor's house before, and had not realized the neighborhood's social wealth.

It was the first time a dance had followed a chopping-bee. But this affair served to wake the valley. After the bee at Miss Brown's, a dance was assumed as a matter of course, and not less than thirty couples took possession of her cottage in the evening.

It had been impossible for either of the three principal disputants, Dale, Burns, and Bunt, to prove that he had cut the most wood, and so when I left at three in the morning, the little hostess stepped outside, to be heard above the fiddle, the merry voices, the rhythmical tread and shuffle of feet, and giving me her hand, said gaily:

"You see it is still my own, Miss Brown's."

"If you had always lived in this valley, you would have lost it long ago."

"How do you know?"

She blushed and smiled, and slipped inside.

"That's not very complimentary to Miss Brown," said Nancy, as we were walking home.

"Why not?"

"You imply that her single state is a misfortune, and that she is unmarried because she has been overlooked."

"There is no reproach to her in that. It is true that in the cities and towns of our day such natures are the ones overlooked. There was a time when domestic ideals and desires overbalanced ambition in this country. Then a simple woman, affectionate, pure-minded, and sincere, was considered the first great treasure a man could possess. In our cities and towns, where the current motives of society are in force, this is no longer so; but here in the Plaaterkill a good home is still the most desirable thing possibility offers. All these girls here owe their beauty and attractiveness to nothing but their good health, their wholesome desires, their pleasure in a natural and useful life. They are adorable because of the unaffected ease with which they give and receive thoughtless tokens of affection. They are all good housekeepers, and they expect to be wives and mothers, and do their own work and have very happy homes. That is what they are living for. They expect to be loved and petted. There were twenty innocent kisses and little hugs and pats taken and granted this evening before everybody's eyes. There was no thought of concealment. And why should there be? These people are honest. The sentiment of affection, when given a natural expression, remains normal and submits to the control of law and order, and to generous conceptions of morality. There is certainly an amazing freedom among the boys and girls here, and yet I understand that in the entire history of the Plaaterkill there has been but one advantage taken of this liberty. And what opportunities are here! The boys and girls ride long distances alone to whatever entertainments they have. Chaperones are unheard of, and it is an understood thing that a girl to be agreeable must nestle cozily to her escort on those long cold drives."

"Yes," said Nancy, "I think the country has been slandered by romancers. They have placed too many of their victims in the rural setting."

"Yes; it has become an easy theme." And I blushed to think how that whistle in my second chapter had tempted me to follow blindly in the well-worn way.

It was a fine, clear night, and a pleasant walk of two miles in the mild light of the stars, over the packed snow of the road, the dry cold of fifteen below zero biting our cheeks and transforming our breath into frozen vapor.

As we turned the second corner and were upon our own side of the valley, the sounds of departing guests came faintly from the opposite mountain-side. A little later were heard laughter, songs, and sleigh-bells, as though a tinkling brook were running after us along the road. Before we reached our bars two cutters passed us.

"Hello!"

"Hello!"

"Good night!"

"Good night!"

The girls, wrapped in shawls, nestled snugly to their companions. Neither of these boys thought of withdrawing his protecting arm. They greeted us and renewed their songs. As we climbed our hillside, we heard the sound of the bells and voices growing fainter and fainter down the valley.

These young people sing the latest songs of the day. The melody that made a hit in New York Monday night is whistled along the mountain roads within two weeks, at least. "I want you, my honey," and "That am the way to spell chicken," are long since worn out. Winnie Gillespie loaned us "Bedelia" in December.

There is nothing musty or mysterious in the life up here. The daily papers are in circulation. A conversation in Jack's kitchen would attract no unusual attention in the Hoffman House café. Japan and Russia have their well-informed partizans there.

The folk-lore of the Plaaterkill and the folk-lore of Broadway are much the same. I have found nothing grotesque, nothing abnormal, and nothing romantic, according to the literary traditions of romance, but I have found, at least, one strange and significant thing.

Most of the young men I know here have been to New York, impelled by the vague aspirations of youth, and they have returned here of their own accord to live. And it was not because they met with poor success. Young men like Will Dale, Mike and Hughie Burns, Tom Seifferth, Will and John Gillespie do not fail. Strong and resourceful in mind and body, hopeful, persistent, interested in the world's affairs, quick to perceive and accurate in their judgments, they are the types of the nation's youth that the Spirit of the Nation has, for a hundred progressive years, tempted to the center of its activities.

Now the Spirit of the Nation no longer tempts them.

"This country is getting too greedy," said Will Dale.

Hughie Burns put it this way:

"At first I thought the city was great. After a while I couldn't tell whether I was really succeeding or had a fever. I would as soon join a stampede of cattle as to go there again."

"There was no end of strain and worry," said Tom Seifferth, "and all at once I got disgusted. I don't want to ride in a coupe, nor live in a house on Fifth Avenue, nor give a five-thousand-dollar ball, nor marry my daughter to a duke, so what am I here for? I sold out my interests and came back to the farm."

John Gillespie has still a year in a New York veterinary college. "I don't know what to do," he said. "I should like to practise in the city for the sake of the libraries and opportunities for attending operations and lectures, but there is so much sham and show and noise in the city, it wears you out."

Will Gillespie is your ideal of an amiable giant, with clear blue eyes, penetrating and mild, and a voice at once deep and persuasive.

We have smoked and talked together up there in that lonely house on the mountain, and a cozy, companionable house it is, with a well-stocked cellar and pantry, a big kitchen, a library, a piano, violin, and horns, comfortable bed-rooms, and a family of five boys and five girls, who romp and sing and dance and play games and read together.

Among many things, Will has said to me:

"I like to have a fine team and take care of it myself." "I like to work in the woods and drive along these mountain roads." "I like to see the day break over the peak back there." "I would rather be free and in the open air than own the Park Row Building if I had to spend my life thinking about it." "What is the good of being rich? Nobody seems to be any better for it."

One day, when he was cutting Christmas trees on my hillside, and we spoke of politics, he said, with a pleasant, earnest humor:

"I guess I'm not patriotic. I don't sympathize with this country since the Spanish War. I can cut a good deal of wood in a day, but, still, I don't seem to be strenuous enough for the life out there."

And so, for all students of men and morals, I offer this community, where robust, alert young men look askant at the greedy, feverish tendency of the times, and where tempting maids may be affectionate, impulsive, and unguarded, and still be safe.

CHAPTER XVII

THE SIMPLE LIFE

OR three months now this stubborn soil has been covered with two feet of snow.

Nature here is always spectacular. The view from my window is like a Christmas card glistening with diamond dust. There is nothing here to soil the purity of the snow. The fields along the river, the little clearings on the knolls of the valley, glisten in the sunlight. The forests that fill the hollows and cover the mountains are flecked with green fir-trees fringed with snow, their boughs bending beneath their fleecy burdens.

There is gentleness in the greatest strength. The year is majestic, for in its round of seasons there is both May and December. In majesty there is the tender and tempestuous. Here, in these mountains, winter is sublime. There is health in the frosty air, vigor in the cold. When the storms howl, men must keep indoors. In the silence of clear, still days, the air is musical with chiming sleigh-bells.

We have seventeen pans of milk in our milk-room. A two-gallon jar is almost full of cream ripe enough to churn. We make our own butter, and it is good. There is always a pailful of sweet milk, and a pan from which Nancy can skim the cream as we want it.

I began this book in the shelter of the balsams on my hillside. My own cows were grazing near me. I could hear the sound of Maggie's tinkling Swiss bell as I wrote. I am closing it before a fire of logs. My cows are dozing at their mangers in a warm barn. My horse is in his stall. In the carriage-house is a cutter, with its sleeping chime of bells. Within an hour we shall be out upon the road, moving swiftly through this sparkling world of snow. There is a barrel of the pork I raised, in the meat-room. In the cellar we fought for, are three barrels of potatoes from the garden we conquered, two barrels of cider from wild mountain apples, eighty-three cans of preserves from wild berry-bushes, and a barrel of Baldwins for pies. It was twenty-three degrees below zero yesterday, and we heard the hens cackling in their warm coop. We took five eggs from the nests.

If I have succeeded in these pages, you must see, between each of these poetical statements, innumerable details of toil.

If we would live in our palace of dreams, we must do the chores. To live, one must labor. Even the mendicant grows weary. The lazy man finds trouble in avoiding his tasks. Now that this place is tamed, we might still be always straining at the treadmill. It requires six hours a day to do the necessary things.

There is no wisdom in laziness. To be happy, however, one must be the master and not the slave of toil. There is the fat, good-natured slattern, and the lean, fastidious shrew.

If we would keep the candles burning at our shrines, we must take the time to light them and to watch them burn.

No one ever rambled through the woods nor lay on the sunny hillsides of to-morrow.

"I am weary of all this work," said Nancy in the summer-time. "It is wearing me out."

I reminded her of that first season when she left the brook-side for her bed, and of the month of idleness she promised me, breaking her word for the brush-heap, dragging at it when she could have passed her days at ease.

"Your restless habits wear you out. Activity in you is something of a disease."

She tried to argue, and I drove her to the hillside for a few hours every day. We took our book and blankets. We preserved our view. Sordid preoccupation is more of an obstruction than a brush-heap before the door.

Nancy loves, and in her generous affection she submits to me. She would like to keep the house in perfect order, but she sometimes lets things go. There are always pies and cookies in the pantry, and once a day we have a hearty meal. She will even forget Necessity and take a walk with me. At a moment's notice she can leave the sink and don a pretty house-gown, red silk stockings, invisibly darned, red satin slippers, a little worn, but dainty still, and sit beside me before the fire, to read.

Every three weeks there is a night of illumination, of music, of abandonment—six hours of rhythmic delight. After the house-warming came the calico ball, then a burlap dance, then Christmas eve, with a great tree for the Plaaterkill, on which the people of the valley exchanged their gifts.

You should have seen those costumes, made of feed-bags, ripped, washed, ironed, and cut by pattern. There were bolero jackets, embroidered with beads; bell-shaped skirts, evenly hung, trimmed with tinsel. There were crimson, blue, and dark-green sashes, pendants, and yokes. Little bells were hidden in the flounces. The girls sought dainty effects. The boys were more fantastic. We are kept busy preparing costumes for these events. Still, our neighbors have excelled us.

On the nights of the dances we hurry through our chores. Once I was milking when the first arrival came. He cleaned the horse-stall and threw down the hay. He used my bootjack to remove his boots, and put on slippers for the dance.

Out of the moonlit valley came, not the ethereal messengers of the vague, poetical contentment I had expected here, but troops of boys and men, that saw wood and pry stones and milk cows, and run timber down the mountains to the sawmill, miles below. They bring their wives, their daughters, sisters, and cousins. They find their sweethearts when the dance begins.

To the House in the Woods came brawny giants from the edges of the dark forests which overhang the mountain-sides, and hay-cutters from meadows traversed by trout-brooks, where city boarders defraud nature by massacring the fingerlings. Men met between whom lay the slow, cold feuds of isolation. Happily the Northern blood does not run to the vendetta. These were not the feuds of the Tennessee mountains, but there were jealousies and petty enmities which sometimes found expression, not over a rifle-barrel, but in an honest Anglo-Saxon fight with fists. Such fights between good fellows had frequently occurred at the public dances of the villages, where passions were fired by whisky gulped in back rooms. Meeting at the burlap dances, the atmosphere was changed. There was at first, perhaps, the slight constraint of those upon new ground; but this was succeeded by the joy of invention, the delight in clever costumes and new forms of cheer, and, best of all, the discovery of a good-fellowship and manhood in others which chased away suspicion and brought a sunnier atmosphere into the mountain life.

Who would exchange these realities for the phantoms that lured us here?

It has become the fashion to long for a closer communion with nature, and to sigh for the Simple Life. Rural landscapes fill our art galleries and adorn the walls of innumerable city homes, but it does not follow that all those who clasp their hands before them would be happy on a farm. To those in whom these desires are vain and superficial, this book will, no doubt, have missed its opportunities; but to sincere pilgrims upon the dusty highways, and to those who, while caught in the tangle of the world's concerns, still cling to the dreams of youth, I offer these pages with confidence, for in them there is, at least, one true picture of possession in the Eden they long for. It will be something to them to know that the poet may tempt us to a homestead, but that the "Farm Journal" must preserve us there. If we run from the city to escape its vexations, we will find the vexations of the country in wait for us. In either place, all is vanity to the vain, saith the Preacher, and Happiness is for him who perceives it where he is.

Beautiful is our House in the Woods, and, though now a thing of timber and of stone, more beautiful than my wistful dream of it. The mighty forest that brushes our eaves and extends from our dooryard in almost impenetrable tangles beyond the distant peak is still an unknown world to me. All life is alike mysterious and beautiful. Sometime, when I know my human neighbors better, and they know me, I shall make advances to my neighbors of the wilderness. You will find many curious and appealing traits in wild creatures, in bushes, trees, and flowers; but, whether in the country or the town, you will find in the meanest man more that is curious and appealing, and something that is sublime, if you will seek for it with half the self-forgetfulness, predisposition, and patience you must use to follow a fox upon a forage, or to watch a partridge drum.

AFTERWORD

Every friend we make helps to solve the
riddle of life and to lessen its tradgedy
while often entangling our own affairs.[1]
Arthur Henry

If the reader has traveled this far, then let him journey further with me. As I turned the book's final page, I determined to come to know better its author and those he had cloaked in anonymity, to learn as much as I could about him who had so informed and enriched my love of this special place, this Mountain Top.

Early in his career, young Arthur Henry wrote an obituary essay on Dion Boucicault, an Irish playwright of some note, an "unabashed wizard of absolute theatrics" said one latter-day critic, but whose marital difficulties apparently had earned him unfavorable notoriety. "Regarding the separation of Dion Boucicault and Agnes Robertson," Henry observes, "we have nothing to say. The world has no reason to be interested in Dion Boucicault as a husband. He claimed their attention simply as a playwright, and as such was well worthy of it."[2] On these same terms, I am certain, would Arthur Henry have us read *The House in the Woods*, judging it solely on its own merits, exhibiting not the least curiosity about its author.

As will become evident as the quilt of his life unfolds, however, such was the personality of Arthur Henry that he wanted, indeed needed, to be known and recognized. Had this not been so, he could have cloaked himself, as he did his two companions, in pseudonymous anonymity, or published a work of pure fiction; but he did neither. And so, we have every right to ask, "Who was Arthur Henry?" With this question, we pass through the Looking Glass into a world of unreality and distorted reality, into a world in which so often fiction became fact and fact fiction.

It may be helpful at this point to suggest a distinction between an idealist and a romantic, for Arthur Henry flew the banner of an idealist when in fact he was a full-blooded romantic. If an idealist is one who sees in reality the potential for perfection, or who works to create new realities in which perfection might be attained, then a romantic is one who, not being able to reconcile reality with the perfection he seeks, rationalizes or ignores reality or creates pseudo-realities. An idealist writes manifestos and builds societies; a romantic spins fairy tales and dreams of ivory towers. However convoluted these definitions might seem, the distinction remains an important one if we are to understand the author of *The House in the Woods*.

Arthur Henry seems to have had more trouble than most with growing up—not to mention growing old. In *The House in the Woods*, he represented himself in terms of struggling youth, and I am certain this is how he saw himself. But what is young? At the time of his first visit to the Catskills in 1899, Henry was nearly thirty-two years old and thirty-six at the end of the year described in the book. Certainly not middle-aged, but hardly a youth.

He was born on November 27, 1867,[3] in Pecatonica, Illinois,[4] a small town forty or so miles west of Chicago, so claims Arthur Henry—and a host of confirming voices that includes *Who's Who*, *The New York Times*, numerous book reviewers, and New York City's Marriage License Bureau. At first blush, there seemed no reason to question either his date of birth or birthplace, and yet a curious confusion clouds the latter. In a segment of his mother's autobiography, she writes that in "August of '65 ... [my husband] was discharged incurable ... Soon after this we went west, and spent the next two years in Pecatonica and vicinity, where our second son [Arthur] was born ... A couple of months later in August of '67, [we] returned to our home on the farm [in East Homer]."[5]

The August date of the family's return to East Homer suggests that Henry's November birth could not have been in Pecatonica, and further evidence is provided by Paul Gill, Clerk of Illinois' Winnebago County, who reported that there was no record of an Arthur (or Baby Boy) Henry having been born there in the years 1862 through 1874.

An essay by Frances E. Willard* on Sarepta Irish Henry in *Woman and Temperance*, an early publication (1883) of the Woman's Christian Temperance Union, reports that Sarepta and James Henry's second son,

---

* Of interest to friends of the Catskills' Mountain Top, Frances Willard was a sometime resident of Haines Falls' Twilight Park; her cousin, Emma, founded the school for young women in Troy that bears her name.

Arthur, was born in East Homer, New York, a tiny village on the fringe of New York's Finger Lakes, as was his sister, Mary, and older brother, Alfred. The latter births are confirmed by both civil and school records; but, as with Pecatonica, there is no record of Arthur's birth in East Homer either.

The resolution of this confusion would not be of great consequence to the tale that follows were it not that Arthur Henry seemed often to stumble in recalling his early years. However, as Miss Willard's essay was written but sixteen years after his birth and during the period of her closest association with his mother, designated the WCTU's Temperance Evangelist, it seems reasonable to accept the accuracy of her chronology.

What is known about Arthur Henry's childhood and adolescence comes from two sources: primarily secondhand recollections of those years reported by others, chiefly critics and reviewers; and his mother's autobiography included in *My Mother's Life*. Of the former, in 1900 as now, biographical grist is provided by the subject, and thus we are told that his mother was a founder and one of the leading voices of the Woman's Christian Temperance Union and that as a child he rode a white horse from Chicago to New York as part of a WCTU crusade. One reviewer writes that "as a boy he was not very strong and, it being necessary for him to live out-of-doors, he never received any regular schooling, his early years being spent in going from one farm to another in search of health, and finally living for some time on a ranch in the Far West."[6] Two years later, another literary journal probably working from the same *curriculum vitae* reported that "Mr. Henry is the product of a small Illinois village of an unpronounceable name. As a child he was delicate and spent his early years on a farm under close maternal supervision, his education being limited to exactly three months in a public school."[7]

To set the record straight, his mother was not a founder of the Woman's Christian Temperance Union;[8] she was, however, the founder of the Women's Temperance Union of Rockford, Illinois that preceded the National's founding. Sarepta[9] was the originator of the Children's Cold War Army into which large numbers of children were conscripted in the fight against drunkenness. Neither did Arthur ride on a white horse from Chicago to New York as part of a W.C.T.U. crusade;[10] although it is possible that he may have participated in a march on the Illinois capital to present the WCTU's Home Protection Petition, said Edith Stanley, President of the WCTU, in a 1976 telephone conversation, "but certainly not to New York City."

In his mother's autobiography there is no indication of either his physical frailty or having to live out-of-doors, although that was Sarepta's remedy for curing her own recurring bouts of illness. There was indeed a fair amount of bouncing from one locale to another in his early years and those of his sister and brother, once even locating on a ranch—but not in search of health; rather, these moves were prompted by his mother's itinerant career as a temperance evangelist.

While the *persona* of Sarepta Henry was a strong presence even when she was on the circuit, the children lived often in the care of relatives or friends— and sometimes that duty was assigned Mary; while neglect was never present, "close maternal supervision" was hyperbole.

Acknowledging his trials and tribulations, one reviewer described him as fortunate in having retained the illusions, enthusiasms, aspirations, and even irresponsibilities of his early youth.[11] *Not* so fortunate, a psychiatrist friend of mine said recently, is he who cannot release his youth, for it often means that he is incapable of growing up. A shrewd observation, as shall be seen.

In *Lodgings in Town*, his autobiographical sequel to *The House in the Woods*, there is no talk of ill health, but there is mention of attending elementary school. There is no reference anywhere, however, that in July 1879 his mother moved to Evanston "to educate her children in our university," as Miss Willard records. "Mary is a sophomore … Alfred is also in the course of the Northwestern University, and Arthur has begun his studies … " in the preparatory school which was then a part of the university.[12] The university's archives reveal that "he was listed as a first year student in the Northwestern University Preparatory School for the academic year 1882/83," but there is no record of his attendance for any subsequent years.[13] Arthur, not yet sixteen at the end of that school year, dropped out and took his first steps down the yellow brick road that led to Chicago, fame, and fortune.

In her biographical essay, Miss Willard concludes her description of the Henry family with these optimistic words: "The boys have made it possible for their mother to do her work by faithfully keeping her words in their hearts … and their promise to be loyal to mother, sister, and God."[14] One reviewer prophesied in 1902 that "her influence is now making itself felt through her sons and daughter in the production of literature of the distinctly constructive sort."[15] For the sake of Sarepta Irish Henry, described as a "magnificent woman" by one who loved both her and Arthur,[16] would that the course of the boys' subsequent histories confirmed Frances Willard's confidence.

Mary Henry Rossiter, the author of *My Mother's Life: The Evolution of a Recluse*, became a teacher and journalist. In fact, it was she who best fulfilled her mother's expectations; but it must have been Alfred Henry who most quickly raised Sarepta Henry's hopes, for he became a Methodist minister of some renown, occupying pulpits in Salt Lake City, Butte, and finally Yakima, and authored *By Order of the Prophet*, a book on the Mormons. He ended his career as president of a successful land and orchard development company in Yakima, which acknowledged his contribution toward its growth by naming the terminating point for one of its trolley lines after him—"Henryb'ro."

But moral indiscretions plagued his pastorates. His former sister-in-law referred to his death in 1945 thus: "And more news. Arthur's brother, Alfred Henry, passed out October 16 … Yes, Alfred has joined the innumerable throng after nearly 60 years of preaching, apple-orcharding and love-making to other men's wives, his dark deeds and maybe a few lighter colored ones preceding him."[17] A few months earlier, this same correspondent observed, "For a cleric, Alfred sure did raise hell."[18]

Arthur Henry apparently did not give his mother even the transitory satisfaction accorded by brother Alfred. Except to report that she took him as a young child to work in Chicago's Bible House where a foreman kicked him, he does not mention her once in any of his published works. If Sarepta was able to set Mary and Alfred on the paths of righteousness, however wandering Alfred's steps along the way might have been, she must have felt that she truly had failed with Arthur who, at all points, professed antipathy if not antagonism toward organized religion and its moralistic strictures.

Yet, however much he sought to be the rebel in his life and writing, the conventional quality of his value system is inescapable, possibly suggesting a greater maternal influence than he was willing to admit. He seemed to acknowledge this in a letter written to "My Darling Momma" on the occasion of Sarepta's 50th birthday in 1889; he was 22. It toasts the accomplishments of her "fifty noble years" and her "noble qualities of character", concluding: "Believe me mother darling that you are the ideal woman of your children. Sometimes our opinions differ but opinions are nothing. Our affections and ideals point the same way and that is everything."[19]

Ranging from sensitive appreciations of the human condition (as in *The House in the Woods*) to the grossly maudlin romanticism of his last published work (a play, *The Night Before*), Henry's views of man and his world were obviously nurtured in the greenhouse of historic Christendom and flourished in the home(s) of his childhood and youth. But the idealistic humanism he propounded as the wave of the future had in fact walked the earth before and would again, blooms severed from their roots—cut flowers, often beautiful and sweet-smelling, yet lacking the sustaining power of growth.

As we shall see, he and Alfred trod nearly identical paths—the latter a rebel traditionalist, Arthur a traditionalist rebel. Both sought to slough off the smothering convictions of Sarepta Irish Henry. Of Alfred's success in freeing himself, we know hardly enough to measure; but Arthur failed—although he never stopped trying.

In *Lodgings in Town*, published after *The House in the Woods* but treating the years that preceded his appearance on the Catskills' scene, Arthur Henry would have the reader believe that the course of his life led directly from days of early youth in Chicago to New York (and thence to the Catskills) with no stops in between—and the literary world bought that chronology. But, however much his romantic mind might have wished this scenario, we cannot permit him so cavalierly to lose a decade.

The youngest member of a family of gifted writers, Arthur was recognized early as perhaps the most talented, a fact which secured him a position on the staff of the *Chicago Globe*[20] in 1884 at age seventeen—probably hastening his abandonment of formal education. He remained with the *Globe* for eight years, writing on politics and coming to know that company of great journalists and writers that abounded on the Chicago literary scene in those years. Apparently he was not happy with his role as a political writer exclusively, for he constantly petitioned his editors that he write fairy tales as a regular feature in the paper,[21] but without success. While with the *Chicago Globe*, Arthur Henry produced his first book, a novel.[22] It was published in 1890; he had not yet turned twenty-three. The story of a freed slave seeking public office in a post-Civil War election, it often displays a maturity of style remarkable for one so young. His eye for lyric detail—except for moments in *The House in the Woods*—was never again to be so sharp.

In facsimile, *Nicholas Blood, Candidate* is included in the Black Heritage Library Collection. A century later, it comes across as a "disgustingly racist book ... to today's African-American students."[23] I'm certain Arthur Henry would be shocked by this appraisal, and I would join him in a denial of intent to offend, for—even at those times when he thought ill of others—he spoke in language sublime.

During his years with the *Chicago Globe*, Henry developed friendships and contacts that were to stand him in good stead. The most abiding was with Brand Whitlock, a fellow member with Henry in the Whitechapel Club,[24] named after the London slum where Jack the Ripper roamed. Like the Gridiron Club of Washington, it had started informally in a saloon where newspapermen could get things off their chests and off the record, but soon it expanded into a formal meeting place decorated with relics of crimes and disasters. The club never had more than ninety members, fewer than forty being newspaper editors and reporters; the rest were from the community—including judges, lawyers, police officials, novelists, politicians, musicians and artists, and "a reformed clergyman or two like ... *Arthur Henry* [italics mine]—and one magician, Alexander Herrmann.[25] *

Whitlock, who was to become America's envoy to Belgium in World War I, remained an intimate friend of Henry's until their almost simultaneous deaths in 1934. It was Whitlock who, in 1892, recommended Henry as City Editor of Ohio's *Toledo Blade*, a position which he accepted with alacrity.

Although he claimed the Toledo/Maumee area as home until his move to New York in 1899, Henry remained in this new post only two years. In the course of his tenure as City Editor, two events of relevance to this tale occurred: first, he met and in March 1893 married Maude Wood, the *Blade's* first woman reporter, and their only child, Dorothy, was born the following year; second, in early 1894, Theodore Dreiser appeared at the *Blade* looking for work, and Henry assigned him to cover a streetcar strike that threatened to immobilize the city.

Dreiser may have been given a job, protests Maude Wood Henry in her April 2, 1945 letter to Professor Elias, "but it was not to cover the strike—I did that!" This claim is denied from many sides, among them the article's TD byline and later by Dreiser himself in *A Book About Myself*. As opposed to Maude's claim made a half-century after the fact, then, it seems difficult to deny Dreiser authorship.

However, there is something so suspiciously "Arthur Henry-ish" about this whole issue. The problem is that Maude, a feminist well before her time, was married to a male chauvinist of romantic proportions, matched I am sure

---

*In her April 25, 1945 letter to Professor Elias, Maude recalls that " ... when he came to 'The Blade', Arthur regaled me with stories of the old Whitechapel Club days ... Dreiser was not one (i.e. a member) then, but later joined the fraternity."

Dreiser's Whitechapel/Bohemian Club membership is acknowledged by scholars. It should be noted, however, that the *Chicago Tribune* 1945 piece on the Club did not mention TD as among its distinguished members, although by that time he was a nationally distinguished author.

by Dreiser's own proclivities. While we are led by scholars to accept his authorship of the article, the distinct possibility remains that both he and Maude may have been jointly assigned the story—but that Dreiser got the gold ring. As we shall see, it would not be the first time Arthur Henry had denied a woman co-authorship.[26]

I found it hard to believe that their paths had not crossed during the Chicago years, for it seemed to me highly improbable that a Dreiser-unknown should just wander into a Toledo newspaper office and immediately be assigned a major news story. Yet, improbable or no, neither man references a prior meeting, and by their silence Dreiser scholars cannot accept that one occurred.

An answer may lie with the Whitechapel Club to which each belonged, but not concurrently, and with Brand Whitlock, whose membership spanned theirs. I suggest that he might be the engine that turns improbability into a possibility to which even Dreiser scholars might give credence: viz. I cannot imagine a New-York-bound Dreiser not being urged by fellow Club member Brand Whitlock to drop in at the *Blade* to see his good friend, Arthur Henry, recently made the paper's City Editor on his recommendation.

That neither man ever alluded to an encounter preceding Toledo lends credence to this conjecture while supporting the research that none ever occurred.

At first, Arthur and Maude lived in Toledo with her mother and sisters, but by 1893 had managed to save enough money to make a down payment on a house in nearby Maumee which they named "House of Four Pillars."[27] The *Maumee News-Bee* of October 27, 1930 states that they bought the house:

> ... because a May sun sank radiantly behind an apple orchard[28] in full bloom ... [They] employed about all the contractors and finishers in Toledo to knock out partitions and inclose several basement rooms in oiled wood panels ... and the workmen weren't worried because they thought newspaper people made a lot of money. As a matter of fact, the combined salaries of the Henrys totaled several dollars less than 50 a week, and the total expenses on the house preparatory to moving in had been something over $5000.

In her correspondence with Dreiser biographer Robert Elias of Cornell University, Maude Wood Henry recalls that those were happy, carefree days—even if days of enforced simplicity:

Arthur and I thought we were living sumptuously on 'cream cheese from the dairy of heaven' which I made from brimming pailsful of sour creamy Jersey milk ... on gorgeous homemade bread and huge sour cream cookies ... on fish caught by us in the nearby river and fresh fruit from our own garden ... Arthur often pounded on the table until the dishes rattled in his delight at our simple but delicious meals, or executed an Indian dance around his chair, or sang in a lusty voice.[29]

Their lust for life was such that they drew to The House of Four Pillars any who would share their enthusiasms. A latter day account of those years reports that during their occupancy the house "developed a name and character, for they were writers and opened their home to their wide acquaintance of authors and artists ... While [they] occupied the house it took on a garish and spectacular aspect; a sort of 'Bohemian life' prevailed within its walls."[30]

Arthur Henry's assault on public sensibilities had begun in earnest.

Arthur and Maude resigned their positions with the *Blade* in 1894, but both continued working. They collaborated as writers during these years, producing a collection of fairy tales (*The Flight of a Pigeon*, 1894), and published a newspaper (*The Maumee Liar*). Together they had developed some business interests in Toledo; but then Arthur accepted a position as publicity agent for a friend from Whitechapel Club days, magician "Herrmann the Great", and Maude a position as Assistant Manager of Chicago's Theodore Thomas Orchestra, soon to become the Chicago Symphony, with Thomas its first conductor.

In my copy of *The Flight of a Pigeon*, the dedication to Herrmann in Arthur Henry's hand reads:

To him who, with a gentle heart and manners of the mystic East,
Combines the power of devils with the virtues of a priest,
Speeds now this book of mine to ask a little of the Author's fate-
How stands my star today oh mighty one—Herrmann the Great?

However stood Arthur Henry's star, Herrmann's was on the wane, for in 1896 he was killed in an automobile accident. Arthur found that he could not work with Herrmann's widow and the magician's replacement, a nephew, Leon, so he and Maude switched jobs: Arthur returned to the Toledo area in the employ of the Thomas Orchestra, and Maude traveled with the magic show.

While Henry's stint with Herrmann undoubtedly fed his appetite for fantasy and illusion, it also provided him with what must have seemed a heaven-sent opportunity to reestablish many of his Chicago literary contacts now relocated in New York, and enabled him to begin sounding out editors and publishers with story ideas. It was during this period that Henry's friendship with Dreiser was nurtured most fully. Their friendship was obviously one of mutual attraction, for Dreiser was to speak of him with an intensity of feeling not shared with any other of his friends: "If he would have been a girl I would have married him, of course. It would have been inevitable … we reveled in that wonderful possession, intellectual possession."[31]

Dreiser described his friend as "one of those idealists who needs someone to look after him."[32] It was indeed an apt description, for Henry had not been long in the service of Herrmann the Great before he found that "someone": Anna T. Mallon, listed in business directories of New York City in the 1890's as the head of "Anna T. Mallon & Co., Stenographers and Typewriters." Her office, located on the top floor of the five-story Mutual Reserve Building on Broadway, was situated on the inner edge of what was then New York's newspaper district; today, although standing within sight of Wall Street, the building looks rather lonely, an OTB parlor occupying its ground floor.

He met Anna Mallon, says Arthur Henry in the romantic chronology of *Lodgings in Town*, by the sheerest accident, by a stroke of fate. On arriving in New York from Chicago, a story was churning inside of him. He had attempted to transfer it to paper but found that thoughts came faster than his hand could write. Seeking a secretary before the muse left him, he chanced upon Anna's establishment and dictated to her well into the evening, long after her staff had gone home:

> … it was past midnight when the work was done. Hand in hand, we walked down Broadway, stopped to watch the fountain in the City Hall Park playing in the moonlight, and then slowly to the bridge. "I have been a long time looking for you," I said. She answered quietly, "And I for you."[33]

Even the most naive researcher might be led to wonder how a new boy in town could "chance upon" an office on the top floor of an undistinguished building; and, if he were so to wonder, he would be correct. That's not the way it happened, says Dreiser. A successful businesswoman with a staff of fifteen or so "stenographers and typewriters," Anna Mallon counted a number of writers among her clients, Dreiser included, and it was certainly he who recommended her to Henry. The compelling inspiration that brought them together came out as "Peter and the Fairies", a story originally included in *Lodgings in Town*, but later published separately.* As Arthur shuttled between Toledo/Maumee and New York, a friendship of more than casual import developed with Anna, one shared with Dreiser—and even with Maude when her travels for the orchestra brought her to New York.

With the appearance of Anna Mallon, we have found Nancy of *The House in the Woods*.

During his years with Herrmann, possibly to reciprocate the hospitality extended him in New York, Arthur Henry began to encourage Dreiser to visit him and Maude in Maumee. In the summer of 1899, Dreiser—now Editor of *Ev'ry Month* and just recently married—succumbed to Henry's constant invitation. The visit, originally planned to be of short duration, soon was extended to include almost the entire summer—and with dire consequences to the Henry's meager resources.

Thirty years later, Dreiser was to describe the Arthur Henry of The House of Four Pillars thus:

> He was brilliant, good-looking, semi-idealistic, in philosophy at least, but useless for almost any practical purpose in life ... As I saw him then and see him now, he was a dreamer of dreams, a spinner of fine fancies, a lover of impossible romances which fascinated me by their very impossibility. Also he was jolly, generous, a lover of life and play, mostly play ... His weakest and most irritating trait was a vaulting egotism which caused him to imagine: first, that he was as great a thinker and writer as had ever appeared; second, that he was at the same time practical, a man of the world, a man of affairs. Let him but give his solemn attention to any muddle and it must come straight. Let him but think seriously, and every philosophic as well as practical

---

* Is it not interesting to note that both Maude and Anna were collaborators with Arthur Henry in the writing of *The Flight of a Pigeon* (MWH) and "Peter and the Fairies" (AM), yet their co-authorship was not acknowledged; I suspect also that Anna, whose obituary notice identified her as "NOTED AUTHOR", probably deserved co-authorship of *The House in the Woods* as well. On reflection, might this pattern not speak tellingly to the authorship of the strike article? Male chauvinism was alive and well!

riddle was solved ... Because I liked him much ... I was inclined to let him have his way in everything. He was too delightful and interesting not to humor.[34]

"Yes, I think it was inevitable that Dreiser should come under the benign influence of the calm, clear gray eyes, the idealism, the reasoning mind of Arthur Henry," wrote Maude Wood Henry, reflecting on that summer, "always ready for adventure, for gay laughter, for hard work when necessary, but ingrained with the ... fairy tale happenings of early youth."[35] Dreiser himself was to recall that summer in Maumee as "the happiest time of my life."[36]

Well, frolic they did during that summer, pondering their futures, spinning ghost and Indian tales for listeners of every age, and ruminating philosophically about God, man, and the world. Henry had developed, Dreiser said, "a 'doctrine of happiness' ... which was little more, as I saw it, than a kind of self-salving, soul-salving, way of escaping a too galling routine of duty. The first rule of his new, cheerful doctrine was to be happy oneself, regardless of others and come what might; only in order to give it a somewhat more humane look it was explained that by so doing one conveyed happiness and sunshine to others." [37]

The major occurrence of that summer was that each pledged to begin a novel, Henry his *A Princess of Arcady* and Dreiser his *Sister Carrie*. While Dreiser scholars claim that *Sister Carrie* was not begun until his return to New York from this summer visit, Maude Wood Henry insists that the start was made in Maumee. "My recollection is exclusively of *Sister Carrie* in the making that summer ... I feel safe in saying that Dreiser wrote a goodly part of *Sister Carrie* in the basement den that summer ... "[38] Six months later, in an interview on Dreiser's death, Maude recalled the Dreiser of the summer of 1899 as one who "laughed little, spent hours in philosophical discussions and arguments [with Arthur] ... and spent most of his time buried in the basement den working on his book. Seated in a big split-cane rocking chair, a thick pad of paper on the wide arms of it, he wrote for hours at a time."[39]

It is a constant regret that Maude "passed out" (her phrase) before this research began, for I believe her to be the drama's most objective observer. While her memory sometimes faltered by the time of her correspondence with Professor Elias, I am inclined to trust her recollections of events in which she was directly involved, her sense of place, and thus her claim for The House of Four Pillars as the book's birthplace.

In the matter of the launching of *Sister Carrie*, therefore, as in the co-authorship of the strike story, I respect the accuracy of her recollections. If this puts her at odds with Dreiser himself, then so be it. But remember, says one Dreiser scholar, "We have caught Dreiser in memory lapses in other instances, so I hold no brief for his infallibility."[40]

When the Dreisers returned to New York at the end of that summer, Henry accompanied them. Although the knot would not be cut for three or four years, for all intents and purposes, Maumee, Maude, and The House of Four Pillars had become a closed chapter in his life.

Describing that summer of 1899, Maude reflected on the impact of the Dreisers' extended stay:

> In due time our funds began to give out, so I notified Arthur ... What he did was to tell Dreiser who (no doubt thinking this was a great way to entertain visitors—I laugh) loaned him a hundred or two dollars. Arthur, without my knowledge or consent, promptly made over a half interest in The House of Four Pillars to him. We had bought this in 1893 and not only had been paying on it regularly to a loan company but had put several thousands in the restoration. Quite a trade wasn't it? ... Behold, soon afterward, they all departed for New York and left me to hold the bag ... [41]

The weight of the bag for Maude increased to the point that foreclosure proceedings were instituted within five years, and The House of Four Pillars became the property of its mortgagee, a Mr. Hiett. Maude and her daughter returned to Toledo.

Such then was the route by which Arthur Henry came to New York City late in the summer of 1899, immediately prior to his first visit to Platte Clove that fall. Rather than the struggling, unpublished, and young writer he claimed to be in *The House in the Woods*, by the time of this move to New York that closed the chapter on nearly seven years in Toledo/Maumee, he had authored two books, at least three magazine articles, was an experienced writer trained in journalism's school of hard knocks, and was married and a father; on returning to Platte Clove in 1903, the year in which *The House in the Woods* was written, another book had been published, as had at least six additional magazine articles. And, as we shall see, one wife had been shed for another.

On arriving in New York in 1899, he settled in with the Dreisers, the two of them working side by side on their novels. It is certainly Arthur Henry's greatest contribution to the history of American literature that he literally baby-sat, bird-dogged, cajoled, and threatened Dreiser until *Sister Carrie* was finished. The inclusion of notes, revisions, and editorial suggestions in Henry's hand in the final *Carrie* manuscript is clear evidence, were such needed, of his close oversight involvement with Dreiser's work during this time. He then played a major role in assuring the book's publication in England after Doubleday reneged on a large first printing because of its sensibility-shattering subject matter. As will soon be seen, Dreiser reciprocated the courtesy.

Dreiser acknowledged his indebtedness and his friendship with Henry by dedicating *Sister Carrie*'s first edition thus:

To My Friend
ARTHUR HENRY
Whose steadfast ideals and serene devotion
to truth and beauty have served to lighten
the method and strengthen the purpose of this volume.

The irony of their relationship during these months of mutual support and encouragement, of course, is that Henry was certain that they each were authoring the great American novel.

However, Henry's return to New York also made possible the renewal of his relationship with Anna. Although their work on the novels continued, all did not run smoothly between the two men. Henry began to disappear from the Dreiser household for a time, return to continue the writing, disappear again, return again, and then finally he moved out to settle into the Mallon household in Brooklyn as a boarder with her widowed mother, an old Irish cook, a maid, and of course with Anna.

Henry's increasingly unequal sharing of both time and attention with Anna engendered a petulant jealousy in Dreiser; but, if it was disturbing to Dreiser, it was apparently no less distracting for Arthur Henry, for Dreiser had to write the conclusion to his *A Princess of Arcady* in order to get it to the publisher on time.

The setting of *A Princess of Arcady* would suggest that his relationship with Anna Mallon during his years with Herrmann was somewhat more than purely professional. The book early shifts from Maumee to a convent school in New York—obviously drawing vicariously on Anna's years as a student in Brooklyn's Academy of the Visitation. Henry acknowledges his indebtedness by dedicating the volume, published in 1900, to Anna, his "tutor in convent education."

Until her dying day, Anna's mother never trusted Arthur Henry, but Anna found him a refreshing, exciting release from the years of spinsterhood spent in the copying office. There were trips to the City, picnics and bicycle excursions to the country, the vacation in the Catskills reported in *The House in the Woods*, and thence to the shore as described in *An Island Cabin*. Much of this, of course, was at Anna's expense, including the purchase of the land in Platte Clove and the renting of the island off the coast of Noank. Except for the fact that he was yet married, all was done with decency and propriety, with "Elizabeth" serving as a chaperone.

An Island Cabin, published in 1902, was written in the interim between the first and second visits to Platte Clove. The book is significant not only as a watershed in Henry's already romantically turbulent life, but also as a turning point in his relationship with Dreiser.

To treat the latter first, the book is Henry's record of a few months spent at the mercy of Nature on an island off the coast of Noank, Connecticut. Although he would have the reader believe the island was located nearly in open sea, in fact it was but a few hundred yards from shore. Central to *An Island Cabin* is a series of long philosophical conversations he has with a visiting friend he had always assumed to be a like-minded liberal idealist, but who—when confronted by Nature without the trappings of civilization to fall back on—proved to be a traditionalist, a conservative, a reactionary of the worst kind. Whether this is an accurate summary of these conversations, the reader can decide for himself; but Dreiser, who quickly and correctly recognized himself as Henry's pseudonymous adversary, read it that way, and his anger shattered their friendship. As one of his contemporaries observed of Dreiser, he had "a gift for estrangement nearly equal to his gift for engagement."

In a burst of self-justification, Henry wrote to Dreiser in 1904: "I have just gone over carefully the chapters ... that have offended you, and, as I read them now ... it is very clear to me that this book is not responsible for the interruption of our friendship. That was doomed before the book was written."[42] The attack on Dreiser's jealousy of his and Anna's relationship that followed merely intensified Dreiser's resentment, and Dreiser's anger raged unabated until he was avenged by the publication in 1929 of "Rona Murtha" in his two-volume collection of essays, *A Gallery of Women*. Assigning him the pseudonym "Winfield Vlasto", Dreiser peels away Arthur Henry's idealism like the layers of an onion until nothing remains but the ashes of his vaulting, destructive egotism.

It is through Dreiser's eyes that we know most about Arthur Henry during the years at the turn of the century, and his observations are valuable and often confirmed by other evidence; but we must remember that he is not always the objective, disinterested reporter. Even Maude, who had just cause to share Dreiser's anger at her husband, rebels. "I am boiling with rage after reading Dreiser's garbled and malicious 'Rona Murtha' ... I personally should like to call him to account for that traitorous treatment of his dear friend Arthur—which is partially correct but which seems to me to have been written in a vengeful spirit ... I consider that story a rotten over-rating of Arthur's weak points."[43] Although a reconciliation of sorts was to occur between them, the friendship of Arthur Henry and Theodore Dreiser was never fully restored.

It was also during that summer on the island that the marriage of Maude and Arthur Henry was ended, although divorce would not come for nearly two years. Here again, the versions of its dissolution are as fascinating as they are varied:

> *Arthur*: Maude and I were not separated until she was happily engaged ... developing and selling suburbs all over the country—a pursuit that was greatly to her taste, and that gave a salary of $2,500 a year, all expenses, and good commissions, which brought her income to nearly $4000. At that time Maude, Anna, and I were on affectionate and friendly terms, and this friendship has increased from then till now.[44]
> *Dreiser*: ... he had married a most charming and intelligent girl, and ... was the father of a child and the putative breadwinner of the family and director of its destinies. But in a Shelleyesque manner (which had he ever achieved great repute would have been forgiven him), he had walked away and left both to shift for themselves. But to be duly truthful in the matter, his wife was essentially capable and better able

to take care of herself than he was of taking care of himself … [45]
Maude: I gave Arthur a divorce after that summer at the cabin … because "he thought he ought to marry Anna". I was lying in the indoor hammock, Anna was sitting cross-legged on the floor sewing and Arthur had been writing on his book, when he told me that. Naturally I was surprised, but I replied that I did not know that I had any objections, except that there was Dorothy. He said, "Lord, I'll take her or you can." And I said, "No, Arthur, you will not take her," adding, "but you told me last year in New York that you were not in love with Anna, any more than you were with your grandmother." "Well, I'm not in love with Anna, but her mother is sitting over there at Noank trying to watch this island with a telescope … and I feel that I ought to marry her" … Arthur rushed over to the hammock and offered himself back to me—but I shook my head no. Anna had run from the cabin and I got up and followed … "I wouldn't have Arthur Henry for a million dollars if you want him," she said pretty wildly. Of course she did want him—although I hadn't been suspicious about this affair while I was there. My reply was that she could have him—but warned her that there would be trouble. Women and finances … He got his friend Brand Whitlock to represent us in a three-minute trial … and Arthur met me in the old Boody House here immediately afterward with a resounding smack and the remark that I would never know how much he cared for me. As Dreiser would say—"so much for romance."[46]

Arthur Henry and Anna Mallon were married on March 9, 1903 in the Office of the City Clerk, Borough of Manhattan. He claimed thirty-four as his age, but was thirty-five; Anna was forty-one. Despite his willingness to encourage inferences to the contrary in *The House in the Woods*, Arthur and Anna returned to Platte Clove that spring as man and wife.

A word must be said about "Elizabeth", the second of the companions "dear" to Arthur Henry during the first visit to Platte Clove, but who was conspicuous by her absence upon their return in 1903; Arthur had written that during the three-year interim Elizabeth had been "lost". Tragic death? Indeed not! Elizabeth was Brigitte Seery (called "Beezie"), a young and pretty Irish immigrant who was taken into the Mallon household in Brooklyn, and who served as chaperone during the days of Arthur and Anna's courtship.

During the stay in Noank, Brigitte met George Main, the town barber, and they were married in 1902; thus was Elizabeth of *The House in the Woods* "lost".

Mrs. Walter Lowe, child of that marriage, remembered Anna as a frequent visitor to their home, always bringing gifts (including "Bob Golightly", the Henrys' collie), and possessing lovely, long hair which she would ask the young child to brush. As she recalled those days for me, Mrs. Lowe paused contemplatively, and then said, "You know, even though I was only a small child, I always sensed something during those visits which only now have I been able to acknowledge. Anna was kind and generous, but I felt something that my mother didn't: she always acted as if she were better than we. Isn't that funny? I've only been able to admit this after all these years."

A final observation will draw these interim years to a close. If the classic example of the Yiddish word, "chutzpah", is that of the girl who murdered her parents and then threw herself on the mercy of the court because she was an orphan, then hardly less classic is the author (Arthur) who, while married to one wife (Maude), dedicates his book (*A Princess of Arcady*) to another woman (Anna); and then, divorced from the first and about to marry the second, he dedicates his next book (*An Island Cabin*) to her whom he had just cast off.

O tempore, O mores, O Arthur Henry!

Meanwhile, back in Platte Clove, having admonished readers of *The House in the Woods* that, "if we would live in the palace of our dreams, we must do the chores,"[47] Arthur Henry found that other sentiments were creeping in: "Toil, toil, toil. Everything to be done, and to be done first ... We had been here almost three months and had not opened a book, nor taken a ramble, nor passed a day upon the hillside, nor slept in the sunny hollow. Every hour seemed to add to the turmoil of our peaceful retreat. We were weary."[48] He even empathized with the personal odor of farmers as he found himself often too exhausted to bathe. Making the characteristic remark that, if you cannot stand reality, then change it, he quickly finished the manuscript, sent it to his publisher, sold their pigs and chickens and cows, let the garden go fallow, hired two helpers to do the chores that remained, and began to enjoy life again. But not for long.

In March 1905, the ink on the book hardly dry, their House in the Woods burned to the ground. The loss he dramatized as total except for a rescued tin box and an unfinished manuscript (most probably *Lodgings in Town*), but in fact more of their possessions than that have continued into the present—including the framed quotation from Dryden, "The Gods to live in woods have left the sky," which yet hangs over the mantel of the house they immediately built, not in replica, but on the same foundations. It is this second House in the Woods that stands today.

The loss by fire of their House in the Woods was a severe blow to Arthur and Anna's once adequate resources, a blow made even more devastating by the fact that Anna's mother—upon her daughter's marriage to a man she had disapproved of from the very outset—had disinherited her. To build the second House in the Woods, a larger and more expensive structure, Anna sold her copying office; but even this was not sufficient to the task, and records in the Office of the Clerk of Greene County indicate a number of chattel mortgages to local craftsmen and tradesmen entered into to complete the reconstruction. For the second time in little more than a decade, a source of support began to dry up on Arthur Henry.

In 1906, faced with insolvency, Arthur Henry accepted an offer from a publishing house, A. S. Barnes, to become General Manager, and both he and Anna moved back to the city. Hardly had they settled there when brother Alfred, now moonlighting from his pastoral duties in land speculation, invited them to join him in Yakima. With little hesitation (on Arthur's part, at least), they went west in pursuit of big, fast money. With Anna lending her business acumen, Arthur and Alfred established Henry Bros. Realty and Investment Company. The trio embarked on this new enterprise with such vigor that Alfred permitted his ministry to fall into an inactive status. With Alfred in the fields and Anna at the books, Arthur was sent east to recruit investors—which he did with notable success; the Dreisers and muckraking author Ida Tarbell were included among his conquests.

But something else was happening at this time also. Arthur began to be seen with increasing frequency at parties and social gatherings with Clare Kummer, a young and successful playwright whose lasting claim to fame, however, may be that she wrote the song "Dearie".* Anna, distressed by the rumors that wafted back to Yakima, went east to retrieve her husband, but to no avail. They were divorced in 1910, and Arthur Henry, age 43, married Clare Kummer, twenty-one years his junior.

Except for one or two weekend visits to the House in the Woods in the

* Movie buffs may be interested to know that Clare Kummer's daughter by a first marriage married Roland Young, Hollywood's redoubtable "Topper".

year following his divorce from Anna, Arthur Henry closed that chapter in his life, and apparently without a pang of remorse. This cannot but come as a surprise to the reader of *The House in the Woods*, for the book commands such a commitment to the simple life, such a love for the mountains and the people who live there, such a sense of place as the essential ingredient in the health of our human condition, that one cannot but feel betrayed by the ease with which that commitment was abandoned; and, in that betrayal, one cannot but identify with both Maude and Anna whose financial and emotional investment in their sense of place was thought to be a shared one, but which was so easily released by him—and which each bore as an open wound to the day of her dying.

"Parallel play" has long been recognized as an important and pervasive pattern of human interrelationship. It can be seen, for example, in a tableau of two children building a sand castle. They work together with joy, cooperate in the design and re-design of the structure developing before them, share the tools of its building, reflect on its beauty with mutual pleasure. How wonderful, says an observer of this scene, that two youngsters are building the castle of their dreams. Suddenly, one of them gets up, kicks down the castle, and walks off, leaving the other in tears at its destruction. Obviously, while the task was a shared one, and even the vision of it, the emotional investment of each was qualitatively different.

They were involved in "parallel play." They had come to a common agreement on place and task. For one, however, the goal was attained in the castle's completion, and he could destroy it without compunction and walk away with nary a backward glance; for the other, the goal was the shared relationship and its continuation through the survival of the structure which symbolized that relationship, and only sadness and pain could result from its destruction. Such is the basis of so many human relationships, that seem to the observer to be so solid but which are so easily destroyed; this is probably a perceptive insight into Arthur Henry and the emotional rubble he left in his wake.

With his marriage to Clare Kummer, the years of Henry's greatest productivity drew to a close. Although some eleven journeyman articles of no consequence were written over the next two and a half decades, no major works of fiction or even semi-fiction (his specialty) were forthcoming. Apparently an autobiographical novel, *The Life of Roger Allen*, was begun in 1937, but lay unfinished at the time of his death.

Spurred possibly by his young wife's success as a playwright, he did take a turn at playwriting, and seven plays were published in the years 1924 through 1932—including four horrendous one-act plays for children written with his daughter. The play that was to be his last tweak of public sensibilities was *The Night Before*, originally titled *Holy Night!*. It was written again with Dorothy and produced by her husband, Dane; it flared briefly, but as with a comet's tail was the last hurrah of a burnt-out star.

The play opened at Werba's Brooklyn Theater on September 3, 1928 for its pre-Broadway run. The theater critic of the *Brooklyn Standard Union* the next day reviewed it thus:

> We can picture Arthur and Dorothy Henry, the authors of *The Night Before* ... discussing how they would write it—
> 'Let's show the naked truth,' one might say.
> 'Let's show that bordellos aren't always blots on the landscape.'
> 'Heck! Let's show one that's an ornament. How shall we do that?'
> 'Well, there'll be a poor girl supporting her brothers and sisters.'
> 'What for?'
> 'Now wait. You'll see what for. She needs money. See? And her friend sends her to Madame Meinart's place. We'll make it a grand place, with all the girls prosperous and educated and contented. We'll portray that as a better life than being married to a selfish, rotten husband.'
> 'And then?'
> 'Well, it will be Christmas Eve, and carolers will sing outside the window, and then let's see. We'll have a young man sent there by his grandfather to be educated, and he'll meet the young girls, and they'll fall in love there in the bordello, and they'll go out and get married. How is that?'
> 'Great. Now where is the typewriter paper?'

The reviews, without exception, were appallingly bad: "It certainly leaves this reviewer cold";[49] it needs "a thorough overhauling;[50] "'The Night Before' is almost unbelievably stupid."[51] The play was rescued from instant oblivion, however, by an over-zealous district attorney seeking to advance his political career by bolstering a reputation for public vigilance—a time-honored political stratagem. He had the police close the show four nights after it opened, and threw the cast and its primary author, Arthur Henry, in jail. One of the cast members, a young woman not yet twenty and appearing in her first professional production, nearly fifty years later recalled Arthur Henry as "gentle, soft-spoken, supportive, but threadbare, lonely", and remembers her incarceration with awe: "Just think," she told me with a sigh, "I spent a night in jail with Franchot Tone," the play's male ingenue.[52]

Defended by Actor's Equity and the Drama League of America, the case reached the State Supreme Court where a Judge Caldwell dismissed the charges on the grounds that the play was "so repellent that it would not tend to corrupt anyone."[53]

For all intents and purposes, the play signaled the end of Henry's literary career. His attention turned elsewhere. "He was greatly interested in current events in the broader social sense, and at one time was active in the movement to improve housing conditions among the poor. He was directly responsible for the 'tenement law' enacted there [Narragansett] and sponsored by William DeForest."[54]

Arthur Henry died on June 2, 1934 at his home in Narragansett Pier, Rhode Island, with his wife at his side. He was in his sixty-seventh year, fulfilling an oft-expressed wish that he would die quietly before the age of 70. His obituary concluded: "Friends say he always loved New England. He cherished particularly the house at Narragansett." How wonderfully "Arthur Henry"!

Dreiser wrote to Clare later that month:

Dear Claire [sic]: The first news I had [of Arthur's death] was from Will Lengel of *Liberty Magazine*, who knew of our friendship and called to say that Arthur was dead ... I assumed you were in Hollywood or elsewhere and in my hurry to say something, I addressed my telegram [to Dorothy] ... I don't think I need to explain or say anything more to you. As I said, Hen's death struck close to me.

How wonderfully TD!

In her May 13, 1945 letter to Dreiser biographer Robert Elias, Maude Wood Henry suggests, "If Dreiser and Arthur interest you, maybe a peek behind the scenes where the women of their books lurk may not come amiss"; for Arthur Henry, the suggestion is equally apt. If full appreciation of *The*

House in the Woods demands that its author be known, then almost more so must the reader come to know his relationship with Anna Mallon—for if he could leave their house in the valley of the Plattekill without so much as a backward glance, she could not contemplate for long a future apart from it.

On the surface, Dreiser and Henry seem to share similar attitudes towards women. Both were accused of being womanizers, Dreiser so much so that Maude warns her daughter's husband on the eve of a trip to California where the couple will visit Dreiser: "I also told Dane ... not to let Dorothy go there alone, if possible, that I had no faith in him, even at the age of 74, so far as women are concerned."[55] Arthur Henry was so remembered by both Maude (" ... he was always having incipient affairs with just about any girl that was handy and sometimes telling me about them ... "[56]) and Anna (who reports in several letters that Arthur was having affairs with other women, and implying that Alfred's character flaw was "congenital").

And yet, there was a significant difference between the two men, for this was not as Henry saw himself, nor as Dreiser saw him. In "Rona Murtha", Dreiser speaks affectionately of his friend's contacts with women, almost as if he were describing an adolescent preparing to burst onto the scene of adult sexuality: " ... he was fascinated by women—almost any young, pretty, and intelligent girl—and he could not see why he should not be allowed to make friends and play with them. And most women he met were inclined to agree with him. Yet, I honestly think that ... quite all of his relations with women were platonic ... Even the normally conservative women appeared to wish to indulge him."[57] This was hardly Dreiser's own posture on sexual relationships, but it is probably an accurate appraisal of Henry's sexual dynamic, one which he never outgrew.

And this wish to play and make friends with women created such problems for him! Henry's inscription in a copy of his novel that followed *Lodgings in Town*, *The Unwritten Law*, given to Margaret Farrell of Platte Clove, reads: "Every friend we make helps to solve the riddle of life and lessen its tradgedy [*sic*] while often entangling our own affairs."[58] Written out of a web of entanglements that had already begun to entrap him, it is a plaintive, yet confirming, statement that separates him from Dreiser.

If he parts company from Dreiser early in comparison, how then *did* Arthur Henry view women? There is little doubt that here as elsewhere in his life he would claim to fly the banner of the idealist, of the modern man who readily acknowledged an integrity, a purity, in the female as have males for generations. What else, he might ask, could one expect of a son born of a lib-erated mother?* What else could have attracted him to Maude Wood who, two years before they met, realized that men were being paid more than women for identical work, wrote an irate letter to the editor of the *Blade* demanding "JUSTICE" for her sex, and was promptly hired as that paper's (and quite possibly Ohio's) first woman reporter—and who gladly joined him in assaulting those shibboleths of public mores that denied equal stature and integrity to women of the New Century?[59] Henry would not know that Maude continued undaunted on that road they so briefly traveled together, taking public stands, writing verse and articles—even though infirm and blind—until her death at age 88 in 1957.

Further, Arthur Henry would certainly have assigned the same motives and values to his relationship with Anna Mallon. In her, he sought not the stereotypical woman of his age, but one who had clearly made her way with notable success in a man's world, exhibiting an imagination and business acumen that would put most men to shame. Anna he also saw as a harbinger of the New Times of which he felt himself a spokesman. And even Clare Kummer, although exhibiting more of the grace and charm of archetypal woman, yet met men of the literary and theater worlds on more than equal terms.[60]

In his relationships with women, then, Arthur Henry laid claim to the mantle of the idealist, assuming almost an asexual posture—as if to exhibit sexual feelings would have been a denial of his idealism. In speaking of Henry's relationship with Anna Mallon on the island prior to their mar-riage, Dreiser writes: "Perhaps a superficial flaw was a ... platonism between [Arthur] and [Anna], which was intended to convey that no intimacies beyond those permissible between wholly affectionate friends were here afoot, nor would be until marriage had united them ... Only what of it, I

---

* Although one might be tempted to restrict appreciation of Sarepta Irish Henry's life to her faith-based ded-ication to temperance evangelism, she could speak with equal fervor to issues that endeared her to Maude and earns her a place in the hearts of contemporary women: " ... the young men of our [Northwestern Academy] class were all preparing for Northwestern University. It was taken as a matter of course that when this year's work was finished we girls must go quietly back to our homes and engage in whatever womanly occupation we might be able to find ... [but] there was just as much need, and even more, that I should be thoroughly edu-cated ... as any one of these young men. 'Ellen,' Sarepta said to a classmate, 'I am going to record a vow with you; if I ever live to grow up and have a daughter of my own, she shall be educated in that university.' Ellen looked at me with big eyes, and said, 'Your daughter will be a girl, and they won't have her.' ... 'You mark what I say: my daughter shall go to that university.' " She kept that vow! Mary graduated from Northwestern University with a Bachelor of Arts degree in 1888.

thought? ... [There was] a marked absence of that salt of desire and especially that intense avidity for exclusiveness which is the mark sterling of all true passion. No, it was not there. He did not enough wish to be alone with her."[61]

Dreiser's estimate seems confirmed by the fact that when their House in the Woods burned hardly two years into their marriage, Arthur and Anna were sleeping apart at opposite ends of the house, a maid's room and an upstairs foyer separating them.

Of course, as we have seen, Arthur Henry was never the idealist he thought he was, but far more the romantic; and it is romanticism—however much it solved for him the riddle of life—that was the force that entangled his affairs beyond repair. Running through his life and work with unrelenting persistence, nowhere is this romanticism—as it relates to his attitudes toward women—better seen than in A Princess of Arcady. Here, he writes of the unrequited devotion of Minot Alexander for Betty, whom he had loved as a young man but who had cut short his hopes for marriage by her decision to become a nun. Thirty years later, the flame of that love yet burning brightly within him, Alexander assumes responsibility for a young orphan whom he enrolls in the convent school in New York of which Betty—now Mother Pelagia—is headmistress. The following correspondence between them ensues, after a silence of three decades:

> "Dear Betty ... For such natures (as ours) love is a flame that may either illuminate or consume the soul. It separated you and me and rendered our lives lonely and desolate ... If, thirty years ago, you and I had known ourselves or understood anything of life or the world, we would not have been separated by a misunderstanding which was significant only because of the intensity of the love that caused it. Perhaps you have found as great a joy in religion ... As for me, I am lonely and my life is empty."

> "Dear Friend," she replies, "The 'Betty' you once knew should be forgotten by us both, and yet I am afraid she will not be altogether still ... Dear friend, believe me when I say that, lonely as you are, it is far better for both you and me that we were so early separated. In such a nature as yours only the virtues grow, and so I know I have become for you a far nobler woman than I could have been had I remained with you in the world ... "[62]

Yet, the memory of the love that had been between them remained undiminished for Alexander, and Arthur Henry describes his anticipation of their first meeting:

> In a few hours he would be again in the presence of his youth; he would touch the hand and look into the eyes of the girl he had always loved. He had never seen Mother Pelagia ... but his Betty was always before his eyes ... He saw a slender, blackrobed figure coming quickly toward him ... When she entered the bright room and stood before him, he saw a little old lady with white hair showing beneath her quaint bonnet ... He started, stood up, stared for a moment into the wrinkled, faded face before him, and, dropping his eyes, said not a word. "I told you she was dead, but you would not believe me." ... "Don't speak unkindly of her," he interrupted. "She is not dead ... [Until I die] I will protect her."
>
> He bent a little as he walked to the carriage, [and] he realized now, for the first time, that he was really old.[63]

Henry, the romantic, has his hero walk away from the reality he cannot accept; yet carrying, still unchanged, the memory of thirty years' standing as if it had not just been denied. Arthur Henry, the author, had obviously created Minot Alexander in the image of Arthur Henry, the man.

In describing her concern at the drain on their limited resources caused by the Dreisers' summer visit to Maumee, Maude writes: "In due time our funds began to give out, so I notified Arthur. He at once looked so injured and abused that one would think I had produce this disaster with malice aforement."[64]

Unable to deal with the harsh reality that had intruded into the romantic idyll of that summer, Henry had first sold half of the House of Four Pillars to Dreiser for a pittance; and, that failing to solve the problem, then walked away from the reality he could neither accept nor change, oblivious to the havoc wrought by his determination to search for new realities that would better suit his romantic nature. Anna, of course, was the next reality he grasped for, and here again the pattern was repeated.

"[Anna] hoped by way of material treasures as well as a very genuine adoration ... to hold him," writes Dreiser in "Rona Murtha". "Intellectually, I am sure he was convinced that [she] was neither his nor my mental or emotional equal ... Her greatest value to him, as I saw, and knew that she knew also, lay in her money and her sensible and practical use of the same in his behalf."[65]

When these resources dwindled, as they did rapidly in the rebuilding following the fire, reactions were triggered in them both that were to prove disastrous. It would appear that, if Arthur were often difficult to live with, Anna in the face of stress was hardly less so. Almost as if in premonition, she recalled that once she rebuffed a client whose amorous advances toward her were cloaked by a need for "someone to understand him": "Ah, sir," she replied, "but you have no idea what unfathomable depths of uncongeniality there are in me."[66]

After their divorce, Anna reflected on the years of their marriage with a disarming honesty in a letter to Delia Farrell Seifferth: "I had not always been loving enough, wise enough, or patient enough ... and then I lost my temper once in a while when things seemed utterly hopeless."[67]

In that same letter, Anna said that, once again betrayed by reality, Arthur's first response was to attempt to sell the House in the Woods: "Arthur would like to sell and forever and forever close up that chapter." That failing, he turned on his heels in a search again for new realities more compatible.

"Somewhere the pleasant paths that seemed leading to a genial world had disappeared," Henry wrote. "I know that in the years between that first summer ... and these later days of care and labor, there have been innumerable occasions when, through fear or greed, through anger, vanity, or resentment, I might easily have lost my way."[68]

Perhaps the hallmark of the romantic is that even when lost he never knows he's lost.

Another ingredient is also present in Henry's romanticism that must have been present in his response to both Maude and Anna: he was obsessed by youth; he romanticized its perfection, and feared its loss. He dedicates *The Unwritten Law* "to the inquiring Spirit of Youth." If every parent knows that selfishness and anger and covetousness and deceit are not the exclusive afflictions of the adult, Arthur Henry never learned that lesson in his brief fling with parenthood. It was innocence and purity of mind and body alone that he saw in the newborn, qualities that continued through childhood and early youth, but so soon to be besieged by the world and the flesh.

In *A Princess of Arcady*, he speaks through Minot Alexander as he contemplates adoption of the young orphan: "If I were to adopt this child, I would want her to grow into womanhood, learning to know herself, but ignorant of the world ... "[69] Such sentiments abound in Henry's writings. The platonic character of his sexual relationships most likely represented an attempt to extend into adulthood that which he saw as the province of childhood and youth, an innocence so easily and inevitably lost.

As in so many things, he conspired to destroy that innocence, that beauty. Illness and aging were for Arthur Henry *bêtes noire* of proportions that expanded with the passing years; as he could not face them in himself, neither could he deal with them in others. There can be no colds, he might have proclaimed, in the Garden of Eden.

But both Maude and Anna were afflicted with ill health. "Remembering that I had all but died when Dorothy was born and had been ill—very ill—for a year afterward,"[70] Maude began one of her letters, and it is the first of frequent references to the ill health that plagued her whole life. And, the first several of the letters of Anna Mallon are written from sanitaria on the West Coast, the earliest barely five years after their marriage; from internal evidence, it can be assumed that the throat, head, and nerve problems that afflicted her were of some years' standing. To Arthur Henry, these were symptoms of a fall from grace that repelled him. So, both of his companions in the search for the Eden he longed for disqualified themselves early, and were abandoned.

There was a consistency in his attitude that must be acknowledged, however. As we have seen, his obituaries recorded his wish to leave this vale of tears before "septuagenarianism" set in. He may have given himself a little more leeway than he extended to others, but he saw aging even in himself as the illness of growing old—and wished to avoid that reality as he had so many others.

What does one come up with, then, when pseudo-idealism is mixed with romanticism in establishing an attitude toward women? ("You're an interesting woman, Maude," Arthur Henry once told her on a moonlit night in their Maumee garden, "but an impossible wife.")[71] You come up, of course, with a male chauvinist.

> For two years now, [Henry wrote Dreiser] Anna and I have lived together alone, and our mutual efforts to realize an ideal in our daily life has resulted in a constantly increasing respect, affection, and happiness. As the years pass, Anna is becoming more generous, more kindly, and less given to resentment and criticism. Instead of my yielding to the influence of whatever is unworthy in her ... we have

remained together only because she has continued always to yield to the best that is in me.[72]

So much for idealism.

In *The House in the Woods* Arthur Henry describes the ideal woman in the valley of the Plattekill, his Eden so unsullied by the world:

> "There was a time when domestic ideals and desires overbalanced ambition in this country. Then a simple woman, affectionate, pure-minded, and sincere was considered the first great treasure a man could possess ... Here in the Plattekill a good home is still the most desirable thing ... All these girls here owe their beauty and attractiveness to nothing but their good health, their wholesome desires, their pleasure in a natural and useful life ... They are all good housekeepers, and they expect to be wives and mothers, and do their own work and have very happy homes. That is what they are living for. They expect to be loved and petted ... These people are honest. The sentiment of affection, when given a natural expression, remains normal and submits to the control of law and order, and to generous conceptions of morality. There is certainly an amazing freedom among the boys and girls here, and yet I understand that in the entire history of the Plattekill there has been but one advantage taken of this liberty. And what opportunities are here!"
>
> "Yes," said Nancy, "I think the country has been slandered by romancers ..."
>
> "Yes, it has become an easy theme." And I blushed to think how that whistle in my second chapter had tempted me to follow blindly in the well-worn way.[73]

Before we leave these speculations, however, a word might be said on Arthur Henry's behalf; for, if he misrepresented himself to both Maude and Anna, neither of them was of a single mind as to who they were either. Maude, playing the role of the liberated woman all her life, yet recalls from their days of courtship: "I had not found marriage too agreeable with a visionary like Arthur and three of my own family ... on the rocks financially and two of them ill and helpless. I refused to marry Arthur at the outset because of them and he had assured me that he didn't mind taking them on jointly with me—which meant that I would continue to write and work also."[74] Maude was more a traditional product of her times than she could ever admit. And Anna, infatuated "with the so-different-from-New-York-men-in-general youth who had invaded her sanctum with his fairy tale book and dreams,"[75] speaks of him not as his wife but as a mother: Arthur is "a poor lost lamb wandering about the world … He is a very dear and loveable fellow, and always means to do the right thing, … [but] he had no discipline in his early years… He had no guiding hand in his youth, and I spoiled him … I cannot help feeling a very great concern for Arthur, just as a mother would for a wayward boy—wondering what the matter can be with him to make him so irresponsible, and caring so little for the feelings of other people."[76]

So Arthur, thinking he had married two women freed from the constraints of their times, found one to be traditional beyond even her understanding and the other to be a smothering, maternal figure. Dreiser, obviously more sympathetic with Maude (of whom he was not jealous), wrote of Anna (of whom he was jealous) that, although Arthur accepted her generosity gladly, "yet even so, I then felt, and still feel, that [Anna] was amply repaid by even the partial presence and affable gayety of so charming a dreamer and poet."[77] A harsh judgment in the light of all that followed, but probably an observation of considerable insight.

What then of Clare Kummer? Known to both Maude and Anna, she is described by them in less than appreciative terms, Anna not surprisingly being the more eloquent in her lack of enthusiasm:

> " … the lady (whom I have met twice—very talented and attractive), a divorced woman, … has a very difficult temper, and is as erratic and unconventional as Arthur himself;" or again, " … the new wife is attractive and talented, but rude to people, very extravagant, witty and cynical, very exacting, very nervous, and all the things that Arthur especially hates in a wife;" and finally, "I do feel sure that this present marriage relation will not last, not beyond a few years anyway, if that long."[78]

If these are even minimally accurate descriptions, why did this marriage last nearly two and a half decades? I would speculate that it was because Clare Kummer proved to be exactly as advertised—an independent spirit with no hidden agenda. Although his literary productivity tailed off dramatically, the years of their marriage were her most productive, Clare Kummer becoming one of the most prolific and successful playwrights of her time. For Henry, it was as if his idealism and romanticism finally were integrated, and he settled back with relief, in a peace he had not previously known.

For Anna, there was no such respite, but only a destructive intensification of feelings toward a past she could not release and a future she could not face. In a remarkable series of letters to Delia Farrell Seifferth, rescued from the dust of his attic by her nephew, Martin J. Farrell of Platte Clove, we have a dramatic record of Anna's final years. Delia Farrell ("Maggie", the Seifferth's chore girl in the book) married Thomas Seifferth, son and namesake of the owner of Meadow Lawn. Although Anna and Delia were separated in age by more than twenty years, their marriages were hardly a month apart, and Anna always viewed Delia in peer intimacy: "Seven years now—April 15, 1903, when you were married," Anna wrote in 1910. "Does it not seem a very long, long time ago? We were both starting housekeeping together, about the same time … "[79] It is to Delia that Anna opens her heart, and provides a glimpse into the resolution of the romance with the valley of the Plattekill that was begun with such high hopes in that fall of 1903.

Anna Mallon was born into a well-established family of more than modest means. Her father, James, was a brevetted (i.e. commissioned in the field) general in the Civil War at the age of 26, and was killed in action during the Virginia campaigns; her grandfather was an officer in the Revolutionary War. Her student notebooks from her years at the Academy of the Visitation are written in a bold, neat hand, with a precision and accuracy that foretells the adult that was to be. Dreiser describes the Mallon home in Brooklyn as a place in which "there was constant entertainment … Hers was truly an agreeable home … the whole place smacked of tradition and means."[80] Although her formal education did not continue beyond the secondary years, she had obviously learned well, for her correspondence is nearly letter-perfect by even the most exacting of standards. And, from the portion of her library that has survived the years in the Platte Clove house, it is apparent that the process of learning had continued, for volumes of philosophy, history, biography—all well-marked and underlined in her hand—remain in testimony to an ongoing intellectual growth. For Arthur, therefore, she was capable of being not merely a sounding board for his literary efforts, but a full partner in them. The headlines of her obituary notice describe her as an "Authoress … Writer of Some Note", and its text states that "for a number of years (she) had engaged in literary work. In collaboration with her husband, Arthur Henry, she wrote *The House in the Woods* and other popular works of fiction. She was divorced about nine years ago and since that time has been writing under her own name."[81] I could find no confirmation for writing done on her own, but it is interesting to speculate whether she was indeed a collaborator with Arthur, as were Maude before her and Clare after. If she was, it is ironic that in this, as in so many other things, she received no credit from him.

By late summer 1908, the date of the first letter we have in her correspondence with Delia Farrell Seifferth, she and Arthur had been nearly two years in Washington in the land and orchard business with Alfred. Arthur had begun his selling treks back in the East. He apparently used The House in the Woods for occasional weekend visits with friends, and had just described for Anna one that included the Dreisers. She tells Delia that Arthur had promised "that he would not permit the Dreisers to go again, because it made me suffer so ... I won't go into all my feelings in the matter. You already know them;" but she does ask Delia to set aside "the little trunk which contains the correspondence between Arthur and the Dreisers."[82] In a year, she will instruct Delia's sister, Margaret, to burn its contents if Arthur came up again. "They're gone, those letters," Delia's nephew told me, "because Maggie was a burner. Delia saved things; but Maggie was a burner."[83] One can feel the shudder that must ripple through the ranks of Dreiser scholars at this bit of homespun information.

It is difficult to explain Anna's obvious antipathy toward Dreiser. Perhaps it was the jealousy he felt for her having intruded on his intense friendship with Arthur. Or possibly, remembering that it was Dreiser who had introduced Arthur to her, she wondered whether history was repeating itself with Clare Kummer and Arthur, Dreiser again being the agent of their encounter.

In any event, although she reports with optimism on their business ventures in Washington, poor health had become an overriding concern for her: "I am not at all well this summer, after all of these wearying things, and many others that I cannot write about ... Now, don't worry about me. I do not get as heartbroken as I used to. It affects my health and sleep a lot."[84] The letter is written from a sanitarium in North Yakima.

This letter concludes with a few words of bitter advice for her young friend back in Platte Clove: "Don't be unselfish, little Delia girl, or make sacrifices. They only make you an easy mark for clever people ... Be cheerful and get all you can out of people." In a similar vein, Maude had written Professor Elias: "Warning—Beware of everyone but yourself. Never expect a return on anything you may do. Friends scuttle away like cockroaches ... "[85] If joy and goodwill were what guided Arthur in his quest, they were certainly not what he left in his wake.

The day following, Anna writes again, telling Delia:

> I have just written Arthur a letter—letters—that will make him feel very sad, but broken promises bring tears ... Arthur rushes in to do fine things for new friends without considering how I feel about it. But I have regained a great deal of my old courage and spirit ... and there is a new Anna to deal with ... I am tired of submitting to unpleasant, unnecessary things. I love Arthur dearly, but I shall no longer be capable, I believe, of being deeply hurt by him ... I have finally made up my mind not to separate from Arthur, unless he is unpleasant or unreasonable, but to have some interest of my own, and to be as free in my movements as he has always been in his.[86]

The marriage is obviously in trouble, and implicitly has been for some time—for this is not new information for Delia. But, as shall be seen, Anna's posture of courage was sheer bravado.

A year later, in mid-September 1909, Anna writes: "I have not been too happy ... [and] the doctor has ordered me to go to California at once—so I leave today for the Napa Valley ... *This is private*—except that I am in California for my throat trouble."[87] But it is more than "throat trouble". The next letter, from St. Helena Sanitarium, reports that, "the doctor wants me to stay here for a year, to see if the relaxing air of California will not help both nerves and throat—both of which have been dangerously affected by the changes, excitement, and responsibilities of the past year or two."[88] In mid-October, a postscript: " ... the doctor has ordered me to Lower California—Long Beach Sanitarium."[89]

Letters in subsequent months confirm the suspicion that Anna's problems were more than physical: "I have had to take very severe treatments for the head ... I have nearly lost my mind, and ... I have to go every day to the treatment rooms here, and have my head vibrated."[90] And then in May 1910: "I feel much better; throat fairly well, but the woman still treats my head. Though the headache is gone, it gets very tired thinking."

In the letters from St. Helena Sanitarium, two themes that will recur appear for the first time. "I told you that if I needed the money, I would let you know. I shall need some of it—$50—by return mail, if possible—and the balance by the middle of November. I have to take some expensive treatments that I had not expected when I first came ... Don't tell Tom why I need the money."[91] It would seem that here Anna is not borrowing from Delia, but merely drawing on loans she had made to the young couple at the time of their marriage; yet, suggested by these and subsequent requests is that financial pressures have become a dominant concern. Anna in the West is but a fading shadow of the successful businesswoman of the copying office who underwrote the building of two houses but a few years earlier.

Although still overawed by the beauty of the Far West, she finally gives voice to a yearning for the valley of the Plattekill: "There was never any air that agreed with me like the dear old Catskill air—where I wasn't conscious that I even had a throat. I often wish that I had never left it. I was never happier than in those two first simple years of living in that first dear old 'House in the Woods' ... Often and often I have longed to drop in and see you, and get a touch of that warm, tender hand of yours. I close my eyes, and see the white house, and the light in your window."[92]

And, five days later: "I can still see the red in the maple leaf now—and by and by, I shall hear the pleasant sound and jingle of your sleigh bells. My heart goes back a great deal." In a Christmas letter that same year, but from a sanitarium in Point Loma, California, the yearning is voiced again: "I have thought, too, a great deal about the House in the Woods. I never want Arthur to sell it. I look at the dear pictures very often, and wonder whether I shall get back there again ... But someday I shall."[93] The grip of memory tightens.

1910 dawns for Anna with a reluctant acknowledgement that her health has not improved, but with no indication that she is aware of the traumatic event that lies but a few months away. On March 12, back in Yakima, she explains to Delia: "I am here to obtain a divorce from A.—*It is his wish.* Ground—incompatibility and desertion ... It will be all over in about three weeks ... do not let it grieve you, I am getting all my punishment for whatever wrong I have done in my life—all at once ... What I shall do, I do not yet know ... I would come back to the House in the Woods, only it seems to me that the loneliness ... would be my finish. Luckily, I believe in God—in you—and a few friends."

Fearful of the loneliness—but probably more so of the humiliation—that would await her in Platte Clove, Anna seeks to make her own way in the West, to regain solvency, so that she might return with at least a semblance of the pride of former years. Disinherited by her mother, erratically and minimally supported by Arthur, she has only Delia's repayments and her own ingenuity to fall back on. She considers first speculating in land, but then settles on establishing a small chicken farm with a young couple in La Jolla; by the end of April the chicks arrived. Two letters in May follow, but the poultry enterprise is not mentioned.

A gap of six years in this correspondence follows, the date of the next letter to Delia being December 11, 1916. Surprisingly, it is Maude who fills this gap:

> When Arthur's only sister wrote me from the West after Arthur had deserted Anna—eight years after their marriage, she told me that Anna was half-crazed ... I re-read one of the letters she [Anna] sat up nearly all night to write me, giving me all the details of their marriage, with A's affairs with other women, his brother Alfred's treatment of them both, and the 'hurry up with the divorce—lovingly, Arthur' end which she did not take as philosophically as I had at the cabin.
>
> She was broken mentally, spiritually and financially, the House in the Woods was heavily mortgaged, but she thought if she could again see her mother she might get some of her own money which was being held up and possibly sell the Catskill mountain place. So I sent her the necessary funds and she came on and first stopped here, then we arranged that Dorothy, my sisters and I would follow her after she had opened the house and made it ready for us ... Anna, however, after she got in touch with her mother who was near death in a Sullivan County sanitarium—(I stayed alone in the House in the Woods when she made that trip ...), brought her mother to this place after I left and she died there ... Anna got all the tied up money and repaid me ... "[94]

It is not only politics that makes strange bedfellows.

Back in Platte Clove, her health and fortunes somewhat restored, Anna was able to set her mind toward the accomplishment of how to keep the House in the Woods not only from being sold but also in her sole possession, a task which from the West had so often seemed an impossibility. Torn by the double fear that either Arthur would sell it or that her financial difficulties would necessitate its sale, early in her correspondence with Delia her mind turned toward how both eventualities might be averted.

In August 1908, to settle debts with local workmen incurred in the rebuilding after the fire, a $3,500 mortgage was placed on the House; it was held by Emma Frances Parker, a mutual friend from New York City. "I should like to go to the House in the Woods this fall," Anna wrote from Yakima, "but I have told A. I shall not return until the debts are all paid."[95] On January 27, 1910, reporting that Arthur "may have to sell the House to raise some money," Anna evidences that despite her physical and emotional problems, her business mind had been hard at work: "You must not feel badly about it—because as I say, it may not come off ... and it may come into my possession. I cannot explain what I mean until later. This is between you and me alone—the possibility of it becoming mine." This is followed the next month, in a letter describing the terms of the divorce, by another cryptic reference to plans she has afoot: "I hate to think of the dear House passing into other hands—Maybe yet something will prevent that ... A. cannot sell it without my knowledge—that is, I have tried to arrange it so as to prevent him from doing so ... A miracle might still happen."[96]

Well, if miracles do not just happen but are made, Anna began work on hers within a year of her return to Platte Clove in 1911. The process of its accomplishment should dispel any doubts that she was an imaginative and facile businesswoman. By the end of March, 1910, the plan was taking shape. "I cannot tell you anything definite yet ... I have had to agree to sell [the House], but I have reserved the right (and A. gives me the right) to live there until it is sold at a price agreed upon by me. If I hold on long enough, it may yet be wholly mine."[97] And, in an April 29 letter, she repeats that "he cannot sell without my consent. That is where his lawyer gave me the advantage." The reference is to the divorce settlement, which provided:

> That Arthur Henry, an unmarried man ... [for] the sum of one dollar ($1.00) to him in hand paid ... by Anna T. Mallon, formerly his wife ... does hereby remise, release, and forever quit claim ... [to the] 'House in the Woods' ... Said property to be held by the parties hereto, as joint tenants and not as tenants in common ... It is further and expressly understood, that until such time as the parties hereto can agree upon a sale of said property, party of the second part shall

have the right and privilege of living upon and occupying said property as her house, without further expense to her, than the payment of taxes and repairs ...

Anna has accomplished three things by insisting on these terms: first, she has gained *de facto* ownership of the House; second, she is assured that no sale of the property can occur without her full approval; and, third, Arthur is solely and fully responsible for the $3,500 mortgage.

And a strange mortgage it was. It was written with a feature akin to double indemnity: until its due date, July 31, 1913, no principal payments were required; but, if for any reason default occurred, a sum of $7,000 became due immediately. This unusual feature had implications that were at the heart of Anna's four-step strategy for repossessing the castle of her dreams:

STEP ONE: In September 1912, Delia Farrell Seifferth purchased the mortgage from Emma Frances Parker for $3,535, continuing its terms, conditions, and due date. It must be assumed that Delia was merely acting on Anna's behalf, and that the funds for this transaction came in whole or in part either from monies still owed Anna by Delia and Thomas Seifferth or from resources made available to Anna by her mother on their reconciliation.

STEP TWO: Since her return to Platte Clove, Anna had intentionally neglected to pay some taxes; outstanding were the 1911 School Taxes ($2.17), the 1912 School Taxes ($1.82), and the 1913 School and other taxes ($15.50). Total taxes due: $19.49. The amount notwithstanding, a principle is a principle says the law, and Greene County, for taxes unpaid, declares Arthur in default and the house and property up for auction.

STEP THREE: By the terms of the mortgage which she now holds, Delia Seifferth forecloses, and $7000 becomes due immediately—all Arthur's responsibility. So finely honed was Anna's scheme that the foreclosure preceded the mortgage's due date by less than two and a half months. Whether Arthur was ever geared to meet the $3,500 mortgage is not known; but certainly he was not prepared to produce $7000 for a house to which he had in effect relinquished both claim and interest.

STEP FOUR—and Shut the Door! On May 16, 1913, Anna Mallon Henry repurchased her House in the Woods at public auction for $2,000.

What a marvelous scenario of poetic justice! Having accomplished the return of the House in the Woods to her sole possession, however, the peace and stability for which she had so hoped and so desperately needed was not to be for Anna. Like a moth to a candle, she returned to Yakima, apparently in an effort to recoup at least a portion of the equity to which she felt entitled from Alfred's business; but it was to no avail. Her resources were exhausted.

On December 11, 1916, in personal service as housekeeper for a Mrs. Charles Fincke in Princeton, New Jersey, Anna writes to Delia, her pride rapidly slipping from her grasp. Bemoaning her inability to borrow money from either family or friends, she then paints this picture of her duties: "It's a constant, unremitting job … This being maid-of-all-work—ready to open the door with a white apron on from 9 A.M. on, and washing dishes, cooking, sweeping, answering phones, waiting on table, watering plants, etc., etc.—is some chore … I'm not going to be discouraged because people think I'm too good for the job … I'll cherish the experience and never be ashamed of it."

What a tragic decline in fortune for a proud woman who, little more than a decade earlier, spoke from a pinnacle of success and affluence. That she shortly exchanged the role of housekeeper for that of companion to an elderly widow must have been of little solace to her battered ego.

With the proceeds from the sale of the house to her niece in 1919, Anna once more headed west—"to be hectored and chased after some more by Arthur's wily ex-Methodist preacher brother."[98] It was again a vain groping for a measure of success that would permit her to return to Platte Clove; but Anna was in a losing spiral that sucked her deeper into frayed emotions and further from the peaceful glades of the Plattekill. This time, the business venture was a tearoom in partnership with an Elon Bowker, whom she describes to Delia in two mid-February 1921 letters that " … explain so many things I could not say last Fall, and why I gave up Tea Room. Shall I say it now? Elon is a paranoiac, and since June last has continually threatened to kill me, and makes a good try at it. He adores me, he thinks, and has at the same time the most malignant hatred. Thinks he is called to be God's instrument to do it. There you are … Going to have him put under order of the Court to stay away 1000 yards from me … [Elon] ill-treated me beyond my telling of it … I was dumb thro' the most terrible fear I have ever known in my life. He is a psychic and clairvoyant … he made me believe in the Devil and the evil spirits that can possess man … he tortured me, mentally and physically (with terrific blows on the back, the head, face, mouth—*even kicked me*) and kept me up until 2-3-4—all night, to torment my mind, insisting I was insane … When my hand trembled and let a dish fall, he would break two or three or four, to make up for lost time, because he said he never broke any … Took food off the stove in pots or pans, threw it at me or on the walls or up on the ceiling … "[99]

Not a week after these revelations of an emotional and spiritual turbulence even more debilitating than her physical ailments, she apologizes to Delia for not having written in so long—as if the two previous letters had never been written. "I'm wonderfully happy," she wrote, "but have been so ill, I thought never to get well again."[100] All these letters begin in her familiar neat hand, but degenerate into an at times illegible scrawl. A March letter asks Delia for a loan of $400; on the bottom of the back page, Delia summarized: "She wanted to borrow $400—I wrote had no money."[101] On April 24, Anna tells Delia: "I am again losing my nerve … I find I am that way to my great bewilderment … I wish I understood my own self better."

On May 7, 1921, Delia Seifferth received a telegram from Alfred Henry: "Anna Henry accidentally drowned today. Evidently fell from high bank into the river. She has been visiting in Yakima for two months. Was at her nephew's ranch when accident occurred. Please notify her relatives and friends. Burial Sunday. Letter follows."

As promised, Alfred writes Delia at the end of May: "We do not know any of the details of poor Anna's death. She loved to walk by the swiftly flowing river bank and to sit there and dream. Whether the bank caved in with her or whether she had a sinking spell (to which she was liable) and fell we do not know. She seemed so happy and contented that we think it must have been pure accident … It is all very sad but we have the satisfaction of knowing that she found comfort and happiness in her visit to Yakima even if it did end disastrously."[102]

Shrouded by these maudlin sentiments and true to form was a request that Delia send him any money still owed Anna by the Seifferths, "as it will require about $500 to pay her funeral expenses and clear up some debts she had contracted at the stores here … [for which] I have become responsible."

One cannot help remembering Maude's words on Alfred: "She told me in that all-night letter that if anything untoward ever happened to her I would know who was responsible for it. What I personally think of Alfred Henry wouldn't sound well in print."[103,104]

Although the thought of suicide, not foul play, must have crossed his mind, Coroner Brown declared her death to be one of accidental drowning, and deemed an inquest unnecessary. Yet, the spectre of suicide haunted Anna's niece, Elizabeth Clearwaters, with whom she often stayed in Yakima: "We surely miss dear little Aunt Anna," she wrote to Delia. "I know she is at peace now but we thought we were making her happy. That's what hurts. The only thing that makes me bitter is that if we'd just been well off financially, I feel sure she'd have been with us now. And then some people say money doesn't count."[105]

Thus ends the saga of Anna Mallon Henry, drowned in the Naches River. The bruises and wounds that caused her death could never have been revealed by even the most meticulous inquest or the most thorough autopsy. She was 59.

* * *

Although I must have driven down the Platte Clove road past its entrance pillars and funky mailbox a hundred times, I was well into my research before I laid eyes on or set foot in the House in the Woods. Its owners, sisters, and descendants of Anna Mallon, confessed that they knew virtually nothing of the early history of the house, nor of the couple who built it; in fact, as it turned out, they possessed only the sketchiest of information. To encourage the continuation of my investigations, they loaned me a picture of Anna Mallon, the first I had seen of her.

Shortly after that visit, Justine Hommel, maven of Mountain Top history and lore, called to ask if I would be interested in speaking with a man who had met Anna Mallon. Interested? Indeed! The next Sunday afternoon, I was in the Hommel's Twilight Park living room facing not the octogenarian-plus I had anticipated, but a hale man in his fifties, frustratingly reluctant to speak about Anna Mallon. Only when my impatience translated into signs of leaving, did he speak.

"All right, but if any of you laugh at what I'm about to say," he said, "I'll be the one who leaves. I didn't meet Anna Mallon herself." He paused, and taking a deep breath continued, "I met her ghost."

I thought, "Oh really now," but no one laughed. He went on to describe having fallen asleep in the Morris chair in his kitchen after supper one evening a few years ago and being awakened by a strange sensation that he was no longer alone.

"There was a woman sitting at the kitchen table with her hands covering her face. Then she looked squarely at me, saying not a word. She had been crying, I think, but it was the sadness of her face that I remember most. It was her, all right," he said solemnly. "It was the ghost of Anna Mallon."

"I shouted at it, 'Get out of my house, you evil thing, and go back where you came from!', and it disappeared."

As he was growing up, he said later, relatives told a lot of stories about that house, and about Anna Mallon and the sad life she lived, but he swore he had never seen a picture of her—and "double-swore" that he had not been dreaming that night. He was wide awake, he said, and he knew it was she.

Two weeks later, I visited him at his house with six or seven vintage pictures of older women, including the Anna Mallon photograph I had recently obtained. I asked whether any of them was Anna, as I wished to include her in my book but had no idea what she looked like.

He took the photographs from me, began to shuffle through them quickly, and pulled out the fourth, saying, "That's her. She's the ghost who sat in my kitchen. That's Anna Mallon, all right." It was the picture of Anna the sisters had given me.

Over the succeeding three years, the apparition in the kitchen had been pushed into the far recesses of memory as the wealth of House in the Woods data accumulated. It was when the first draft of the Afterword had just been completed that an invitation from the sisters for a second visit was received.

I can yet recall clearly driving down the Platte Clove road that afternoon, past the overgrown foundations of Meadow Lawn which had burned to the ground a quarter of a century earlier. I turned through the gates and saw that giant pines, planted as a protective screen by subsequent owners, blocked the view of the valley of the Plattekill and the mountains beyond that Arthur and Anna had worked so hard to expose. A bend in the road, and then the House in the Woods—looking hardly different than in its earliest photographs taken seventy years earlier. Only Bob Golightly, their Scotch collie, lying by the entrance, was missing.

My anticipation at this second visit was more than matched by the sisters, whose love of the House in the Woods seemed gently buffed by its sombre charm. I was led into the living room, past the fieldstone fireplace with the framed Dryden quotation resting on its mantel, a silent survivor of the first house which had been built with such shared hope for the future.

Chairs had been set in a circle, and I was directed to a large oak rocker in which surely Arthur and Anna had sat in the days of their togetherness. I was

introduced to three weekend guests—the head of a small religious community dedicated to prayer and meditation and two of his associates. All three,
even less informed than the sisters, shared in their anticipation.

"Before you begin," said the head of the Order, "might I ask a question?
Are you going to tell us of a woman who had suffered greatly, and who met a
possibly suspicious but certainly tragic end?"

I acknowledged that I was.

"She's here, you know."

Ignoring my look of disbelief, he continued. "I saw her last night at the
end of the upstairs hall. We looked at each other for the longest time; but,
when I spoke to her, she vanished."

"How remarkable," said one of his associates. "I hadn't had time to tell
you, but late last night I sat reading in that chair," indicating the chair on
whose edge I now sat, "and I felt a presence. Standing behind my left shoulder was a middle-aged woman. A sad, sad look—a look of anguish, of pain—
was on her face. But as soon as I too attempted to speak to her, she was gone."

"Perhaps that explains the fighting," one of the sisters suggested
hesitantly.

"What fighting?" I asked quickly.

"Well, every so often in the years we've had the House in the Woods, we'd
be awakened in the middle of the night by the sounds of a man and a woman
fighting. Shouting. The words were never clear, but the argument was vicious.
It seemed to come from out on the lawn, but as soon as we'd turn on the
floodlights, the sounds would stop—and there'd be no one there."

The room was smothered in the sounds of silence.

"She's here, all right," said the male religious.

"They're both here," said his associate, and the others all nodded in
agreement.

* * *

With the deaths of Anna Mallon and Arthur Henry, the tragic tale of the
House in the Woods ought to have come to a close. But, as in that tale's
telling, reasonable expectations were rare; so it came as no surprise to this
chronicler that the unexpected would be present in its ending as well.

Donald T. Oakes
January 1, 2000

APPENDIX I

THE SUBSEQUENT HISTORY OF THE HOUSE IN THE WOODS

It may be fitting to conclude this tale by tracing the ownership of the House in the Woods to the present. It is a trail with twists and turns, to be sure, but one which never loses sight of its goal of keeping the House within the protective shade of the Mallon family tree.

By September, 1916, Anna had again fallen on hard financial times, and she sold the House in the Woods to Margaret Farrell (Delia's sister) for $1.00, undoubtedly to provide collateral for loans made to her. Three years later, on September 11, 1919, Anna repurchased the house and property from Margaret for $3,000, the price certainly reflecting her indebtedness to Margaret and not its market value. Less than a week later, on September 16, Anna sold the house and property to her maternal niece, Elizabeth Riley Smith, for $6,000. Without question, this transaction—while assuring that the House in the Woods would stay within the family—was designed chiefly to provide Elizabeth Smith with collateral for a personal loan, part of which Anna used to settle with Margaret; by personal agreement with her niece, Anna retained *de facto* possession, and until her death always considered the House in the Woods her home.

In June 1935, Elizabeth Smith transferred title to her daughter, Angela Marie Smith Weisbrod. On her death, it passed to Antoinette Walker Martignoni and Elizabeth Walker O'Brien, sisters, nieces of Angela Weisbrod, and granddaughters of Elizabeth Smith.

In December 1979, Antoinette Martignoni transferred her one-half interest in the House to Julie and James Lemaire, children of Anne and Mallon Lemaire (Antoinette and Elizabeth's half-brother) and to Thomas Lemaire, Julie and James' cousin and nephew of Mallon Lemaire. In 1980, Elizabeth O'Brien followed suit, naming Julie, James, and Thomas beneficiaries of her one-half interest as well.

With Elizabeth's death in December 1991, then, the House in the Woods had three owners, all descendants of the founding family. Julie, James, and Thomas Lemaire share equally in the title and are so listed on the Town of Hunter tax rolls.

In course of the past nearly two decades, the relationship of its owners with the House was diminished either by geography (Julie settled on the West Coast, James in Nevada) or by career (Thomas in eastern Massachusetts, immersed in data processing). Although the children continue as owners of record, the mantle has been passed to Mallon and Anne Lemaire who, describing themselves simply as "visitors in residence", have become resident caretakers of the House in the Woods and stewards of its tragic history.

APPENDIX II

THE ARTHUR HENRY LITERARY CANON

Books
1890   *Nicholas Blood, Candidate*
1894   *The Flight of a Pigeon*
          (w/Maude Wood Henry)
1900   *A Princess of Arcady*
1902   *An Island Cabin*
1904   *The House in the Woods*
1905   *Lodgings in Town*
          (includes "Peter and the Fairies", published separately in 1913.)
          The Unwritten Law
1937   *The Life of Roger Allen*
          (unpublished—in progress at the time of his death)

Plays
1924   *Time* —produced in 1928
1927   "Boastful Benny," "The Eagle's Feather," "The Happy Birthday," "Mother's Day" (One-act plays for children written with his daughter, Dorothy van Auken)
1928   *The Night Before*
1932   *The Beloved Vagabond*
          (written with Mary Ward—date is approximate)

Articles
          1890   "Dion Boucicault," *Harpers*
          1895   "The Good Laugh," *Ev'ry Month*
                    "The Philosophy of Hope," *Munsey's*

1900   "The Outdoor Recreation League," *Outlook*
       "The New Spirit of Education," *Munsey's*
1901   "Among the Immigrants," *Scribners*
       "New Manual Training," *Munsey's*
1902   "Mr. Jerome's Official Home on the
       East Side," *Outlook*
       "The Tombs Angel," *Outlook*
1903   "The Life of Teasle," *Outlook*
1912–1927 Five articles were written for *Radio
       Broadcast*, three for *Hampton Magazine*, and
       one each for *Ladies Home Journal*, *Colliers*,
       and *Canadian Magazine*.

(I cannot claim the above to be a definitive or complete listing, but for the time frame that is the focus of this study, it probably serves the purpose.)

ENDNOTES

Foreword

1. *The House in the Woods*, p.2.
2. *Ibid.*, p.39.
3. *Ibid.*, p.16.
4. *Ibid.*, p.22.
5. *Ibid.*, p.271.
6. *Ibid.*, A blending of quotations.
7. *Ibid.*, p.90.
8. *Ibid.*, p.120.
9. *Ibid.*, p.150.
10. Confirmed by the House's owners in 1978 as part of an oral tradition passed on to them by their grandmother, Elizabeth Riley Smith, niece of and successor to Anna Mallon Henry as owner of the House in the Woods.
11. *The House in the Woods*, p.10.
12. *Ibid.*, p.153.

Afterword

Please note: the majority of Afterword/Endnote references are drawn from five primary sources; references or quotations from these will be identified beyond pagination and date only to provide text clarity.

Arthur Henry: *A Princess of Arcady*, Doubleday, Page & Co., 1900; *An Island Cabin*, McClure Phillips & Co., 1902; *The House in the Woods*, A.S. Barnes & Co., 1904; and *Lodgings in Town*, A.S. Barnes & Co., 1905.

Theodore Dreiser: "Rona Murtha," a portrait in *A Gallery of Women*, Volume II, Horace Liveright, 1929. Permission to quote was graciously accorded by The Dreiser Trust.

Mary Henry Rossiter: *My Mother's Life*, Fleming H. Revell Company, 1900.

Personal letters: Maude Wood Henry to Professor Robert Elias, author *Theodore Dreiser: Apostle of Nature*, Cornell University Press, 1970, now in the archives of the Cornell University Library, Ithaca, New York.

Personal letters: Anna Mallon Henry to Delia Farrell Seifferth and her sister, Margaret Farrell. Permission to quote granted by Martin J. Farrell of Platte Clove, New York.

1. Arthur Henry's handwritten inscription in the copy of *The Unwritten Law* in the library of the House in the Woods.
2. "Dion Boucicault," *Harper's Weekly* 34:760, September 27, 1890.
3. Although there seems little reason to question this date, it must be noted that Henry shaved a year-plus off his age on the certificate of his marriage to Anna Mallon on March 9, 1903, claiming a youthful 34 to her 41.
4. *My Mother's Life*, p.111. This volume is comprised of autobiographic material from Sarepta Irish Henry's writings (SIH) and her daughter's reflections (MHR) on her mother's extraordinary life.
5. *Ibid.*, p.111 (SIH).
6. Pre-publication review of *A Princess of Arcady*, *The Book Buyer Magazine*, 21:845, September 1900.
7. In "Chronicle and Comment", 15:11, March 1902, and a review of *An Island Cabin*, 15:478-80, July 1902, *Bookman Magazine*.
8. In August, 1874, at a Chautauqua Assembly a handful of women organized the National W.C.T.U, and in October Frances E. Willard, recently resigned as Dean of the Woman's Branch of Northwestern University, accepted the presidency of the Chicago Central Union; in November she was elected Corresponding Secretary of the young National. Although she and Sarepta were acquainted by correspondence and reputation, it was not until the following December that the two first met.
9. "Sarepta" is the anglicizing of "Zaraphath", a Phoenician city midway between Tyre and Sidon, where Elijah lodged in the home of a widow and restored her son to life. I Kings 17:18-24.
10. This historical exaggeration continued through his entire adult life, and beyond: it was included in his *New York Times* obituary, June 5, 1934.

11. In "Chronicle and Comment", 15:11, March 1902, and a review of *An Island Cabin*, 15:478-80, July 1902, *Bookman Magazine*.
12. *Woman and Temperance*, Frances E. Willard, Woman's Christian Temperance Union, 1883, p.191.
13. Patrick M. Quinn, University Archivist, May 20, 1976 letter.
14. *Woman and Temperance*, Frances E. Willard, WCTU, 1883, p.191.
15. From a September 1902 review of *By Order of the Prophet*, Northwestern University Archives.
16. Maude Wood Henry letter, December 17, 1945.
17. *Ibid.*, December 17, 1945.
18. *Ibid.*, June 5, 1945.
19. Appended in *My Mother's Life*.
20. An April 4, 1978 letter from Dreiser biographer Robert Elias informed me that, although all references to Arthur Henry's newspaper days speak of his being on the staff of the Chicago *Herald*, it was in fact the *Globe* before Henry quit.
21. MWH letter, December 17, 1945.
22. *Bookman Magazine*, 15:11, March 1902, chronicled that, following an unappreciated apprenticeship on the Chicago *Daily News*, Henry "drifted to New York and wrote his first novel." All subsequent reviewers adopted some variant of that scenario. Arthur Henry's first novel, *Nicholas Blood, Candidate*, was written in Chicago while with the Chicago *Globe* and published by Oliver Dodd in 1890.
23. Letter from Marjorie J. Walker, Arthur Henry's granddaughter, March 29, 1993.
24. At some point, its name became The Bohemian Club, perhaps because it was more acceptable to be known for victimizing traditional social values rather than innocent streetwalkers.
25. Excerpted from an article by Delos Avery in the Graphics Section of the January 28, 1945 issue of the *Chicago Tribune*. I can only assume that bestowing clerical orders on Arthur Henry was a research error, confusing him with brother Alfred.
26. Note should be taken that Dreiser published Henry's "The Good Laugh" in an 1895 issue of his *Ev'ry Month*. One good turn deserves another?
27. The house today is entered in the National Register of Historic Places by virtue of its Civil War use as a station in the underground railway.

28. There seemed to be implications for "putting down roots" in the setting sun for Arthur Henry, for it was an autumn setting sun behind Hunter Mountain that confirmed the site of the House in the Woods.
29. MWH letter, June 5, 1945.
30. "Maumee Homes", November 7, 1951, courtesy of Toledo-Lucas County Public Library.
31. Quoted from "Rona Murtha" by F. O. Matthiessen in his *Dreiser*, William Sloane Assoc., 1951, pp.33-34.
32. *Ibid.*
33. *Lodgings in Town*, p.140.
34. "Rona Murtha", pp.567-8.
35. MWH letter, April 2, 1945.
36. "Rona Murtha", pp.567-70.
37. *Ibid.*
38. MWH letter, April 2, 1945.
39. Toledo *Blade*, December 29, 1945.
40. Neda Westlake letter to DTO, May 3, 1985.
41. MWH letter, June 5, 1945.
42. Arthur Henry to Theodore Dreiser, personal letter, February 17, 1904.
43. MWH letter, May 13, 1945.
44. Arthur Henry to Theodore Dreiser, personal letter, February 17, 1904.
45. "Rona Murtha", p.568.
46. MWH letter, May 13, 1945.
47. *The House in the Woods*, p.152.
48. *Ibid.*, p.105.
49. *The Brooklyn Standard Union*, September 4, 1928.
50. *Brooklyn Daily Times*, September 4, 1928.
51. *Brooklyn Daily Eagle*, September 4, 1928.
52. A 1976 conversation with Betty Rinehart, re. the photo of the cast of *The Night Before*: "The haughty creature on the [back step] left is I, 5 ft 4$^{1}/_{2}$ without heels. What a dowdy looking group!"
53. *The New York Times*, November 23, 1928.
54. *Providence Journal* obituary, June 5, 1934.
55. MWH letter, May 13, 1945.
56. *Ibid.*, May 13, 1945.
57. "Rona Murtha", pp.577, 584-85.

58. Arthur Henry's signature had been erased, reflecting Margaret Farrell's empathy for her friend Anna's suffering.
59. Sarepta Irish Henry autobiography, *My Mother's Life*, pp.68-69.
60. At one point, she was reported to "have several plays running simul taneously on Broadway."
61. "Rona Murtha", p.592.
62. *A Princess of Arcady*, pp.29-30, 80-81.
63. *Ibid.*, pp.170-171, 184-187.
64. MWH letter, June 5, 1945.
65. "Rona Murtha", pp.577, 584-5.
66. MWH letter, August 22, 1947.
67. The first of Anna Mallon Henry letters to Delia Farrell Seifferth, February 28, 1910.
68. *The House in the Woods*, p.128.
69. *A Princess of Arcady*, p.56.
70. MWH letter, May 13, 1945.
71. MWH letter, May 13, 1945.
72. Arthur Henry to Theodore Dreiser, personal letter, February 17, 1904.
73. *The House in the Woods*, p.148.
74. MWH letter, August 23, 1947.
75. *Ibid.*, August 23, 1947.
76. AMH letters, February 10 and 28, March 12, 1910.
77. "Rona Murtha", p.585.
78. AMH letters, April 29 and May 3, 1910.
79. *Ibid.*, May 1, 1910.
80. "Rona Murtha", p.582.
81. *Yakima Herald*, May 8, 1921.
82. AMH letter, August 1, 1908.
83. Jack Farrell observation.
84. AMH letter, August 1, l908.
85. MWH letter, April 4, 1946.
86. AMH letter, August 2, 1908.
87. *Ibid.*, September 16, 1909.
88. *Ibid.*, October 6, 1909.
89. *Ibid.*, October 11, 1909.
90. *Ibid.*, April 12, 1910.
91. *Ibid.*, October 6, 1909.

92. *Ibid.*, October 6, 1909.

93. *Ibid.*, December 16, 1909.

94. MWH letter, May 13, 1945.

95. AMH letter, August 6, 1908.

96. *Ibid.*, March 12, 1910.

97. *Ibid.*, March 24, 1910.

98. MWH letter, May 13, 1945.

99. AMH letters, February 15,19, 1921.

100. *Ibid.*, February 25, 1921.

101. Delia Farrell Seifferth, in a note on AMH letter to her, March 2, 1921.

102. Alfred Henry letter to Delia Seifferth, May 23, 1921.

103. MWH letter, May 13, 1945.

104. Is it not ironic that on February 20, 1915 Arthur and Alfred's sister, Mary Henry Rossiter, also died in Yakima!

105. Letter to Delia Seifferth, undated, but probably written immediately subsequent to Anna's death.